A Few Thoughts From DAD

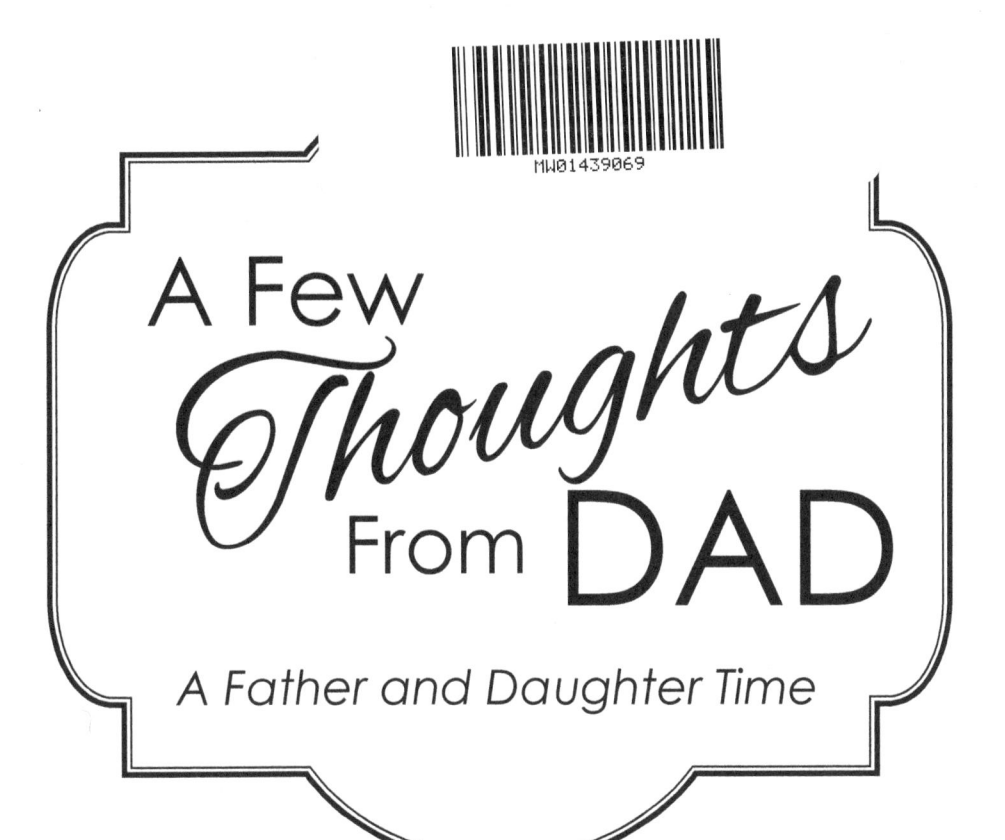

A Father and Daughter Time

KIP JACKSON

ISBN 978-1-63903-960-9 (paperback)
ISBN 978-1-63903-962-3 (hardcover)
ISBN 978-1-63903-961-6 (digital)

Copyright © 2022 by Kip Jackson

All rights reserved. No part of this publication may be reproduced, distributed, or transmitted in any form or by any means, including photocopying, recording, or other electronic or mechanical methods without the prior written permission of the publisher. For permission requests, solicit the publisher via the address below.

Christian Faith Publishing
832 Park Avenue
Meadville, PA 16335
www.christianfaithpublishing.com

Any quotes without stating who wrote or said them are all my own saying.

Printed in the United States of America

Contents

Introduction ix

"The Words I Would Say" 1
How Fast the Years Have Gone 3
The Note 16
Where Are You Heading? 17
Red Robin 19
I'm on Guard while You Are Out 21
More than Just a Pretty Face 23
A Smile 26
Don't be a Grinch 27
Always Remember to Laugh 32
"Laughter Just Like a Medicine" 33
The Power to Cause Laughter 36
"Laugh Out Loud" Song 37
You Are a Treasure 39
XOXO 40
You Are Beautiful 42
May I Have the Next Dance? 43
Cinderella 44
A Place Called Home 46
Can I Help You? 48
You Might Not Know 50
You Are Matchless 53
There Is Only One You 54
"God Made You Special" 57
You Can Always Try 58
"Beauty Will Rise" 61
Remember to Accept the Differences in People 64
What Will It Cost to Do That? 66
Count the Cost 71
To Buy or Not to Buy 72
You Are Changing the World 82
The Hand-Shaped Hole 84

You Are My Daughter 87
Fathers and Daughters..88
God Made You Good, Smart, and Beautiful 89
Daddy's Little Girl..91
Ask Your Questions 92
"Why, God" 94
Let Me Make It Easier 96
Franklin D. Roosevelt...99
It's Possible 100
When You're Scared, I'll Comfort You 101
When You're Afraid, I'll Protect You 104
"Daddy's Don't Leave" 107
You Are on a Journey..109
I Enjoy My Work and What I Do, but I Love My Family Most.....111
Love in Any Language 114
A Safe Haven Called Home..116
Love Isn't Just a Word or a Feeling...118
I Am on Your Side!...120
Live Your Life with Honesty and Integrity...............................122
You Are More than Capable 125
There Is Only One You! 126
A Woman of Character...128
Always Hold Yourself to a Higher Standard 130
Whatever You Are Going Through 133
Sometimes the Best Things in Life Come in Threes.................136
You Are Never Alone 138
I'm Already There...140
You Are Imperfect (and That's Okay) 141
Rights, Wrongs, and Reasons..143
Decide Wisely 145
What Does Politics Have to Do with Anything? 148
Everybody Needs Somebody Sometime....................................159
In My Daughter's Eyes..161
A Kiss Good Night...162
Good Night, My Little Girl, I Love You the Most 164
Your Own Special Song..166
"The Father's Song" 169

"Singing Over You"	170
"Sing Over Me"	170
Because I Love You So Much	171
You Are Loved Just as You Are	174
I Believe in You!	176
Judge with Wisdom	178
Be Careful Where You Get Your Information	181
Respect Has to Be Earned	182
You Are Forgiven	184
To Err Is Human, to Forgive Is Divine	187
Stubbornness vs. Determination	189
Never Let Your Words Demean Your Character	191
"Words"	193
Be Careful to Not Allow Anger to Characterize You	194
Whatever You Face, Just Remember "I Believe in You!"	198
You Are the Center of My World	201
My Little Girl song	202
Put Your Past in Your Past…	203
Be a Woman of Integrity, Purity, and Honor	205
What I Want in a Son-in-Law	208
We Are Not an Island	209
Do Your Best to Become a Proverbs 31 Woman.	211
Integrity and Character Forever	212
You Are More Than You Know	214
If You Need Me, I Will Be There for You	215
"I Will Be There for You"	216
Let Patience Guide You	218
What Makes a Person Strong?	222
Being Honest Is Being Best	225
Live Life as a Faithful Steward	227
A Good Steward of People	228
A Good Steward of Your Work	232
Making the World a Better Place	233
A Good Steward of Your Possessions	236
Be a Good Steward of Your Wealth	238
You Are Blessed	241
Never Compromise on What Is Right and True.	242

Preferences and Convictions	244
Why Do We Compromise Our Convictions?	246
When We Fall Down, We Get Back Up	250
"We Fall Down"	251
What I Remember I Never Forget	252
I Will Be There to Help You Keep Going	254
I Will Be Here for You	255
To Help You Find Your Way	256
I Will Be That Voice You Hear	257
You Are the Moon That Shines in My Night Sky	258
Your Tears Wet My Eyes	259
Why Do You Carry Me?	261
Find Your Moral Compass	263
You Can Make a Difference	265
Stand on My Shoulders	268
Look, Daddy, Look at Me!	271
The Value of a Hug	274
What Hugging Can Do	276
"Butterfly Kisses"	278
Home of the Wise and Free	280
Be Free	283
Seriously Silly	284
Live with a Proper Perspective	287
Is Fair Really Fair	292
I Want You to Learn to Be Strong	295
Be Who I See You to Be	299
Welcome Home	301
"Welcome Back"	302
Hands	303
Find Someone to Help	307
Comfort in the Storms, and Share in the Stressed	310
What to Do When You're Feeling Stressed	311
Character and Integrity Are Everything	312
Learn How Things Work	314
You Got This	315
You Can Fix it	316
My Love for You Is Unconditional	317

Always Love God First and Family Second 318
Our Love Needs to Be 320
Dear Father in Heaven 321
Always Value Your Parents and Grandparents 322
Honor Your Parents and Grandparents 325
Neither Ignorance nor Grace 328
Push to the Future 331
Test What Is True and Don't be Gullible 334
Urgent or Important 336
Be Willing to Try Something New 339
Choose Joy and Peace 342
To Date or Not to Date 344
A Real Man Is Also a Gentleman 346
Who Is Good Enough for You? 349
"I Loved Her First" 350
There Is a Man Who Is Right for You 351
"Daddy Dance with Me" 354
Develop a Sixth Sense 356
Friend or Acquaintance 358
Have As Many Good Friends As You Can 359
Everyone Is Valuable and Is a Gift from God 362
What Can I Do 364
Prayer Is How We Connect with God 366
Learning Happens Everywhere 370
A Great Father for Your Children 373
A Wise Woman Will… 375
Be the Best Mother You Can Be 377
Build Your Home, Strengthen Your Family 379
Be the Best Wife You Can Be 381
Be the Best Mother You Can Be 383
Be the Best Domestic Engineer You Can Be (Housewife/
Home Care) 388
Be the Best Cook/Dietitian You Can Be 390
Set the Best Mood You Can 392
Be the Best You That You Can Be 394
I Am Here to Help You Raise Your Children with Strong
Family Connections and Values 397

It's Who You Are That Counts	401
Find the North Star and Let It Lead You to Safety	403
"True North" Song	405
Never Be Afraid of Hard Work	406
You Are Very Blessed	408
"Gifts from God"	410
Gifts of Love and Affection	412
Don't Forget Your Mom	414
Be Very Responsible with Your Money on Good Days	416
Give with a Generous Heart	419
I'll Be Here to Help You Finish Your Work When You're Too Tired to Finish It Yourself	421
Trust Only Those Who Are Trustworthy	423
Remember How to Love	425
If I Could, I Would Give You the World	427
Just a Few Thoughts I've Been Wanting to Share with You…	428

Introduction

I didn't start out with an intent to write a book or even a long letter to you. I was really just thinking of sitting down and jotting down some of the things I have talked with you about over the years that I think are very important and worth saying again. Then I thought about those things that we maybe never did get around to talking about. Then there are always those things that later, after thinking about them or as time went on, I thought of a much better way to say them. Before long, there were more and more things I really wanted to say and stuff I really hoped you knew. I also wanted to give you my reasoning for my convictions and why I believed the way I do.

As a father, I, too often, didn't get around to saying many of the things that really needed to be said or many things that I really didn't know how to say. All those things that I really should have said but for some reason didn't or at least didn't say well enough, I hope they will give you insight into my heart through my beliefs and convictions. I pray this will end up being a treasure for you as you get to know a part of me that maybe you didn't know before. I hope it will be an encouragement for you to know just how much I really have always loved you even when I didn't know how to say it or didn't do a good-enough job at showing it. I hope it will become a practical resource or a reference manual for you as you live your life when you may need to know what to do in certain circumstances or what we as a family believe or have done in the past. I hope it might even be a means of finally answering that number one question you and your siblings always had as you were growing up, WHY! It might even give you an opportunity to stop and have an occasion for a good thought or memory.

Then, too, if this ends up having a bigger value than just me taking time to talk with my daughter and it lives beyond to my grandchildren or if it turns out to be a help to other fathers to share those important points of love and concern for their daughters, that will just be amazing. That would then go on to prove that we fathers have more in common than we might have first thought. All of us struggle with knowing what and how to say what needs to be said to that little girl who, since the first moment we saw her, has had her little fingers wrapped so tightly around our heart—the one we would so quickly give our life for but have such a hard time trying to communicate that with.

To my daughter, please read this one section at a time, as if you and I were sitting down and I just said, "By the way, I've been wanting to talk to you about…" Then read one section at a time, and please hear my heart and how much I love you in each thought.

If this was to be helpful for another father out there, I could see you using it as a devotional to go through with your teenage daughter (on through adulthood), and then you could personalize those memories I have into one that would be meaningful for you and your daughter, or you could read it together over the phone or rewrite a section at a time in a letter, changing it to be what you would say to your daughter.

As you are going through this, read the passages; laugh at the funny stories; read the quotes, the antics, the poems; and listen to the songs that are mentioned. It's all part of trying my best to communicate the "What, How, and Why" we do what we do, as well as "the way we believe." So take whatever time you need to go through all my thoughts and feelings, page by page, point by point; and I hope and pray that my heart will be heard clearly through all that is said.

If you were to ask me what this was all about or how I would summarize this book, I would have to say it is an attempt to communicate how much I Love you, I Believe in you, and I want you to be safe. It's also a means of sharing my heart and soul with you and trying to explain why I do and believe the way I do. All of this is in the hopes that you will not just understand but also take to heart the beliefs, the whys, and the hows that make our family, I believe in many ways, unique; that having a real living and growing relationship with Jesus Christ is at the center of everything; and that He loves you so much too.

I love you,
Dad

See what great love the Father has lavished on us, that we should be called children of God! And that is what we are.
—1 John 3:1

"The Words I Would Say"

Artists: Sam Mizell, David Frey, and Ben McDonald
Sung by the Sidewalk Prophets

Three in the morning,
And I'm still awake,
So I picked up a pen and a page,
And I started writing,
Just what I'd say,
If we were face-to-face,
I'd tell you just what you mean to me,
I'd tell you these simple truths,
Be strong in the Lord and,
Never give up hope,
You're going to do great things,
I already know,
God's got His hand on you so,
Don't live life in fear,
Forgive and forget,
But don't forget why you're here,
Take your time and pray,
These are the words I would say,
Last time we spoke,
You said you were hurting,
And I felt your pain in my heart,
I want to tell you,
That I keep on praying,
Love will find you where you are,
I know 'cause I've already been there,
So please hear these simple truths,
Be strong in the Lord and,
Never give up hope,
You're going to do great things,
I already know,

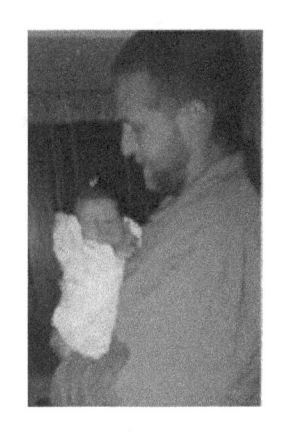

God's got His hand on you so,
Don't live life in fear,
Forgive and forget,
But don't forget why you're here,
Take your time and pray,
These are the words I would say,

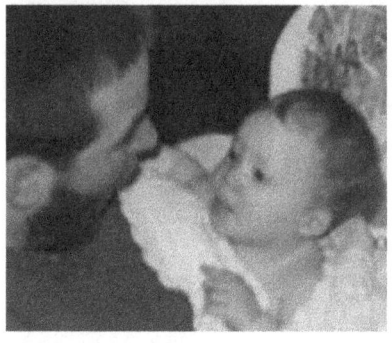

From one simple life to another,
I will say,
Come find peace in the Father,
Be strong in the Lord and,
Never give up hope,
You're going to do great things,
I already know,
God's got His hand on you so,
Don't live life in fear,
Forgive and forget,
But don't forget why you're here,
Take your time and pray,
Thank God for each day,
His love will find a way,
These are the words I would say

How Fast the Years Have Gone

I was just sitting here thinking about you and remembering in just how short of time and yet how much my world has changed…

It seems like it was just yesterday when your mother and I were newly married and just a couple of happy kids starting our lives together. It wasn't long before we started thinking how nice it would be to have a little one running around here that we could love and nurture and share our world with…and with that thought, I knew my world was about to change.

It seems like it was just yesterday when your mother and I were so excited to find out you're coming. We could hardly wait to tell everyone. I knew you were going to be my little girl even before the doctor told us. Your mom said I was silly and kept telling me "we just needed to be thankful for whatever you turned out to be," but I knew. We could hardly wait to see you. We started buying little things we thought you'd like and fixing up your room, decorating it to make it just right for you… The crib, curtains, the little mobile over your crib, the little baby booties sitting ready on your dresser… Looking around in that room so excited, hopeful, and ready, I knew my world was about to change.

It seemed like it was just yesterday when your mother told me, "I think it's time!" We rushed around and loaded up your mother's suitcase and everything she needed, got in the car, and rushed off to the hospital. Looking back, I don't remember if there was anyone else in the hospital that day. All I knew was that your mother was there and you were coming. If anyone else was there or anything else was going on, I wouldn't have known. I took off work and stayed at the hospital with you and your mom. I helped the doctor bring you into the world. I was the first person you saw. I was the first one to hold you. I cut your cord and tied it. I was so nervous the nurse was there to make sure I didn't drop you (smile), but I was there from the very beginning. It wasn't long before they said I had to give you up so your mother could have a chance to hold you too. Before long, they had to take you to get your measurements and make sure you were healthy. But I stayed at the hospital with you and your mom until we all came home together. Now that I stop to think about it, I might have even been the first one to change your diaper. We didn't like it when the nurse said that you had to go back into the nursery so they could do their blood work and other tests. I didn't want you or your mom out of my sight and made them promise as soon as they were done to bring you back to us. I didn't trust them and followed you down to the nursery and kept an eye on you and what they were doing. You were definitely the prettiest baby in the nursery. While I sat there proud as a peacock, rocking you there in the hospital room, just looking at you with your little hand wrapped around my finger, I knew my world was about to change.

It seemed like it was just yesterday we brought you home from the hospital. I didn't want to let go of you or make you sit all alone in that seat. Did I have to let go of you? You were so little for that big car seat. I had to help your mother into the front seat. She was tired and sore. She said she felt that she had just given birth to a watermelon. I said at least we know you were healthy, not like one of those skinny little babies the other parents had. I had to drive so carefully and slowly, bringing you home. No speeding tickets that day! Everybody had better get out of our way because I was bringing my little girl home. As I was driving, I was thinking, *I'm really your dad*, and I knew my world was about to change.

It seemed like it was just yesterday when people were coming over to see you and hold you. All the aunts, the uncles, the grandparents, the cousins, the friends, and the neighbors. Everyone was wanting to hold you, and before long, your mother was starting to get a little frustrated. She was telling me, "That's my baby, and I want to hold her!" Yup, you were an instant star, the center of attention, and I knew my world was about to change.

It seemed like it was just yesterday when we were trying to teach you how to crawl and then to walk. You would be there on your hands and knees teetering back and forth, just grinning and giggling. One of us would have your hands, and the other would be moving your legs. There we were both crawling back and forth across the floor with you in the middle, and we looked like a couple of crazy people, laughing hysterically. You wouldn't believe how fun and tiring it is to crawl on the floor with you, and as I finally lay there on the floor holding you over my head laughing together, I knew my world was about to change.

It seemed like it was just yesterday your mother and I were trying to see who can get you to say your first word: *Momma* or *Daddy*. "Ma...ma... Ma... Da...da... Da... Come on, you can do it. Da... da... Da... Come on, you can do it. I'll give you some ice cream if you say it, Da...da... Da..." I think I won. Then you started talking...constantly...not just full words, sentences, phrases, complete thoughts. You were amazing! You never stopped... I thought, *Is this normal? Or did I just have an exceptionally smart daughter?* Then listening to you talk away, learning to say all the stuff you were trying to say, I knew my world was about to change.

It seemed like it was just yesterday when we were trying to teach you how to walk. It wasn't long before you would stand up to the couch and then take steps along the couch or chair. Then we started encouraging you to walk while hanging onto our fingers, and we would lead you around the room or have you stand on my feet while I would walk holding your hands. Later, we would prop you up beside the couch, and we would both start calling to you to see who you would try to come to. I think it was me most of the time. You would take a couple of shaky steps and then plop down on your bottom. Then we would stand you back up by the couch again. Your mom and I would argue about which one you were trying to walk to. You were there just laughing, all grins and giggles; and then we would do it all over again and again and again. Pretty soon, you would make it all the way, and we would cheer and laugh and roll around on the floor together. Then finally sitting there on the floor with you still holding my finger, all of us tired from laughing, I knew my world was about to change.

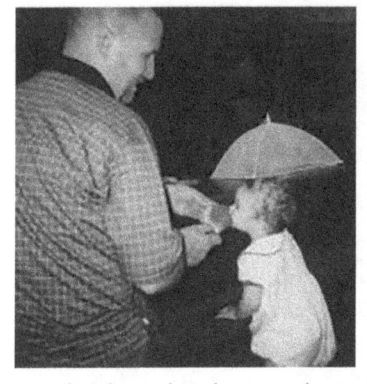

It seems like just yesterday that we got you your first bike and I was helping you learn to ride it. At first, we would work to teach you to pedal. "Forward, no, not break. Forward, yes, no, not break...," I would say. Before long, when the time was right, it was time to learn to ride with just two wheels. You were very nervous and kept telling me, "Don't let go, Daddy." We would practice in the backyard or on the street (when there were no cars). I would run alongside you. ("You're doing good, honey. You're doing good." "Don't let go, Daddy." "You're doing it." "*Don't let go.*" "You got it." "Don't let go.") Then when you weren't looking and I thought you were doing good enough, I would slowly let go but stay close enough to grab on if you started to tip or fall. A couple of times, you fell, but I caught you and kept you from getting hurt. Then we would try it again and again. Faster and faster you would go…until I couldn't keep up with you, and I realized you no longer needed me to run alongside you to keep you safe. "*I can do it myself,*" you would tell me. As I stood there watching you go and thinking about those words ("you can do it **all by yourself**"), I knew my world was about to change.

It seemed like just yesterday that you and your sisters would be coming up to the house soaking wet after going swimming in the back field, sometimes forgetting some of your clothes by the swimming hole, like shoes, socks, shorts… (A couple of years ago, I was back there, and I happened to find what was left of a pair of shorts by your old swimming spot.) Once in a while, we would have company, and we'd see you girls walking up from the back field. Your mother or I would try to run out there with a towel for you before our company would see you climbing over the gate, and if they did, we would just shake our heads and say, "It's a good thing we live in the country." You loved playing in the stream so much. Sometimes, you guys would make us just shake our heads and laugh, and I knew my world was about to change.

It seems like just yesterday we would have our baby ducks or baby chicks and you would love holding them. "*Daddy, come see. They're so soft and cute!*" you would say. Or the baby goats we got, you would have so much fun feeding them with a bottle. You kids always wanted more baby animals around. Maybe not so much the big adult ones but definitely the little ones. I have to admit I was a big pushover for letting you kids talk me into getting more and more critters. That was okay because I knew my world was about to change.

It seems like just yesterday we would go out in the field together on long walks to collect things that you were interested in or sometimes needed for school or sometimes for another project you had in mind. Sometimes, it was just because you were always interested in things like butterflies, lightning bugs, rocks, or frogs; and you would put them in a box or jar so you could look at them. Or you would put the fireflies in a special container so you could have them in your room and watch them all night long, lighting up your room with their light. You were so inquisitive and interested in everything, seeing something beautiful or wonderful in everything around us. Watching constantly curious and learning, I knew my world was about to change.

It seemed like it was just yesterday when we were taking the sleds out to go down the hills out back, getting cold, going too fast, falling off, getting our faces full of snow, then lying there just laughing or making snow angels, and then hearing you say, "Come on, Daddy, let's do it again!" So then we would hold hands, or I might even let you ride back up the hill on the sled while starting to climb back up the hill just to do it all again. There we were—tired, wet, laughing, and having fun and having a really good time together; and I knew my world was about to change.

It seems like it was just yesterday when we would all get to church and start cleaning and setting it up to be ready for the service. It was a lot of work; and we would all get tired with all the cleaning, vacuuming, printing, and cooking. I don't know if I told you or not, but I was really proud of you being there helping me, no matter if we were painting or shoveling snow or planting flowers. I was proud to have my little girl there with me... There we were sometimes just the two of us working to get ready for Sunday, or even early Sunday morning. There setting up and seeing you there with me, I knew my world was about to change.

It seems like just yesterday after working hard plowing out the driveway and then shoveling the snow into piles, we would start digging through the piles to build the best snow forts ever. When we had a lot of snow, we would end up with a fort big enough for all of us to be inside of it, and you would want to have our lunch in there together. Even just cookies or chips would be fun eating in the snow fort. I remember when you were shoveling the snow, you would toss the snow up in the air, and the dog would try to catch it and get a face full of snow, and we would laugh, and you would do it again and again. There we were, getting soaking wet, having a snowball fight, building a snowman, making snow angels, and having fun; and as I lay there in the snow with you kids piled on top of me, it was so much fun, and yet I knew my world was about to change.

It seemed like just yesterday that you were doing your first sleepover staying away from your mom and me. Of course, it was at Grandma and Grandpa's house, but still that was a big deal for us.

Somehow, you really wanted to do it even if it was just overnight. "My little girl, away from me?" I thought you needed me every day to protect, care for, and keep you safe. Now you thought someone else could do it for a day or two, and you said you'd be okay and I didn't need to be there... We took all your things you needed: a blanket, toys, clothes... last-minute instructions for Grandma and Grandpa of how to take care of our girl (as if they had no idea); and then we left you there and drove home... I didn't sleep much that night. I never slept very well when you were away, and I still don't if I don't know that you're okay...but I lay there in my bed wishing I could hear you or go check on you in your room. As much as I wished it I could have stopped it from happening, I knew I couldn't, and I knew my world was about to change.

It seems like it was just yesterday when I was first putting the toddler seat on the back of my bike. I was excited because I was finally going to get a traveling buddy. Your mom was a little unsure about the whole idea, and to tell you the truth, I was too. Biking can be dangerous, and I already had a few close calls in all the thousands of miles I had traveled on the roads through America and Canada. However, the fun of a long ride with the wind and seeing all the scenery where it's quiet enough to hear the birds and other animals as we pass...I couldn't wait to share all that with you. When you were little, you almost always fell asleep before we would get back home. Later, I bought a bike trailer; and you or you and one of your siblings or cousins would ride back there with you, with snacks and toys, having a good time, laughing, and bouncing along. Then I bought a tagalong bike, and you had to start pedaling and riding like a big girl. You weren't as crazy about that at first, but you got to liking it after a while. Finally, the day came when you were on your own bike, and we started doing the rides together. To be totally honest, once again, I was a little scared. There was a lot that could go wrong riding on the edge of the road as far as we were going. So I went over the rules of the road with you to make sure you knew where to ride, what to watch for, and what the law was pertaining to biking. Then we headed out; you were a real trouper. You did great. We had fun, and of course, we always stopped at least once to get ice cream or something special to drink. I really loved our bike rides together. Yet as good as it was, I had a subtle realization, and I knew my world was about to change.

It seems like it was just yesterday when we would go swimming and I would coax you into the water. You would be there on the side with your water wings on and life jacket and face mask…and I'd say, "It's okay. I'll catch you." Then you would jump into my arms. We would laugh, and I would toss you in the air. Then you'd run to your mother and have her watch you do it again. Before long, you would want me to chase you and throw you into the air or just let you climb up on my shoulders so you could jump into the water. Again and again and again, you never got tired of it. Sometimes I did, but I never wanted you to know it or to limit our fun together. But sometimes you guys would wear me out chasing you under water, picking you up and throwing you into the air until I could hardly move. I loved hearing you laugh; and at the end of the day, we were all sunburnt, tired, and happy. Those were such fun times together, and yet in the back of my mind, I knew my world was about to change.

It seems like just yesterday that we were all standing out in front of the house waiting. You were all dressed up and looking really pretty with your backpack on, and your mom was there holding her camera. I wasn't sure we were ready yet and almost said, "Let's just wait another year," but then that big yellow bus pulled up in front of the house. You were so excited and ready to go. There you were trying to climb up that first step on the school bus (it was so high for your little legs) and then pose for your mother to take your picture. The doors closed, and we waved until we could no longer see you. Then as we turned to go back in the house, the tears trickled down my cheeks, and once again, I knew my world was about to change.

It seems like just yesterday you were needing help with your schoolwork, reading your lesson, getting frustrated trying to figure out how to add numbers together, and needing help to make your shredded paper project and have it ready for school the next day. Next, you needed help to memorize your multiplication facts, the periodic table for science class, and your lines for the school play. You once again needed me. Yah, it made life hectic and busy, but it was great, because you might not have known it, but I needed you too. I was so glad to be your dad. Then, too, in the midst of that when you said, "Dad, I need it by tomorrow. Can you help me?" I had this nagging feeling that I knew my world was about to change.

It seems like it was just yesterday when we were all going out canoeing together. You were concerned but not scared. I don't think you were ever really scared about anything. You wanted to be in my canoe because we were the fastest and they could never tip us over. "Get them, Dad." "Catch them, Dad." "Go faster, Dad." Then before long, you were big enough to learn how to paddle so you would be in the front and I would be in the back... It was great being together, talking about anything and everything. Splashing each other, and racing your siblings in their canoes. There on the river with my little girl in my boat, as good as it was there together, floating, splashing, spinning, and racing the others, somehow, I knew my world was about to change.

It seems like just yesterday when I finally said okay and thought you were old enough. So I began teaching you to drive the lawn mower, then the four-wheeler, and later (even though you didn't really like it) the tractor, I would have you ride with me. Then later I'd have you sit in front of me, and then you would steer. Next, I would let you sit in the seat, and I'd sit on the back. Soon I would stand there with my heart beating out of my chest praying for God's angels to protect you while you were driving it solo. Your mom always thought you kids weren't quite ready and could never watch. I wouldn't let it show, but I would have my heart pounding in my chest and could hardly breathe, but there you were, and you were doing it. I was **so** proud of you, and, oh, how I knew my world was about to change.

It seems like just yesterday you wanted me to do one of the scariest things for me, teach you to drive the car. So you and I went out into the field with the old truck. Some people wondered why we always had an old stick shift truck. Well, I knew If I could teach you to drive a stick shift, you could drive any automatic vehicle. Round and round we went, clunking, grinding, and stalling the truck; but after a while, you were getting it. "Equal gas and clutch." "More gas, less clutch." "Let's try it again." "Go smoothly, and you can get it."

"You almost got it. Don't give up." Then later we went out on the road we would go and then practiced more. You soon were doing pretty good. Next thing, before I knew it, you had your permit and then your license. Then before I could grasp all the changes here, the thing I was dreading the most, you were driving off down the road on your own. "Why did I get suckered into that!" I didn't want to teach you something that would take you away from me. I just wanted to teach you because you needed me. You needed me, and I needed that. You didn't know it, but I would be so nervous until you finally pulled back into the driveway again. Then once again, after thanking God for keeping you safe, I knew my world was about to change.

It seems like just yesterday when all of a sudden you started saying things like those boys are cute. It shocked me! It caught me off guard. I didn't know what to say. "What was my little girl doing noticing boys?" "She is way too young." I was your dad, the only guy in your life. NOOO! Not now, not yet! I tried to get you to wait until you were…thirty years old before you thought about boys, but you would only laugh and think I was joking, but I wasn't. Then in the cold grips of reality, I knew my world was about to change.

It seems like just yesterday when you asked me if you could go out on a date with some boy—a boy whom I didn't know or trust; and I didn't know what to say. *I don't like him. I don't trust him, not with my girl. I know what he is thinking. I know what boys want. Why is he looking at her like that? I think I need to go along with them, if I even let them go at all. Why can't they be happy just being here at our house with us where I can watch them and keep my girl safe from that punk? I think we are fun enough here. She is My Little Girl. I would talk with him and try to hopefully scare him away.* I'll show him my guns, knives, swords. If that doesn't work, I'd let him know I still have some open holes in the back field that are very deep *that no one knows about...* Sometimes, you would catch me staring at him, trying to make him sweat, and you'd give me "that look." I didn't really care. He was not good enough for you! As far as I'm concerned, no one is good enough for my little girl... Yet I'd finally give in, and off you would go with **HIM**; and once again feeling a little jealous and brokenhearted, I knew my world was about to change even more.

It seemed like just yesterday when all of a sudden, I realized you were growing up. When did this happen? Why wasn't I informed? I looked for you, and you weren't here. I searched in your room thinking you might be in there, but you were gone; your clothes were gone. I went to the window hoping I might see you riding your bike or playing in the yard, but you weren't there either. I ran through the backyard, the back field. I called for you, but you weren't there... *Where did you go? How long were you going to be away? Who is going to protect you? To care for you? To watch out for you? Who else loves you as much as I do? I waited by the phone hoping to hear from you, but it didn't ring. Don't you realize You still need me...? Don't you realize I still need you?* I knew my world was about to change forever.

So here I am, sitting here and wondering, "Where has the time gone?" I'm once again thinking about my little girl, wishing at any moment you would come running around the corner with your pigtails bouncing and climb up into my lap. Maybe you would bring a book you want me to read. Or you would show me some neat treasure you just found, or you would ask me, "Why don't chickens talk?" Or maybe you would sit next to me and ask me to help you with your math or tell me about your day or ask me what I thought of that boy. I looked out at the swing swinging in the breeze and for a second hoping I'd see you there and hear you call out, "*Daddy, come push me!*" I was walking through the Quonset building the other day and saw the bike you used to ride and wished I could see all you kids hurting around getting ready for one of our bike rides again and hear you say, "*Dad, can you fix my chain?*" I don't know what you are doing right now, but maybe, wherever you are right now, you might just remember one of our good memories together and remember just how much I love you. I am proud of you, and you might even feel right now wherever you are, a gentle hug I'm giving you. But whatever you are doing or feeling or going through right now, once again I realize my world has really changed, and I miss you more than you will ever know!

The Note

Once there was a dad who found a note from his daughter that she had written after a bad day at school. She wrote, "*Today, I got a 'C' on my test. At lunch, they ran out of pizza, and my friend wouldn't play with me during recess. This was the worst day of my life!*" Many years later, on her wedding day, Her dad presented that note back to her, framed it, and added the note "I hope this always remains true. That, that was truly the worst day of your life." No matter how bad things seem to us today, once we get to the other side of our problems and look back on them, we will see how simple our problems really were.

Where Are You Heading?

The outcome of every situation depends on which way you are heading, and if you are heading the right way, it will all be okay soon.

And we know that for those who love God all things work...know that all things work together for good to them that love God, to them who are doing what God has called them to do.
—Romans 8:28

Always remember not to make promises that you cannot keep.
Or say you'll do things you have no intentions of doing.
Don't build false hope just to make it easier for you.
Or tell an intentional lie.
Remember to be thankful, listen to encouragement, and hold onto hope.
Don't believe every compliment that comes your way, especially if they are selling something.
Don't take a critic's words to heart, but if you can learn something from what they say, use it.
One who does their best is better than one who does good without really trying.
Think on what is good.
Hold fast onto what is true.
Try to think the best of everyone, and yet expect them to live up to it.
If you say you will do something, then try your best to follow through and do it.

*****

I know there have been times when I forgot. There were times when other things have happened that kept it from happening or things changed where it was no longer relevant. Other than that, I have always tried to keep my promises. However, I do want to apologize to you for those promises I didn't or couldn't keep. Promises are important. I am sure there were some that I didn't realize how important it was to you and you felt hurt when it didn't happen. I am sorry for those! I didn't mean to hurt or disappoint you. Please forgive me.

Remember, no matter how bad, how serious, or how severe our current situation may currently be, our troubles don't last forever.

There's a sign I want to make that said, "Beware, this family is protected by a slightly crazy, overly aggressive, and highly protective father" (me)!

> *Hypocrisy can afford to be magnificent in its promises, for never intending to go beyond promise, it costs nothing.* (Edmund Burke)

> *Promises are like crying babies in a theater, they should be carried out at once.* (Norman Vincent Peale)

> *Losers make promises they often break. Winners make commitments they always keep.* (Denis Waitley)

> *Blessed is she who has believed that the Lord would fulfill His promises to her.* **(Luke 1:45)**

> *I thought about the wrong direction in which I was headed, and turned around and came running back to you.* **(Psalm 119:59–60 TLB)**

> *There's a way that looks harmless enough; but look again—it leads straight to hell.* **(Proverbs 16:25 MSG)**

Red Robin
Artist: Clark Richard

She is just a baby
She's my little girl
She looks like her mommy
Sporting little curls
She's got lots to learn
Though she is sure to know
That I'll quietly spot her
Anywhere she goes

Now our little lady's out with Daddy for the day
She fought the yawns but couldn't stay awake
As I place her in the car
She's out like a light
'Cause she knows I'll get her home all right

She went from the backseat
To hands at ten and two
College came too quickly
Her leaving feels too soon
Now I swore I'd be strong but
These are happy tears
'Cause I get even prouder
With every passing year

Now her weekends will be full of hanging with her friends
But someone needs a call before night's end
She knows I'll toss and turn
No chance I'll sleep tonight
Till I know she's made it home all right

If time could only give me
A moment to reflect
To smile on all that has been
To treasure what is left
Though I won't always be here
This you surely know
That I'll quietly spot you
Anywhere you go

And when we are apart remember it is not the end
You know enough to know we'll meet again
I'll be waiting by the gate
Standing just inside
Till I know you've made it home all right
Till I know you've made it home all right
Let's go home

I'm on Guard while You Are Out

I sleep best when I know you are safe and well.
I will risk everything to keep you safe as long as you're alive.
If you're sick, I'll care for you.
If you're sad, I'll cheer you up.
If you're crying, I'll hold you.
If you're lost, I'll find you.
I will never give up on you!
If you're in need, I'll help you.
If you're attacked, I'll defend you.
If you're in danger, I'll protect you.
Nothing or no one will ever be able to stop me.
If you're ever in need of me I'll be there.
I will go through a brick wall with my bare hands to save you from danger.
If the house was on fire and you were in there I would get you out.
I will fight a grizzly with my bare hands to keep you safe.
My warning to the world,
"Don't mess with my family if you know what's good for you."
I should have a sign made for our property with "Forget the Dog, beware of the Dad!"
Even on your worst day, you will always be a beauty queen winner to me.

*****

> *No need to worry about your teenagers when they're not at home. A national survey revealed that they all go to the same place—"out"—and they all do the same thing—"nothing."* (Bruce Lansky)

Every father's first and highest calling is "Protector" of his wife and daughter, from danger, and perceived dangers, and he won't eat or sleep or do any normal activity until he knows they are safe, and God help anyone that looks like a threat or danger to them.

Getting home before curfew is a way to protect your boyfriend from an overly tired guard with a hairpin trigger from mistaking him as the enemy. Oh and here, Father/guard/soldier all mean the same thing.

For I am sure that neither death nor life, nor angels nor rulers, nor things present nor things to come, nor powers, nor height nor depth, nor anything else in all creation, will be able to separate us from the love of God in Christ Jesus our Lord. **(Romans 8:38–39)**

The Lord is near to the brokenhearted and saves the crushed in spirit. **(Psalm 34:18 ESV)**

Discretion will protect you, and understanding will guard you. Wisdom will save you from the ways of wicked men, from men whose words are perverse. **(Proverbs 2:11–12 NIV)**

More than Just a Pretty Face

Always remember that your value is more than the way you look.
Always know your value goes far beyond anything you could ever do.
I knew you before almost anyone else knew anything about you.
I prayed for you and wanted you before you were conceived.
You definitely were not an accident. You were planned and wanted.
You will always be wanted,
Always be valued,
Always be my precious treasure,
Always be my daughter,
Always be my little girl.
I will still believe in you even when you don't believe in yourself.
I will still always believe in you even if no one else does.
You will always be worth the world to me, because
You are and will always be my little girl.

*****

It was my father who taught me to value myself. (Dawn French)

You are much more than just a pretty face, a very smart thinker, a leader, a skillful crafter, strong, brave, and resourceful, a free spirit, a fun person to be around, a good friend... You're my Daughter! (Me)

> *The beauty of a woman is seen in her eyes, because that is the doorway to her heart, the place where love resides. True beauty in a woman is reflected in her soul. It's the caring that she lovingly gives, the passion that she shows and the beauty of a woman only grows with passing years.* (Audrey Hepburn)

> *Momma always said that "beauty is only skin deep but ugly goes all the way to the core."* (Unknown)

> *It's what is filled into the balloon that takes it high and not its colour.* (Shreya Gawde)

> *Momma always said that Beauty is as Beauty does.* (Forest Gump)

When I see my daughter, I see someone beautiful,
She has a beautiful spirit and is easy to get along with and a joy to be around.
She has a beautiful heart and is considerate, kind, helpful, giving, and loving.
She has a beautiful personality and is one who can laugh at anything, including herself.
She has a beautiful mind and is constantly learning and takes control of her thoughts.
She has a beautiful soul and she thinks deeply about her actions and the world around her.
She is spiritually beautiful and she knows God and the way to find peace with God.
She is also, of course, physically beautiful and always keeps me on my guard

watching out for her. And I'm proud of her because she is my daughter.

She is worth far more than rubies. **(Proverbs 31:10)**

Since you are precious and honored in My sight, and because I love you,
I will give people in exchange for you, nations in exchange for your life. **(Isaiah 43:4 NIV)**

Are not two sparrows sold for a penny? Yet not one of them will fall to the ground outside your Father's care. And even the very hairs of your head are all numbered. So don't be afraid; you are worth more than many sparrows. **(Matthew 10:29-31 NIV)**

A Smile

A smile brightens your eyes
Makes you look nicer
Makes you more approachable
Smooths the wrinkles
Makes you age more beautifully
Changes your outlook
It positively affects those around you
Releases endorphins
It can even make you healthier
Even a good fake smile has great benefits
for you and everyone around you
You almost always get one back
whenever you give one away
So don't forget to put a smile on your pretty face

Don't be a Grinch

Cranky, crusty, crotchety, crabby, cantankerous, curmudgeonly, churlish, cross, cynical, critiquing, criticizing, or complaining person.

I have a friend that believes that cynicism is his special gifting or his superpower. He is someone who can pick apart anyone and anything. If someone sings a song, it was too loud or soft, too dramatic or not passionate enough, off-key or off tempo, not as good as the original, not the right song, or not done the way he would do it. When I would tell a joke, it would never be funny enough or as good as he would tell, or he would tell me I at the very least had to practice a lot more before I could be as good as he would do it. When we would go see a movie, it was never good, because it could have been better if only they would have done it differently. It's always frustrating to share or do anything fun with him, because he will be critical or even seem grumpy about anything that everyone else might think is great, funny, and well done. He would always try to tell you how anything that is done could have been better. All we wanted to do was to enjoy it for what it was, not to learn how to improve it or what they should have done differently. His attitude made it hard to enjoy being around him or to want him to be included in whatever we were doing. He was always trying to "one up" what everyone said or did, or he would try to knock everything that was done or said down a notch. Even though we liked the guy as a person and knew he was smart, we just didn't like him always trying to prove it.

It's really the same with a person who always grumbles or complains about everything. Nothing is ever good enough for them. They can never just enjoy what anyone is

| 27

doing or just try to do their best they can with what they have to work with. It's difficult for them to ever say that was good, because they are thinking it really wasn't very good or I could have done it much better. They definitely wouldn't do the accepted courtesy laugh over a "Dad joke" if it wasn't the absolute funniest joke ever.

I have always tried to find a way to enjoy every job I have ever done, no matter how hard or frustrating it is. Find a way to enjoy it, as much as possible, anyway. Some things are really difficult, and some situations are very difficult, but there can always be something interesting or fun in pretty much everything. Sometimes, you might even have to bring your own good thoughts or fun into a situation, like spending your time thinking about something or some place that is more enjoyable (as long as you can still get your job done well and safely, that is). If you are thinking about sitting under a coconut tree on the beach in Hawaii while you are cleaning a pen in the barn and keep finding yourself sitting in the corner, you might have to find a different happy thought.

Most grumbling, nitpicking, and complaining are just bad habits that bother everyone but the person doing it. Ask the people around you if you do that very much or at all, and try to change it with God's help. I know that I love you and enjoy being around you, but if you are careful to make sure you are being as positive and encouraging as possible, then others will enjoy being around you too.

> *Do all things without **grumbling** or questioning (some versions say **complaining**).* (Philippians 2:14 ESV)

> *You haven't been **complaining** against us, you know, but against God.* (Exodus 16:6–8 MSG)

> *Look! The Master comes with thousands of holy angels to bring judgment against them all, convicting each person of every defiling act of shameless sacrilege, of **every dirty word** they have spewed of*

> their pious filth. These are the **grumpers**, the **bellyachers**, grabbing for the biggest piece of the pie, **talking big, saying anything they think will get them ahead**. (Jude 1:14–16 MSG)

> But understand that with an **attitude** like that, there'll be no glory in it for you. (Judges 4:9–10 MSG)

We need to have the same **attitude** in our everyday life as Christ had. Although He came from heaven and deserved all the glory and everything good, **He didn't complain or grumble** about everything or how unfair it was for Him. He lived His life full of love and compassion, fully content in following the plan set before Him ("For the glory set before Him" [Matthew 12:1–2].) no matter where it led. Worse yet is He already knew where it was leading Him.

> *Think of yourselves the way Christ Jesus thought of Himself. He had equal status with God but didn't think so much of Himself that He had to cling to the advantages of that status no matter what. Not at all. When the time came, He set aside the privileges of deity and took on the status of a slave, became human! Having become human, He stayed human. It was an incredibly humbling process. He didn't claim special privileges. Instead, He lived a selfless, obedient life and then died a selfless, obedient death—and the worst kind of death at that—a crucifixion.* (Philippians 2:5–8 MSG)

"The Fruit of the Spirit" (Galatians 5:22–23) is not just in action that we need to emulate, but it's even more the attitudes that we need to have and show through our everyday way we interact with people. Nowhere in that list do you find anything that would encourage us to be grouchy or grumpy, or respond in a cynical or complaining manner. It seems that the more we are like Jesus, the more we are filled with the Holy Spirit, and the more kind and congenial we tend to be with others. I guess that is why not only did the adults crowd in around Jesus and follow Him everywhere but also the children always wanted to be near Him (Luke 18:16).

People who are critical or quick to put down others are really judgmental of those people or let people think that they think that they are better. It's a real bad attitude for a Christian to display, if not completely sinful, that we are warned to beware of it: *"And whoever demeans and insults a fellow believer is answerable to the congregation"* (Matthew 5:22 TPT). Even if you can do it better or the other didn't do it as good as someone else could, "Does It Really Matter?" Unless you are trying to help the person and the person is wanting to get your help, you are just causing needless harm to that person. If it's very important or vital that the person is corrected or helped, go ahead and share your knowledge, but be careful to do it in a way that builds the other person up and doesn't tear them down. *"Don't say anything that would hurt another person. Instead, speak only what is good so that you can give help wherever it is needed. That way, what you say will help those who hear you"* (Ephesians 4:29 NOG).

It's okay to not show all your knowledge or ability when it really doesn't matter or benefit anyone. Then, too, it is always okay to let someone think they did a good job even if you really think it wasn't as good as it could have or should have been. Especially if there is no big reason to criticize or critique their effort or if it will only cause hurt feelings, keep it to yourself. *"Humble yourselves before the Lord, and He will exalt you"* (James 4:10 ESV). It won't make you less of a person if you don't show your superiority in every given situation. It will actually make you a better person just because you helped them to feel better about themselves.

> *I want to work with happy, good people, who have a positive outlook. Not those who are grumpy, complaining and throw diva behaviour.* (Vaani Kapoor)

> *I like to have everything smiley and happy for my husband. Men don't want to see a grumpy face at the end of a hard day.* (Nita Ambani)

> *You don't criticize or critique your teammates if they're having a hard time. You try to encourage them just like you hope that they'll encourage you.* (Mookie Betts)

Always Remember to Laugh

Laughter is not just a means to respond to something funny.
It is also a way to cope and deal with difficult situations and people.
It is a quick way to change our perspective and outlook in life.
It changes the mood of a difficult situation.
It can help us find hope in a situation.
It changes the people around us.
It can help us calm down.
It changes our outlook.
It can bring healing.
It helps us not to take ourselves too seriously when we can laugh at ourselves.
It can help heal relationships that are broken or hurting.
It can even be as helpful to our physical bodies as taking medicine when we are sick and it also releases chemicals into our blood system that boost our immune system.

"Laughter Just Like a Medicine"

Artist: BeBe Winans

Now tomorrow may bring
One or two things
That you don't like, oh
And if it does
You can rise above
And win the fight
One way of winning is a laughter
(Laughter does good, just like a
medicine)

Does good
Just like a medicine
(Just like a medicine)
Yeah, yeah
Oh yeah
(Just like a medicine)
So keep on laughing
(Laughter does good, like a
 medicine)
(Just like a medicine)
And it works y'all
(Just like a medicine)
So when they lie on you

(Laugh about it)
When they talk about you
(Laugh about it)
When they scandalize your name
(Oh, laugh about it)
That's when you take your
(Take your medicine)
Let it go down, let it go down
(Laugh about it)

Let it heal your broken heart
(Laugh about it)
Laughter will heal your broken heart
(Oh, laugh about it)
When you take your
(Take your medicine)
Now let me hear you laugh, say...

So don't forget how to laugh. Practice it even when you don't feel it. It's contagious. Even when you feel like fighting, find a way to laugh and not at someone else. (Even though it might help you feel better, that might not help the situation.)

A day without laughter is a day wasted. (Charlie Chaplin)

Life's better when you're laughing. (Unknown)

Laughter is poison to fear. (George R. R. Martin)

There is nothing in the world so irresistibly contagious as laughter and good humor. (Unknown)

I have not seen anyone dying of laughter, but I know millions who are dying because they are not laughing. (Unknown)

She is clothed with strength and dignity; she can laugh at the days to come. **(Proverbs 31:25)**

Blessed are ye that hunger now: for ye shall be filled. Blessed are ye that weep now: for ye shall laugh. **(Luke 6:21)**

He will once again fill your mouth with laughter and your lips with shouts of joy. **(Job 8:21)**

For the despondent, every day brings trouble; for the happy heart, life is a continual feast. **(Proverbs 15:15)**

The Power to Cause Laughter

I like to laugh and I like to be with you because you can make me happy or cause me to laugh.

The world today is full of seriousness, fears and drama at every turn, and there is good reason to keep your eyes open and never let your guard down. I'm not wanting you to let your guard down and put yourself in danger. I just want you to make sure that you never forget how to laugh and always try to wear a smile.

I'll always try to bring a smile to your face or make you laugh even if you think it's embarrassing or makes me look foolish.

To make you happy makes me happy.

To make you smile makes me glad.

Your laughter lifts my heart, brightens my day, and gives me hope.

You have a contagious laugh and a beautiful smile that fills my world with sunshine.

"Laugh Out Loud" Song
Jason Gray

He said bring to me your heavy heart
Take my hand and we'll go whistling in the dark
Here we go now!

Ha, don't it make you wanna laugh out loud?
Ooh, ooh, and shout, "Hallelujah!"
Oh yeah, if you got joy go and let it on out
Ha ha ha ha, laugh out loud…

*****

After a while you just want to be with the one who makes you laugh. (Mr. Big)

You can tell how smart people are by what they laugh at. (Tina Fey)

They laugh at me because I'm different. I laugh at them because they are all the same. (Unknown)

If you lose the power to laugh, you lose the power to think. (Clarence Darrow)

Do you want to know how to make God laugh? Tell Him your plans. (Marian Keyes)

I have no greater joy than to hear that my children are walking in the truth. **(3 John 1:4 NIV)**

Finally, my friends, keep your minds on whatever is true, pure, right, holy, friendly, and proper. Don't ever stop thinking about what is truly worthwhile and worthy of praise. You know the teachings I gave you, and you know what you heard me say and saw me do. So follow my example. And God, who gives peace, will be with you. **(Philippians 4:6–9 CEV)**

See what great love the Father has lavished on us, that we should be called children of God! And that is what we are! **(1 John 3:1a)**

The Lord your God is with you, the Mighty Warrior who saves. He will take great delight in you; in His love He will no longer rebuke you, but will rejoice over you with singing. **(Zephaniah 3:17)**

God has given me cause to laugh, and all who hear of it will laugh with me. **(Genesis 21:6)**

We celebrated with laughter and joyful songs. In foreign nations it was said, "The Lord has worked miracles for His people." A joyful heart makes a cheerful face, but with a heartache comes depression. **(Proverbs 126:2 CEV)**

You Are a Treasure

Every treasure has a great value to the one it belongs to. It is precious to them, and they feel it is worth keeping forever. The value of a treasure doesn't just decrease over time nor does it decrease because of a change in one's circumstance. A real treasure only increases in value as time goes by and the desire to have it or be with it continues to increase.

You are a treasure to me. A special gift from God. "*A woman of virtue is worth far more than jewels*" (**Proverbs 31:10**).

XOXO

I will always have time to give you hugs and kisses
I might not know how and I might feel awkward or even a little afraid that I might offend you, but I always enjoy sitting next to you on the couch or putting my arm around you while I sit next to you. I will always want to hold, hug, and kiss my little girl no matter how old she gets.
I am here to calm your fears
I am here to hold you
I am here to hug
I am here to share your tears
I am here to listen to you
I am here to encourage
I am here to help you when you stray
I am here to care for you
I am here to bandage your hurts
I am here to make the pain go away
I am here to defend you
I am here to fight for you
I am here to keep you safe and then
I am here to support you
I am here to pick you up
I am here to help you run again
If life is rough for you
And Times get tough
Just remember I'm here for you
And no matter what may come your way
I am here for you.
Because ILU

*****

Dad, your guiding hand on my shoulder will remain with me forever. (Unknown)

The father of a daughter is nothing but a high-class hostage. A father turns a stony face to his sons, berates them, shakes his antlers, paws the ground, snorts, runs them off into the underbrush, but when his daughter puts her arm over his shoulder and says, "Daddy, I need to ask you something," he is a pat of butter in a hot frying pan. (Garrison Keillor)

To her, the name of father was another name for love. (Fanny Fern, *Fresh Leaves*)

When I was a boy of 14, my father was so ignorant I could hardly stand to have the old man around. But when I got to be 21, I was astonished at how much he had learned in seven years. (Mark Twain)

Steadfast love and faithfulness meet; righteousness and peace kiss each other. (**Psalm 85:10 ESV**)

So he got up and came to his father. But while he was still a long way off, his father saw him and felt compassion for him, and ran and embraced him and kissed him. (**Luke 15:20**)

He left the oxen and ran after Elijah and said, "Please let me kiss my father and my mother, then I will follow you." And he said to him, "Go back again, for what have I done to you?" (**1 Kings 19:20**)

He kisses the lips. Who gives the right answer. (**Proverbs 24:26**)

You Are Beautiful

You, my daughter, are a beautiful woman whom any man would feel honored to be seen with. You are second to none. You are beautiful when you are all dressed up and still look nice when you are just bumming around with your grubby clothes on. Don't ever think you are less than anyone else or let anyone tell you that you are not as pretty as someone else. You are perfect just the way God made you, and I'm very proud to be your dad!

> *Thou hast been beautified above the sons (daughters) of men, Grace hath been poured into thy lips, Therefore hath God blessed thee to the age.* **(Psalm 45:2 YLT)**

> *Nowhere in all the land were there found women as beautiful as…(My) daughters, and their father granted them an inheritance along with their brothers.* **(Job 42:15 NLT)**

May I Have the Next Dance?

I will never mind how my toes may feel
    As long as you are dancing with me.

    There have been a lot of different kinds of dances in my life time, and I used to be a pretty good dancer in my day, but what I liked best was the slow dances of the '70s and '80s (and "NO" you didn't have to be slow to dance it). I would have to say that the flashy disco dancing was the most fun. I'd be glad to show you if I could just find my high-rise shoes, bell-bottom pants, and silk shirt; and, oh yes, I need my fro too.

    Just being with you does me better than your stepping on my toes could ever do me harm. I'll always save a dance for you.

Cinderella

Artist: Steven Curtis Chapman

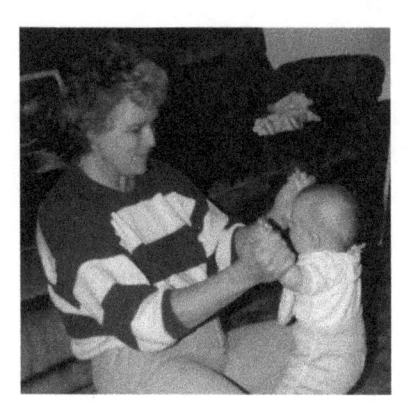

She spins and she sways
To whatever song plays
Without a care in the world
And I'm sitting here wearing
The weight of the world on my shoulders

It's been a long day
And there's still work to do
She's pulling at me saying

"Dad, I need you
"There's a ball at the castle
"And I've been invited
"And I need to practice my dancing
"Oh, please, Daddy, please"

So I will dance with Cinderella
While she is here in my arms
'Cause I know something the prince
    never knew
Oh, I will dance with Cinderella
I don't wanna miss even one song
'Cause all too soon the clock will strike midnight
And she'll be gone…

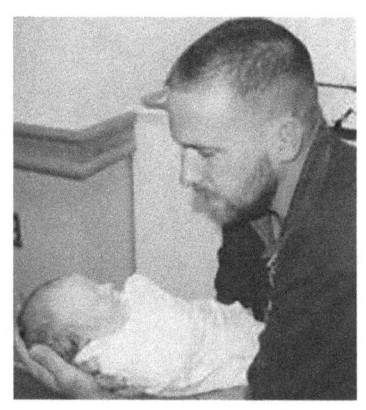

*****

You are the most important thing to me now. The most important thing to me ever. (Stephenie Myer)

Only the hug of a daughter can melt the hardest heart and make the biggest, baddest Daddy cry. (Me)

Put music to our troubles and we'll dance them away. (Unknown)

I don't remember the song and I don't remember the place or when it was but I do remember who I was with, He was my Daddy and I was his little princess. (Unknown)

A time to weep and a time to laugh; A time to mourn and a time to dance. **(Ecclesiastes 3:4)**

You have turned for me my mourning into dancing; You have loosed my sackcloth and girded me with gladness. **(Psalm 30:11)**

Let them praise His name with dancing, making melodies to Him with tambourine and lyre! **(Psalm 149:3 ESV)**

Then shall the young women rejoice in the dance, and the young men and the old shall be merry. I will turn their mourning into joy; I will comfort them, and give them gladness for sorrow. **(Jeremiah 31:13 ESV)**

Praise Him with tambourine and dance; praise Him with strings and pipe! **(Psalm 150:4 ESV)**

A Place Called Home

I hope you will always know that you have a place to come home to.

The *Oxford Dictionary* says that a *home* is "an enjoyable, happy place where you can live, laugh, and learn. It's somewhere where you are loved, respected, and cared for."

Home is a place where time seems to stand still, though years may pass and many things may change; yet everything still seems to be the same, familiar, comfortable, and safe.

Even when I went away to join the Marine Corps, it was very important and comforting for me to know that no matter how I felt or what I was going through, I could always come home and be welcome. There was no real reason required, and I could stay at least for a while with no questions asked. Oh, I still had to follow their rules and not be assuming of them or their time. But I was always welcome, and it always felt like home to me. That gave me a sense of peace and a place of rest if I ever needed it. A Safe Place, a Haven, a Home.

I hope my house, wherever it is at the time, will always feel like home to you so it will always be a warm, inviting, and safe place where the door is always open for you and where you will always know you are welcome and wanted.

> *When I was growing up, we always had a big family dinner at around noon on Sunday. I still love that whenever it is possible to gather the family together.* (Samuel Alito)

> *There is no mile as long the final one that leads back home.* (Katherine Marsh)

> *It is amazing how all our paths of rebellion tend to lead us straight back home.* (Kristine Hunter)

A story about family, first loves second chances, and the moments in life that leads you back home. (Nicholas Sparks)

I think you travel to search and you come back home to find yourself there. (Chimamanda Ngaozi Aidichie)

My people will live in peaceful dwelling places, in secure homes, in undisturbed places of rest. **(Isaiah 32:18)**

The LORD's curse is on the house of the wicked, but He blesses the home of the righteous. **(Proverbs 3:33)**

There are many homes up there where My Father lives, and I am going to prepare them for your coming. When everything is ready, then I will come and get you, so that you can always be with Me where I am. If this weren't so, I would tell you plainly. **(John 14:2–3 TLB)**

Can I Help You?

I hope there is never a day that you think you are too old to need me.

I hope between my person, my knowledge, my skill, my wisdom, or my experience you will always value my opinion, my input, my help, or at least our time together.

I will always value my time with you and desire to be with you and always hope that you still think of me as still being valuable to you. Because you will always be valuable to me.

When my daughter says, "Daddy, I need you!" I wonder if she has any idea that I need her a billion times more. (Stanley Behrman)

To a father growing old, nothing is dearer than a daughter. (Euripides)

The commandment to honor parents was given to ensure that the elderly, although they may not feel wanted by family or society, are still given their appropriate reward. (Laura Schlessinger)

The elders are the history and mirror of the living past. Study them to brighten your life and future. (Ehsan Sehgal)

It's only when you grow up, and step back from him, or leave him for your own career and your own home—it's only then that you can measure his greatness and fully appreciate it. Pride reinforces love. (Margaret Truman)

Even when you're old, I'll take care of you. Even when your hair turns gray, I'll support you. I made you and will continue to care for you. I'll support you and save you. To whom will you compare Me and make Me equal? To whom will you compare Me so that we can be alike? (Isaiah 46:4–5)

Is not wisdom found among the aged? Does not long life bring understanding? To God belong wisdom and power; counsel and understanding are his. (Job 12:12–13)

What do you know that we don't know, or that you understand and that isn't clear to us? We have both the gray-haired and the aged with us, and they are far older than your father. Are God's encouragements inconsequential to you, even a word that has been spoken gently to you? (Job 15:9–11)

You Might Not Know

Just because you are my daughter, you make my world more complete.

My world is a much better place just because you're in it.

Though I have made many mistakes in my life, you definitely are not one of them.

There was a time when I was very happy about a truck I thought I really wanted, and so I purchased it; however, before long, I started to have a lot of problems with it. I had it towed to the mechanic to be fixed. He had to repair, replace, and rebuild things on it. Then soon after that, I noticed that all of the joy and happiness I once felt about getting this dream truck that I really wanted and had to have was gone. Over the years, there were other vehicles that I really wanted and then purchased, yet after a few years, it came down with a bad case of our Wisconsin car cancer, and all my pride for owning and driving it was gone. There are also all of those things we all have bought: computers, cell phones, or other gadgets that at the time we thought we really needed or wanted yet later came to strongly dislike. Most of the time, the same strong feeling we had when we liked, wanted, and even had to have it, in the beginning, over time, we would soon have a similarly strong but opposite feeling of dislike, then a feeling that you don't want, and then finally an equally strong desire to get rid of that very same thing we once had to have; in the end, we loathe it.

However, family should always be a different story. Family members might at times be difficult, be challenging, be frustrating, be exasperating, and make you crazy; yet in the end, I always love them and am thankful for them. I might wish that they would change the things they do, the lifestyle they have chosen, or the choices that have made; but I still love them and desire to be with them.

If I could go back and change all the stuff in my life, I would definitely have chosen better vehicles over the years. However, more importantly, I would have chosen to be a much better husband, father, grandfather, uncle, brother, nephew, grandson, friend, student, pastor, teacher, interpreter… But there is one thing I still wouldn't change, and that is you! I would still want to be your father. No matter how screwed up, messed up, or bad things can be, just having you makes my life more complete.

> *You are not a mistake. You are not a problem to be solved. Treat yourself with outrageous kindness beginning today.* (Geneen Roth)

> *You are loved. You are valuable. You are crafted with beauty and purpose. I treasure you and this world needs you. There is no one like you. You don't need to look like the rest or talk like the rest or be like the rest. This world needs you as you are. There is no truth in the lie that you don't matter. You are loved. You were put here for a reason. You were not an accident. You are not a mistake.* (Curt Mega)

> *You are not important because of how long you live, you are important because of how effective you live.* (Myles Munroe)

> *You are important and you matter. Your feelings matter. Your voice matters. Your story matters. Your life matters. Always.* (Unknown)

I may not be perfect but when I look at my children I know that I got something in my life perfectly right. (Unknown)

I knew you before I formed you in your mother's womb. Before you were born I set you apart and appointed you as My prophet to the nations. **(Jeremiah 1:5)**

For we are God's masterpiece. He has created us anew in Christ Jesus, so we can do the good things He planned for us long ago. **(Ephesians 2:10)**

But you are not like that, for you are a chosen people. You are royal priests, a holy nation, God's very own possession. As a result, you can show others the goodness of God, for He called you out of the darkness into His wonderful light. **(1 Peter 2:9)**

You Are Matchless

My dear daughter never forget that
You are like nobody else on earth
You are created exactly right
You are one of a kind
You are unique with your personality,
You are unique with your talents,
You are unique with your abilities,
You are unique with your strengths,
You are unique with your weaknesses,
You are unique with your looks,
You are unique with your quirks,
You are completely unique in every way!
God has specific plans for your life based on all the unique combinations of who you are. This is so exciting! And I can't wait to see what God has planned!

> *"For I know the plans I have for you," declares the Lord, "plans to prosper you and not to harm you, plans to give you hope and a future."* **(Jeremiah 29:11 NIV)**

> *But when He who had set me apart before I was born, and who called me by His grace.* **(Galatians 1:15 ESV)**

| 53

There Is Only One You

Not only is your thumbprint unique,
Each one of your fingers is also unique
And even if it was possible that someone could have one of the same prints as you have is something like less than one in sixty-four thousand millionths of a chance; it's basically imposable that anyone could have two matching prints,
Beyond that, the prints on your palms and toes and feet are also unique to you,
Then there is your smile, your teeth, and the shape of your face is uniquely yours
The shape of your ears is only yours
The color, the count, and the makeup of your hair is uniquely yours
The color, pattern, and scan of your eyes are yours alone
Even your talents, interests, skills, joys, likes, and humor are not the same as anyone else's
And as we've learned in recent years, your DNA is so uniquely you and detailed that it would take one thousand six-hundred-page books just to record all the details of how unique you are.
There has only been one you in all the history of the world. No one else has ever even come close. There will never be another you, and so no one can ever take your place or do what you can do. You were made specifically for this time and for a specific reason and purpose.

*****

What sets you apart can sometimes feel like a burden and it's not. And a lot of the time, it's what makes you great. (Emma Stone)

When you embrace your difference, your DNA, your look or heritage or religion or your unusual name, that's when you start to shine. (Bethenny Frankel)

In order to be irreplaceable one must always be different. (Coco Chanel)

*Oh yes, You shaped me first inside, then out; You formed me in my mother's womb. I thank You, High God—You're breathtaking! Body and soul, I am marvelously made! I worship in adoration—what a creation! You know me inside and out, You know every bone in my body; You know exactly how I was made, bit by bit, how I was sculpted from nothing into something. Like an open book, you watched me grow from conception to birth; all the stages of my life were spread out before you, the days of my life all prepared before I'd even lived one day. Your thoughts—how rare, how beautiful! God, I'll never comprehend them! I couldn't even begin to count them—any more than I could count the sand of the sea. Oh, let me rise in the morning and live always with You! And please, God, do away with wickedness for good! And you murderers—out of here!—all the men and women who belittle You, God, infatuated with cheap god-imitations. See how I hate those who hate You, G*OD*, see how I loathe all this godless arrogance; I hate it with pure, unadulterated hatred. Your enemies are my enemies! Investigate my life, O God, find out everything about me; Cross-examine and test* *me, get a clear picture of what I'm about; See for Yourself whether I've done anything wrong—then guide me on the road to eternal life.* (**Psalm 139:13–24 MSG**)

"God Made You Special"
Artist: Greg Fritz
Sung by Deniece Williams and VeggieTales

He picked out my smile,
My eyes, and my nose.
He was very particular
From my head to my toes.

I'm just what He wanted,
And I think it shows
That He's really creative
And all of heaven knows…

He thought it all over.
He made me just right.
I make Him happy—
I am His delight.

When I look in the mirror,
I see His touch…
'Cause God made me special,
And He loves me very much!

Sometimes I feel down.
Sometimes I feel blue,
Don't like something about me—
It's sad but it's true.

But then I'm reminded that
God had a plan.
He wants me to be
Just the way that I am…

He thought it all over.
He made me just right.

I make Him happy—
I am His delight.

57

You Can Always Try

"So what" if you fail! "So what" if you have made mistakes!

So what if you only fall and have to get back up and do it all again?

If you can learn something from the experience, you have succeeded.

The mistakes don't automatically equate to failure or an act of stupidity or rebellion.

Mistakes in many ways can even be successes if we allow ourselves to learn from them and become a better, smarter, or wiser person because of what the experience taught us.

Don't just waste the opportunity, let all those learning experiences teach you. From those difficult experiences and the lessons they will teach you, you will come to know more than you thought you knew. You will find out that you are better at more things than you believed you were. With these new skills, you will make yourself more valuable in more diverse areas than you ever thought possible, and because you make every failure into a new success, you will have earned respect in the eyes of your peers and be held in greater regard than you knew.

I know you are not a quitter; and, therefore, I know you won't quit trying. That alone will increase your odds of succeeding and give you infinitely more worth than you will ever know. I believe in you and know you can do whatever you set your mind to doing. I know you can make wonderful and amazing things happen if you just keep trying and never give up.

You are more important to me and more valuable than anything I have, and I would quickly give up everything in trade for your safety, including my life.

Survival can be summed up in three words—Never Give Up! That's the heart of it really. Just keep trying. (Bear Grylls)

When you have exhausted all possibilities, remember this: you haven't. (Thomas Edison)

When I look back on my life, I see pain, mistakes, and heartache. When I look in the mirror, I see strength, learned lessons, and pride in myself. (Unknown)

Your success is determined by how much you can really learn from your failures. (Joel Brown)

You only fail when you stop trying. (Unknown).

You may encounter many defeats but you must not be defeated. (Dr. Maya Angelou)

A river cuts through rock, not because of its power, but because of its persistence. (Unknown)

I want to inspire people. I want someone to look at me and say, "Because of you I didn't give up. (Unknown)

I've failed over and over and over again in my life and that is why I succeed. (Michael Jordan)

Do not gloat over me, my enemies! For though I fall, I will rise again. Though I sit in darkness, the Lord will be my light. **(Micah 7:8 NLT)**

For though the righteous fall seven times, they rise again, but the wicked stumble when calamity strikes. **(Proverbs 24:16 NIV)**

*The steps of a man are established by the L*ORD*, when he delights in His way; though he falls, he shall not be cast headlong, for the L*ORD *upholds his hand.* **(Psalm 37:23–24 ESV)**

"Beauty Will Rise"

Artist: Steven Curtis Chapman

It was the day the world went wrong
I screamed till my voice was gone
And watched through the tears as everything
Came crashing down
Slowly panic turns to pain
As we awake to what remains
And sift through the ashes that are left
Behind

But buried deep beneath
All our broken dreams
We have this hope

Out of these ashes, beauty will rise
And we will dance among the ruins
We will see Him with our own eyes
Out of these ashes, beauty will rise

For we know, joy is coming in the morning,
In the morning, beauty will rise
So take another breath for now,
And let the tears come washing down,
And if you can't believe I will believe
For you.

'Cuz I have seen
The signs of spring!
Just watch and see:

Out of these ashes, beauty will rise
And we will dance among the ruins
We will see Him with our own eyes

Out of these ashes, beauty will rise
For we know, joy is coming in the morning,

In the morning,
I can hear it in the distance
And it's not too far away.
It's the music and the laughter
Of a wedding and a feast.
I can almost feel the hand of God
Reaching for my face
To wipe the tears away, and say,
"It's time to make everything new."

"Make it all new"

This is our hope.
This is the promise.
This is our hope.
This is the promise.
That it would take our breath away
To see the beauty that's been made
Out of the ashes,
Out of the ashes,
That it would take our breath away
To see the beauty that's been made
Out of the ashes,

Out of the ashes,
Out of these ashes, beauty will rise
And we will dance among the ruins
We will see Him with our own eyes
Out of this darkness, new life will shine
And we'll know the joy is coming in the morning,
In the morning, beauty will rise!

Oh, beauty will rise
Oh, beauty will rise
Oh, oh, oh, beauty will rise
Oh, oh, oh, beauty will rise
Oh, oh, oh, beauty will rise

Remember to Accept the Differences in People

Red and yellow, black and white, each is so different but made just right.

Even though people can at times be really stupid and some do really dumb things, they can often make us very upset, and even cause us harm; and although we can become very upset with and even hate what they do, we still must always care for and want the best for them as people. We especially cannot put down those who are different, because of their cultural differences, language, background, economic status in life, history, or race. We all have unique backgrounds and other differences that we can learn from and about each other and grow from our shared experience. We all have a history and have done things we are proud of and even made choices that we later lived to regret. However, morality, integrity, and character are a different story; and on that, each person stands alone. One must prove himself and show that they know what is right or wrong. There is no difference of opinion in what is moral or immoral, right or wrong. That is something we all must just submit to and learn. However, the other types of differences, like styles, colors, textures, and flavors…all do better as they complement, contrast, and highlight each other together as they were meant to be.

It would definitely be a boring world if we didn't have all the different varieties of people and colors and interests and personalities and talents…

If two people were not different, one of them wouldn't be necessary.

Alone we can do so little; together we can do so much. (Helen Keller)

Darkness cannot drive out darkness; only light can do that. Hate cannot drive out hate; only love can do that. (Martin Luther King Jr.)

Don't be afraid of being different, be afraid of being the same as everyone else. (Unknown)

Be different so that people can see you clearly amongst the crowds. (Mehmet Murat ildan)

Do nothing out of selfish ambition or vain conceit, but in humility consider others better than yourselves. **(Philippians 2:3)**

There is neither Jew nor Greek, there is neither slave nor free, there is no male and female, for you are all one in Christ Jesus. **(Galatians 3:28 ESV)**

In His grace, God has given us different gifts for doing certain things well. **(Romans 12:6–8)**

As it is, there are many parts, yet one body. **(1 Corinthians 12:20 ESV)**

What Will It Cost to Do That?

Always think through every decision, weigh the consequences of each action, and make your decisions accordingly.

Everything costs something; nothing is free. Everything cost someone to do it, to get it, to make it, to buy it, to secure it, to bring it. Everything will cost you something—money, time, job, commitment, friends, family, character, health, salvation... Sometimes, they cost one person a lot or a lot of people a little, but there is always someone who paid something for everything you have, do, or enjoy.

The real decision on every good deal or anything I want to have or do has to be based on sound reasoning and the consideration of the following:

First, will the value of the benefit it will bring me be worth the cost I will have to pay for it?

Next, is it actually worth my time to do it, get it, or enjoy it?

Then, will the effect (or cost) of doing it or having it be worth the benefit or enjoyment it will bring?

Even what will the long-term cost or effect be of taking care of it, paying for it, maintaining it after a year? Five years? Ten years? And will the benefit or enjoyment I receive still be worth it?

It's easy to see the cost equating the money paid or payments made for something. It's not too hard to see the care, upkeep, or even the maintenance being a cost that needs to be considered. However, the cost of things can also be the negative effect it will have on me or the people around me.

There has been medicine the doctor had given me that later when I looked over the list of side effects from taking it, they were more dangerous than the problem I got the medicine for. So to me, it wasn't worth taking it, so I didn't take it. As a builder and general contractor, I've had to look at jobs the same way. There were different buildings I had to turn down even though they would have been good financially, yet because of the environment or the group I would have to associate with, it would make my personal cost too high. There were many times I was requested to interpret for different LGBTQRS groups, democratic candidates, even abortion clinics that wanted my help and would have paid very well; but when I weighed the cost to me personally and the people around me, I just couldn't do it, no matter how much they would agree to pay me.

Remember, every action has a reaction, and nothing we could ever do or say will affect or impact only ourselves but also, in more ways than we will ever know, everyone else around us. Our friends and family, both now and in the future, will somehow or another be affected. So even if we think we personally can pay the price, could our family or friends? What effect will my decision have on them? What will be the price that will be paid in the future?

Now don't get me wrong or misunderstand what I am saying. That doesn't mean we should never take any risks or not risk any new ventures. We just need to count the cost and make sure we can afford it at this time and figure whether or not the benefit or return is worth the cost and risk. If it is and you want to or feel led that it's the right thing to do, then do it. However, always remember to pray for God's direction first, not just to tell Him your plan but to ask for His plan and direction and not just that it's a good idea but that it's the right one for you.

As I've said before, there isn't any real success or accomplishment you will ever achieve that could make me love you more or less, and I am already very proud of you. Nor will there be any loss or failure you will experience or go through, but what I, too, will feel the sorrow and loss with you.

Did you know that Thomas Edison failed over ten thousand times in his attempt to invent the first light bulb filament? He tried everything—hair, thread, yarn, string, rope, wool, fur, skin, even plant material…from every kind of animal or plant from all over the world. However, when asked about this, he said he didn't fail but succeeded to discover ten thousand things that wouldn't work. Then it was one of the next few tries that finally did work; he invented the light bulb, and from then on, we finally didn't have to watch TV in the dark anymore…

We will all fall sometimes, but when you do, always fall forward. Then hopefully when you have considered everything that happened, and learned all you can from it, and again weighed all costs with any benefits, you will have gained a lot of knowledge in the process. So even when you once again fall and miss the mark, and at times we all do, you will hopefully still fall in your favor and be able to turn it back around and end up further ahead than when you started.

Always remember that everything has costs involved; things do, jobs do, relationships do, and even what you do with Jesus has a cost. However, with Jesus, He is worth more than any cost there ever is involved in following Him. There is even a cost involved in not doing what we know we should or taking advantage of every option that is given us too.

Count the cost, and know what you'll have to pay before you decide to do it and get it, or tell me how good of a deal you're getting.

Life is 10 percent what happens to you and 90 percent how you react to it. (Charles R. Swindoll)

Get action. Seize the moment. Man was never intended to become an oyster. (Theodore Roosevelt)

Count the cost of your calling, find the value of your dream, and most of all find your place in His love. (Deborah Brodie)

Count the cost first. Don't pay too big a price for pursuing minor values. (Jim Rohn)

But don't begin until you count the cost. For who would begin construction of a building without first calculating the cost to see if there is enough money to finish it? **(Luke 14:28 NLT)**

For what does it profit a man to gain the whole world and forfeit his soul? **(Mark 8:36 ESV)**

Don't build your house and establish a home until your fields are ready, and you are sure that you can earn a living. **(Proverbs 24:27 GNT)**

So here's what I want you to do, God helping you: Take your everyday, ordinary life—your sleeping, eating, going-to-work, and walking-around life—and place it before God as an offering. Embracing what God does for you is the best thing you can do for Him. Don't become so well-adjusted to your culture that you fit into it without even thinking. Instead, fix your attention on God. You'll be changed from the inside out. Readily recognize what He wants from you, and quickly respond to it. Unlike the culture around you, always dragging you down to its level of immaturity, God brings the best out of you, develops well-formed maturity in you. **(Romans 12:1–2 MSG)**

A **job** is a labor or service one provides for payment.

A **career** is a job one intends to keep or maintain for many years.

A **vocation** is one's principal occupation one is trained to perform.

An **avocation** is a hobby or what one does for personal interest or enjoyment, not as a primary source of income.

A **career** may give you satisfaction, but a **vocation** brings you joy.

Your job is what you are paid to do.
Your calling is what you are made to do.

Count the Cost
Artist: David Meece

You gotta count the cost
If you're gonna be a believer
You gotta know that the price
Is the one you can afford
You gotta count the cost
If you're gonna be a believer
You gotta go all the way
If you really love the Lord
He never said it would be easy
He never promised a free ride
There's a costly fee
If you want to be on His side
Oh, the Father knows the cost
His only Son was the price
And when He says to "Follow Me"
He's asking of a man His life
You gotta count the cost…

To Buy or Not to Buy

Major purchases can be a difficult decision to agree on.

One of the hardest things about going from being single to being married is experienced in our buying power. Not only does our money not go as far, but there is also a difference when you realize you used to be able to purchase anything you wanted and you alone would decide if you could afford it or not. However now, once you are married, you have to work it out with one more person. Then worse yet at times, it may seem like one of you are always in disagreement on whether you "both" really "want it" or if you really "can afford it."

Small purchases should not be a problem, and both of you should be able to agree on a realistic budget and be able to work within that budget to buy normal everyday products you continually need. Even the occasional larger purchases could be budgeted and already agreed on, so no real discussion is needed for those.

However, when and how you decide whether or not to make a major purchase and what equates to a major purchase need to be handled differently. The two of you need to sit down and discuss what equates "a major purchase" or what types of purchases should the both of you be involved in making the decision. Sometimes, it's not just the dollar amount but the kind of purchases, or even when to purchase too.

> *Don't build your house and establish a home until your fields are ready, and you are sure that you can earn a living.* (Proverbs 24:27 GWT)

> *Two are better off than one, because together they can work more effectively. If one of them falls down, the other can help him up. But if someone is alone and falls, it's just too bad, because there is no one to help him.* (Ecclesiastes 4:9–12 GNT)

> *All things will be clear and distinct to the man who does not hurry; haste is blind and improvident.* (Livy)

> *Never scuba dive, skydive, ski, hike, travel, or camp without a partner to watch out for you and keep you safe; and if at all possible, avoid making any significant legal, medical, or financial decisions without your partner either.* (Me)

For the most part, your mother and I haven't had any real problem here that I can remember. We have had a few revisits of budget and mutual input discussions after some controversial purchases, but all in all, we have done pretty good.

One thing that has helped us with deciding on our big purchases is that we have always seen our money as "our money" no matter who was the one bringing it in. We have not had separate savings accounts or large stash funds to avoid being accountable to the other. A lot of that has to do with "Trust" on both sides. Just how much do I trust my spouse, and how much do they trust me? The Bible says that as a married couple, *"And the husband and wife will be joined as one flesh, and after that they no longer exist as two, but one flesh"* (Mark 10:8 TPT). They are one in every way in their goal and purpose—physically, emotionally, spiritually, socially, and, yes, even financially. As husband and wife, we are not the same, but we are to be one (look at Paul's explanation of the Church as a body in 1 Corinthians 12:12–31 and further in Romans 12:4). The family is also set up the same way, just in a smaller size. All together and working as one.

Again, let me say, we need to have a budget. We have it worked through and agreed upon for (in general) all our spending. Next, we need to decide on the parameters of what we can purchase without the other one being able to give input on. Of course, there are all the normal necessities such as gas, groceries, housing, phone, insurances... Then there are those things beyond that like fast food or restaurants, gifts, tools, minor appliances, and home decorating items... Those need to be discussed and budgeted. However, anything beyond that agreed budget should always be discussed and agreed on before going ahead with it.

Some of the reasons I have had people tell me they had separate accounts was that "He earns his money and pays his bills, and I earn my money and pay my bills." I have also seen those who keep money aside to have a means of escape, like thinking in the back of their mind that "if this marriage goes south, I will have enough money set aside to give me a new start." Another reason I've seen is "this way I can do what I want without my spouse knowing what I'm doing." All of these reasons are bad reasons! They divide the marriage and show that both are not wanting the marriage to really make them one. The only thing that might be okay is if you are saving up to surprise your spouse with a special gift that you otherwise wouldn't be able to afford. Money issues will either make or break a marriage. So in general, all money in the marriage must be mutual no matter who is leaving the house to earn them. That way, we both have a stake in the game and a right to have input in the budget and buying decisions.

The same goes for you husbands: Be good husbands to your wives. Honor them, delight in them.

As women they lack some of your advantages. But in the new life of God's grace, you're equals. Treat your wives, then, as equals so your prayers don't run aground. (1 Peter 3:7 MSG)

And that a man should leave his father and mother, and be forever united to his wife. The two shall become one—no longer two, but one! And no man may divorce what God has joined together. (Matthew 19:5–6 TLB)

I don't see anything degrading about marriage or homemaking, but my husband and I pool the money we earn, along with the jobs around the house. (Valerie Harper)

Money gives a married couple a great opportunity for two people to practice becoming one. (Me)

Another thing that always helped us is that whenever there was an unusual purchase, a large or unusual one, we would always use the other one as our escape to give us time to think about the necessity of getting it or not. It really worked well when we would get a sales call or a door-to-door sales person trying to pressure us into purchasing something. To be quite honest, I enjoyed listening to a good sales pitch whether it's a vacation package, truck, vacuum, or encyclopedias. I could be sucked into signing on the dotted line and getting it. *"Though one person may be overpowered by another, two people can*

resist one opponent. A triple-braided rope is not easily broken" (Ecclesiastes 4:12 GW). However, we worked out a system that we would always say, "We never make any spur-of-the-moment purchases, and we always talk it over with our spouse first." That always gave me an out, no matter how much I liked the guy or what he was telling me. So make that an agreed-upon practice that you and your spouse will always talk about everything before you purchase anything (out of the ordinary or large purchases, anyway).

> *It is dangerous to have zeal without knowledge, and the one who acts hastily makes poor choices.* (Proverbs 19:2 NET)
>
> *Do you see someone who is hasty in his words? There is more hope for a fool than for him.* (Proverbs 29:20 NET)
>
> *Take time for all things: great haste makes great waste.* (Benjamin Franklin)
>
> *Unreasonable haste is the direct road to error.* (Moliere)

Then, too, we also never make any quick decisions on purchasing anything, because it usually is something that later we would regret if we did. Buying a car or even buying a set of encyclopedias. (Yes, there used to be a bunch of books every good parent would want to purchase. They were very expensive, thousands of pages of information and pictures that would be outdated every other year, and you would sit them on a big shelf so everyone could see how good of a parent you were. No, it was not a computer program.) We would always tell the person "we never buy anything spur of the moment" and at best "we always needed a day to think and talk about it together." That would give us some time to do some research on it first. "*It's stupid and embarrassing to give an answer before you listen*" (Proverbs 18:13 CEV). (Or check out all the facts first.) I'm sure that there were times we did lose out on a few good deals, but more times than not, it saved us a lot of regret from purchasing a bad car or some other not-so-great deal. "*It is a trap for a person to say impulsively, 'This is a holy offering!' and later to have second thoughts about those vows*" (Proverbs 20:25 GWT). It means don't be quick to make a decision and then live to regret it later. It's been proven that if you give a person a waiting time on big decisions, they will tend to make better decisions when they do make them. That's why many states have mandated a twenty-four-to-forty-eight-hour waiting period before having an abortion. Many decisions are made by emotion and not by logic, but when you take time before you make them, you can start to think about the pros and cons of a decision with less emotion to distract you. So take at least twenty-four hours before you jump into any big purchases. If that deal is supposed to be for you, it will be there at the right time.

> *The plans of a hard-working person lead to prosperity, but everyone who is always in a hurry ends up in poverty.* (Proverbs 21:5 GW)

> *A faithful person will have an abundance of blessings, but the one who hastens to gain riches will not go unpunished.* (Proverbs 28:20 NET)

> *A greedy man is in a hurry for wealth; he doesn't know that poverty will come to him.* (Proverbs 28:22 HB)

There also is the help that is available from others. As much as possible, find people who know about that item or thing you are wanting to purchase and ask for their advice. Proverbs 11:14 (AMPC) says, "*Where no wise guidance is, the people fall, but in the multitude of counselors there is safety.*" When my dad was alive, I would always talk things over with him, and he always gave me good counsel and help. He didn't always say what I wanted to hear, but I always knew he would tell me the truth and guide me in what's best for me. Then when there were things I was needing advice on that he didn't know or when I needed to get another opinion, I would find other people I respected and who knew something about the subject. It always helped me to have a better understanding of what to do or if a car was a good one or what a particular tractor was like… Always try to find good people you trust who might know a bit about what you are needing advice on to bounce your ideas off; it could really save you a lot of trouble.

> *A stubborn fool considers his own way the right one, but a person who listens to advice is wise.* (Proverbs 12:15 GW)

> *Pride only breeds quarrels, but with ones who take advice is wisdom.* (Proverbs 13:10 WEB)

> *My mother gave lots of good advice and had a lot to say. As you get older, you realize everything she said was true.* (Lenny Kravitz)

> *To accept good advice is but to increase one's own ability. (Johann Wolfgang von Goethe)*

> *They that will not be counseled, cannot be helped. If you do not hear reason she will rap you on the knuckles. (Benjamin Franklin)*

Then there is listing the pros and cons of a purchase. Do this separately at first and then together. It's really simple—just get some line paper, and draw a line down the middle from top to bottom, and on one side, write all the reasons you should do it or get it, including all the benefits it will bring. Then on the other side, list all the negatives and reasons you shouldn't do it or get it. "*Suppose one of you wants to build a tower. What is the first thing you will do? Won't you sit down and figure out how much it will cost and if you have enough money to pay for it?*" (Luke 14:28 CEV). Then sit down with your spouse, and compare your lists and talk about it. Your mother and I have done this many times with major purchases to help us have confidence in whatever decision we needed to make. It really helps once you get past the emotional reasons (it will be fun, and it will make us happy, and it's my favorite color…). Then the logical reasons can be listed, and a trustworthy wise decision can be made.

> *Sensible people will see trouble coming and avoid it, but an unthinking person will walk right into it and regret it later. (Proverbs 22:3 GNT)*

> *Lincoln had no such person that he could talk with. Often, as a result, he debated with himself, and he would draw up a kind of list of the pros and cons of an argument, and carefully figure them out, and he might test them in public. (David Herbert Donald)*

> *I'm slow to make a decision. I need to think things over for a long time, to weigh the pros and*

> *cons, to look at issues 10, 20, or 30 times. But when that's done, I'm quick to act. (Martin Bouygues)*
>
> *I know that there's pros and cons to everything. (John Morrison)*

Finally, there is always the first and best means of deciding, and that is by praying about it. *"Don't worry about anything; instead, pray about everything. Tell God what you need, and thank Him for all He has done"* (Philippians 4:6 NLT). Quite often, we think that "After I have done all I can do myself then, if there is nothing else I can do, or if I get in some sort of trouble, then all I have left that I can do is pray." But that is totally the wrong idea. That is like saying, "After I pushed my car as far as I can (and I don't know where I'm going) and there is nothing left I can do, then I'll ask God for gas and directions." Why not just start out by asking God for His help in the beginning? *"If any of you needs wisdom to know what you should do, you should ask God, and He will give it to you. God is generous to everyone and doesn't find fault with them"* (James 1:5 GW). If God truly knows everything, has the answer for every question, and wants to be involved in our everyday lives, why not talk to Him to get His directions and guidance? *"Why not ask Him if this is a good idea and to give you wisdom to make the right decision? Ask Me and I will tell you some remarkable secrets about what is going to happen here"* (Jeremiah 33:3 TLB). Why not always pray first? "Never stop praying" (1 Thessalonians 5:17 GW).

> *I hear the Lord saying, "I will stay close to you, instructing and guiding you along the pathway for your life. I will advise you along the way and lead you forth with my eyes as your guide. So don't make it difficult; don't be stubborn when I take you where you've not been before. Don't make Me tug you and pull you along. Just come with Me!"* (Psalm 32:8 TPT)
>
> *Trust God from the bottom of your heart; don't try to figure out everything on your own. Listen for*

God's voice in everything you do, everywhere you go; He's the one who will keep you on track. Don't assume that you know it all. Run to God! (Proverbs 3:5–6 MSG)

All wisdom comes from the LORD, and so do common sense and understanding. (Proverbs 2:6 MSG)

Be careful about rushing God's timing. You never know who or what He is protecting you or saving you from. (Unknown)

You Are Changing the World

It may not have happened yet, and you might not see how it could, but one day YOU are going to change the world. You might be already changing the world in big and small ways and not even know it yet. You don't have to wait until you're older to make a difference.

Every day you are making a difference by the words you say to your family and friends, in the way you smile, the kindness you share, even the way you can encourage a friend brings a lasting change. You are constantly making a difference in the acts of service you do for others in need, in volunteering your time to show you care, even in praying for others can really make a difference in their situation. You're not on this earth to change it someday. You're definitely changing it today!

You have definitely changed my world since the first day your mom told me, "We're going to have a Baby!" until today and every step in between. Make as many changes you possibly can to make this world a better place, as often as you can, for as many as you can, and as many ways as you can.

As you obey and serve the Lord, He will make His purpose for you crystal clear. **(Tony Evans)**

Good words are worth much and cost little. **(George Herbert)**

Even so, let your light shine before men; that they may see your good works, and glorify your Father who is in heaven. **(Matthew 5:15–16)**

I will bless those who bless you, and whoever curses you I will curse; and all peoples on earth will be blessed through you. **(Genesis 12:3)**

And through your offspring all nations on earth will be blessed, because you have obeyed Me. **(Genesis 22:18)**

But I have raised you up for this very purpose, that I might show you My power and that My name might be proclaimed in all the earth. **(Exodus 9:16)**

The Hand-Shaped Hole

There once was a city that had a beautiful stonewall that went all the way around it to protect the good people of the city from the bandits or invaders that used to pillage them and keep them in poverty. The wall was a beautiful artistically crafted stonewall that had a curious hand-shaped hole in it set in it right by the main city gate. As legend would have it and the story was told, it was made by a kindhearted man who helped the people of a poor city survive.

No one knew who this unknown helper of the city was. For many years, whenever there was someone in desperate need somehow, some way, without anyone knowing who, or when, during the middle of the night, someone would help and take care of that need.

Now these were not simple things that anyone could do but great gestures of kindness and help—things like what happened for one old lady, the roof of the house where she lived leaked. She was in desperate need for someone to help her fix it but had no money to pay anyone with. It was bad enough that soon she wouldn't be able to live there any longer. Then one night, someone fixed it as good as new. There was also someone else who had to finish hauling some lumber, or they would be in danger of a breach of contract and lose their business. Then in the morning, there they were—all delivered and stacked. Another farmer needed his field cleared, and then when he all but gave up, there it was cleared and planted with the rocks all off to the piles of rocks near the crumbling city wall.

These acts of kindness continued for many years, and no one knew who it was or why he was helping so many or how he did such good work. Then it was all cleaned up, and if there was any rock, they were all tossed into the growing piles of rock by the city wall. The people were just so thankful for this mysterious answer to their prayers that was helping them. They often wondered if it was an angel of God sent by God, but no one knew. For no one ever saw who it was or who was doing the work.

Then the last great act of kindness was an important section of the city wall that needed to be built to finally protect the people of that city and stop the invading marauders from terrorizing the people. The old man who was the city's wall builder became very sick and unable to finish the wall. Then word came that the marauders were seen sailing within striking distance of that city. All the people were scared, crying, and praying to God for help. However, that night once again, the kind unknown man who always helped all the people was once again there, trying to get the wall built; but it was such a big job and such hard work, and he was so tired that he thought he would just sit down and close his eyes for just a minute. When he woke up, he found out that he had set down with his hand still holding the last rock he was setting in the wall. The problem was that as he drifted off to sleep, his hand still holding that rock sunk deep into the wet mortar of the wall, and now the mortar was beginning to set up hard.

He pulled and he pulled desperately to get free. Then just before the sun came up and the people came out of their houses, he pulled one last time, and his hand squeezed out of the concrete wall. With his hand and arm torn and bleeding from his escape from the wall, he ran away into the woods just before anyone could get a glimpse of him. Never to be heard from again.

The people came out to see the beautiful city wall, which was now finished to protect them; and as if by some miracle, their prayers were answered, and they were saved. The people of the city walked around thanking God for answering their prayers and sending the unknown helper. As they were admiring the beautiful workmanship, they noticed the strange hole right near the right side of the main gate where the kind stranger's big hand was stuck, and they all wondered about this.

Now this story is similar to the Cinderella story in that it became tradition to place your hand in the hole before entering the city gate to see if your hand fit the big hand shape of the kind stranger. If your hand happened to fit, then the townspeople would believe that just maybe you just might be the unknown stranger who helped so many and rebuilt their wall and saved their city come back to visit them. In all these years, no one has had a hand quite big enough or strong enough or kind enough to fit the hole the kind strangers left behind.

Some believe that maybe the stranger damaged his arm very badly and went to seek help in some far away country. Others think he might have gotten sick from it or even captured by the marauders who would have been very mad at his saving the city. Still others say the hand that made that hole had to be from an angel, for no man would have such a big strong and yet kind hand… Whatever the case, the funny thing is that the mysterious acts of kindness have never stopped happening in that city. They continue still today. When there is someone in desperate need and praying for God's help, mysteriously and miraculously, in the middle of the night, someone would do what is needed, and nobody would ever know who did it.

You might say, it's the kind unknown helper of the people who has come back. The problem with that is it's been well over two hundred years since the city was saved that day. Another strange thing is that the city wall (mostly just for history and beauty these days) has had to have been repaired many times over the years, yet nobody knows who did it or when it was. Although today, there are many strange hand-shaped holes in all different places in the city wall. The difference from the first one is all the others were made from all different-size hands.

Many people live their lives as if they are the only concern and the only focus, and when they leave or die, it's like pulling your hand out of a bucket of water. Other than the water maybe being at a slightly different level, no one would know that anything was different, has changed, or is missing. Instead, live your life like you're working with concrete, and when your hand is removed, there is a hole that will be there forever, and people from now on will be stopping to wonder whose hand formed that concrete and why the mark they made still continue on!

Find a way to make a difference. Somehow, someway find a way to make the world a better place for you being here!

You Are My Daughter

And you will always be my favorite little girl in the whole world!

I have always wanted you and prayed for you since before you took your first breath, and I will continue until after I take my last. After that, I will be waiting to see you again. So remember that follow God and always choose what is right because I'll be waiting for you. I will always love you!

I smile because you are my daughter,
I laugh because there's nothing you can do about it.

*****

My little girls are the most beautiful women in the world. I am a lucky, lucky man. I will spend every day making sure that they know this. (Russel Simmons)

I pray every day for my little girls. It's hard out there for the younger generation. (Angie Harmon)

Guns don't kill people. Dads with pretty daughters kill people. (Unknown)

I will declare the Lord's decree:
He said to Me, "You are My [daughter];
 today I have become Your Father." (Psalm 2:7)

"Though the mountains be shaken
and the hills be removed,
yet My unfailing love for you will not be shaken
nor My covenant of peace be removed," says the
Lord, who has compassion on you. (Isaiah 54:10)

Character is everything.

Fathers and Daughters
Artist: Michael Bolton

If I could catch a star for you
I swear I'd steal them all tonight
To make your every wish come true
And every dream for all your life

But that's not how the story goes
The world is full of perfect plans
If there's a promise that I broke
I know one day you will understand

When times are hard, I know you'll be strong
I'll be there in your heart when you'll carry on
Like moonlight on the water, and sunlight in the sky
Fathers and daughters never say goodbye

An angel I will read to sleep
Gave me one dream of my own
So learn to love and spread your wings
And find the one to call your home

When times are hard, I know you'll be strong
I'll be there in your heart when you'll carry on
Like moonlight on the water, and sunlight in the sky
Fathers and daughters never say goodbye

God Made You Good, Smart, and Beautiful

> I don't care what you think or what you feel like or what anyone else has said. To me, you will always be the most beautiful of all.

I remember the first time I saw you, and I was the first one who did see you and to hold you. From the first sight of that tiny baby in my arms with those big eyes looking up at me…you have always been my beautiful little girl that I love with all my heart.

The beauty the world seeks is fleeting, and even beautiful jewelry does eventually tarnish. However, the beauty of one's character and love does nothing but grow more beautiful as time goes on. Trying to look your best is good, and we should always try to put our best foot forward and try to make a good first impression. I always try to not to make the children cry when they see me (I have to start somewhere. Haha.) And that is all good and well, but don't put the most effort and concern into what is only good and doesn't last. Work on having the most beautiful character you can—one that makes a difference wherever you go and then people will always be glad to see you come and sad to see you go.

I truly believe God has made you a beautiful and smart young lady; the rest is up to you.

> *It was my father who taught me to value myself. He told me that I was uncommonly beautiful and that I was the most precious thing in his life.*
> (Dawn French)

> *This woman is a loving mother, a gorgeous daughter, and beautiful angel of imagination.*
> (Debasish Mridha)

I have the most beautiful daughter in the world and I'm grateful for her. (Bethany Frankel)

You are altogether beautiful, my darling; there is no flaw in you. **(Song of Solomon 4:7)**

In all the land no women were as lovely as the daughters of Job. And their father put them into his will along with their brothers. **(Job 42:15 NLT)**

*Charm is deceitful and beauty is vain, But a woman who fears the L*ORD*, she shall be praised.* **(Proverbs 31:30)**

Do not let your adorning be external—the braiding of hair and the putting on of gold jewelry, or the clothing you wear—but let your adorning be the hidden person of the heart with the imperishable beauty of a gentle and quiet spirit, which in God's sight is very precious. **(1 Peter 3:3–4 ESV)**

Daddy's Little Girl

Artists: Livy Jeanne and Victoria Banks
Sung by the Shires

The smell of Old Spice
A flat cap on the dash
Windows rolled down in the wind
While birds fly past
Singing along with the radio
A little latitude
Hanging onto that steering wheel
Was the man who hung the moon

He always used to tell me, "Don't grow up too fast
"Love will come, love will go, your first won't be your last."
I didn't always listen when he gave me advice
Though I hate to admit it, but that man was always right

When I count my blessings, I know where to start
He might not hold my hand no more
But he'll always, always hold my heart

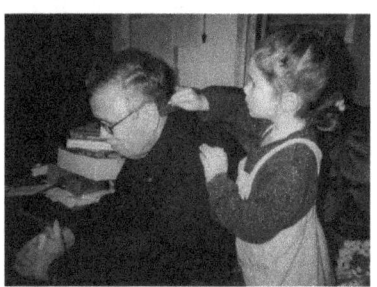

Used to wrap my hands around his little finger
Turns out he was wrapped around mine
He said, "You can be anything you want to in this great big world."
But I'm always gonna be
Yes, I'm always gonna be Daddy's little girl, Daddy's little girl

Ask Your Questions

If I don't know the answer you need,
    I will do my best to find the answer you seek.

You used to have so many questions: "Daddy, are we there yet?" "Why is that the front of the car and not that side?" "Why are the trees so tall and the grass so short?" "Why can't we see the car's horns, but it's so noisy, but we can see the cow's horns, but they don't make any noise?" "Why is the snow so cold and fire so hot?" "Why can't we have a new car like…?" (To which I'd say, "Because it takes lots of money.) "Why don't we have lots of money?" (To which I'd say, "Because we're not rich"; then you'd say, "Then we can get Uncle Rich to help us…")

If you ever need me, I am here. If you need to know something, I will find the answer for you. I will only be, at the most, a phone call away.

I know you are smart and an avid reader. You are very well adapted to the use of technology and using the internet. I can't imagine anything you wouldn't know or couldn't find the answer to, but if there was a time you needed help knowing what to do or where to find the answer, I'll be available to help. Even if my name isn't Rich.

If you can't find the answer, maybe it's time to change the question. (Dr. Shawne)

We shall find the answer when we examine the problem. The problem is never apart from the answer. The problem is the answer. Understanding the problem dissolves the problem. (Bruce Lee)

There are always answers. We just fail to notice them. (Sahina)

It's better I find You, God, and leave the questions unanswered than to find the answer and without finding You. (Saint Augustine)

Don't dwell on what went wrong. Instead focus on what to do next. Spend your energy moving forward to finding the answer. (Denis Waitly)

If any of you lacks wisdom, you should ask God, who gives generously to all without finding fault, and it will be given to you. **(James 1:5 NIV)**

Ask, and it will be given to you; seek, and you will find; knock, and it will be opened to you. **(Matthew 7:7)**

This is what I want you to do: Ask the Father for whatever is in keeping with the things I've revealed to you. Ask in My name, according to My will, and He'll most certainly give it to you. Your joy will be a river overflowing its banks! **(John 16:23–24 MSG)**

The reason you don't have what you want is that you don't ask God for it. **(James 4:2b NLT)**

"Why, God"
Artist: Austin French, from the album *Wide Open*

Why, God, do people have to die,
a daughter or a son so sudden and so young long before their time?

Why, God, do people fall apart,
a promise a ring becomes a broken thing, a road that got too hard?

I don't understand,
but I understand...

Why, God, I need You
It's Why, God, I run to Your arms
over and over again
It's Why, God, I cling to
Your love and hold on for dear life
and I find You are right by my side

Why, God, do we feel so alone?
Every single day Fighting through the pain Hoping there is hope.

I don't understand
but I understand

Why, God, I need You.
It's Why, God, I run to Your arms
over and over again.
It's Why, God, I cling to
Your love and hold on for dear life
and I find You are right by my side.

Give me a faith stronger than I have.
I need to know when it hurts this bad
That You hold my heart when it breaks. And I'm not alone in this pain

It's Why, God, I need You.
It's Why, God, I run to Your arms
over and over again
It's Why, God, I cling to
Your love and hold on for dear life
and I find You are right by my side.
Always right by my side.
Even here in the Why, God.

Let Me Make It Easier

*I am here to help make
the complicated simple and the painful bearable.*

If ever you feel overwhelmed, don't know which way to go, or feel all alone, I will be here to help you get through it, whatever it is you are going through.

There are times when what we are faced with is soo difficult and or life becomes soo painful that we just don't know how to get through it. Sometimes, all you need is just to have someone come alongside you who understands that you are facing a difficult situation and to be reassured that what you are feeling is normal. Then again, sometimes, you need someone who has been in your situation to tell you how they got through it or to give you an idea of what to do to get past, around, and through it, or at least to share with you how to put up with your situation.

With my different surgeries I have gone through, it was helpful to find someone who had gone through the same surgery who could tell me about their recovery and pain they experienced. Therapists and others all would tell me that I should be feeling better and it should only be a few weeks for the pain to be gone. Just do these exercises or stretches, and you will be better…so much so that I was really wondering what was wrong with me and why I still was hurting so badly. I was starting to wonder, *Was there something else wrong with me? Did the doctor not do the surgery right? Am I going to need another surgery now?* I was even thinking, *Or was this all some psychosomatic pain that was all in my head, and I'm really just going crazy?* But then when I found someone who had the same surgery that I had and they could tell me of their experience, then I knew I wasn't crazy, and I had a real reason for feeling the way I was feeling. The amazing thing was, after that, I started feeling much better. I just needed to know I wasn't crazy and what I was feeling or going through was real and it was okay to feel that way. Just that alone changed everything I was going through for me.

Sometimes, we just need to know someone understands and believes in us, and just knowing that can change everything.

Many years back, I was working in the back field, brush hogging the pasture. We had a record crop of thistles and other invasive weeds growing eight to ten feet tall, and I had to mow them all down. Everything was going fine except my allergies were going crazy; and all of a sudden, I ended up with a horrible pain in my eye worse than my normal allergy pain when my eyes would get all red, itchy, and swell way up. I rinsed my eyes several times. I asked several people to look into my eyes to see if they could see anything. No one could see anything. I went to my doctor. He couldn't see anything. I went to the hospital, and they couldn't see anything. Then I went to an eye doctor, and still nothing… Everyone just told me, "There is nothing there, just dust. You're fine. It's just your allergies." And yet I was really hurting bad. I felt like I was losing my mind. It hurt so bad, and yet nothing.

Finally, I called an eye surgeon I knew personally and asked her to look at my eye. Thankfully, she agreed to see me and got me in the next day because she found a half-inch-long thistle embedded in my eye that no one else could see. She removed it, and the whole world changed. The biggest relief was just knowing someone else didn't think it was just in my head and really believed that something was there and then found it.

It felt great to have it out of my eye, but the biggest relief was just to know I wasn't just imagining all the horrendous pain I was feeling.

> *Pain insists upon being attended to. God whispers to us in our pleasures, speaks in our consciences, but shouts in our pains. It is His megaphone to rouse a deaf world.* (C. S. Lewis)

> *It takes courage to live through suffering; and it takes honesty to observe it.* (C. S. Lewis)

> *Crying is how your body speaks when your mouth can't explain the pain you feel.* (Alison Tracy-Perez)

In life, I have made a lot of mistakes, and I have felt a lot of pain, but mistakes make me wiser, and pain makes me stronger. (ChiKat)

Come to Me when you are hurting, and I will share your pain. Come to Me when you are joyful, and I will share your Joy—multiplying it many times over. (Sarah Young, *Dear Jesus*)

I will NEVER *stop bringing this person to Jesus. I will tell my loved one every single day,* **"I will carry your burden. I will take you to Jesus. Just rest and know that you are loved."** (Susan Eaton)

This is all that I have learned: God made us plain and simple, but we have made ourselves very complicated. (**Ecclesiastes 7:29 GNTD**)

The unfolding of Your words gives light; it gives understanding to the simple. (**Psalm 119:130 NIV**)

God is our refuge and strength, an ever-present help in trouble. (**Psalm 46:1 NIV**)

Franklin D. Roosevelt

In 1921, at the age of thirty-nine, FDR came down with polio and lost the use and control of everything below his chest. He developed persistent recurring nightmares relating to his overwhelming fear of being trapped in a burning building without anyone being there to help him get out. Eleven years later, in 1932, he was elected the thirty-second president of the United States and served from 1933 until 1945, when he died. During his inauguration speech, he said, "We have nothing to fear but fear itself."

It's Possible

There is no obstacle which cannot be overcome,
There is no mountain which cannot be ascended,
There is no river which cannot be forded,
There is no ocean that cannot be navigated,
There is no desert that cannot be crossed,
There is no wild beast that cannot be tamed,
There is no monster that cannot be hunted, and
There is no fear which cannot be conquered.
Whatever you can envision and believe, with God's help, you can achieve.
(Genesis 11:6; Philippians 4:11–13; Ephesians 3:20)

When You're Scared, I'll Comfort You

I will always be there whenever you need me,
to protect you from what scares you.
There will never be anything too dark, too scary,
or too dangerous; but what I will risk everything
to keep you safe and calm your fears.

That is one reason we didn't allow horror movies or even scary movies at our house or wherever you kids went. (Unless you would count *ET* as a scary movie... I never did understand how that was scary.) We didn't want you to grow up with any more fears, phobias, or nightmares than we had to. It was important to us to make sure you didn't grow up with your heart and mind full of fearful things; nor did we want you to become numb to the things you should be afraid of. Both being too fearful and not being fearful enough at the right times are a danger to your mind and emotions. It's also dangerous because when you can trick your emotions to think those things are not scary, then it doesn't allow you to recognize the real dangers in the real world around us that should scare us. That would hinder or impede one's ability to quickly respond to dangers to run or fight.

They say that to escape from being attacked by a lion, you don't have to run faster than the lion; you just have to run faster than your slowest friend.

We should never be controlled by fear. Although, it isn't wrong to have some fears. Everyone feels fear from time to time. Fear is good when it gets our attention and keeps us and our loved ones safe. However, when it begins to control us, it doesn't allow us to do what we need to do, or when our fear puts us in danger or we are fearful of things we shouldn't be afraid of, then our fear is out of balance and needs to be overcome.

There will be things that come our way that make us fearful, whether it be health, financial, vocational, legal, spiritual... And we can run from them or ignore them. Neither one is necessarily wrong, but more times than not, we need to face our fears head-on. Then we need to confront it, address it, work through it, fix it, and get rid of it; and sometimes, we need to be willing to stand and fight it. If and when it ever comes to that, then fight with all your might, fight for keeps, and fight to win. When something makes you afraid, always pray about it because God knows what it is and how to deal with it. Whenever you find yourself backed into a corner and needing to fight and you need someone to stand by you, I will.

I've had a lot of worries in my life, most of which never happened. (Mark Twain)

My father gave us inner confidence. He taught us, as young girls, never to be scared. (Geeta Phogat)

There is nothing like staying at home for real comfort. (Unknown)

Do not be afraid of them, for the Lord *your God will personally fight for you.* **(Deuteronomy 3:22 NET)**

God is our refuge and strength, a very present help in trouble. **(Psalm 46:1)**

You who fear the Lord*, trust in the* Lord*; He is their help and their shield.* **(Psalm 115:11)**

Fear not, for I am with you; be not dismayed, for I am your God. I will strengthen you, yes, I will help you, I will uphold you with My righteous right hand. **(Isaiah 41:10)**

When you go out to <u>(where are you going that is making you fearful, i.e., school or work?)</u>

against your (who is it that has come against you, i.e., classmate or coworker?) *and see* (what is it that they have that makes you fearful, i.e., more talent, bigger muscles?) *than yours, do not be afraid of them; for the LORD your God, who* (what is your testimony that God has done for you in the past?) *is with you.* (Deuteronomy 20:1; *rephrased for you when you feel afraid*)

When You're Afraid, I'll Protect You

I'm here to protect you from the bright
lights and loud noises and
whatever else catches you off guard and scares you
Whenever you are scared, are worried, are afraid, or
just need someone to be with, you will never have to
be alone, because I will always be here for you.

You and your siblings were never really scared of too much except for maybe snakes and bats. Remember when we used to get a bat in the house every once and a while, and all of you guys would go crazy screaming and head outside, I'd go in and do my best to try to catch it without hurting it? Then I would let it go outside. It was hilarious. I always felt good to save my family from those big scary bats.

When you kids were young, in the middle of the night, there would occasionally come a loud noise, a flash of light, or a bad dream, you kids would come running into our bedroom and jump up into bed with us and fall fast to sleep. No matter how scared you were just moments before, you were now at perfect peace, curled up there between your mother and I, without a care in the world. Sometimes, without knowing anyone else was there, I'd wake up in the morning with the surprise of having someone's butt or feet on my pillow and someone hogging all the blankets...

As Christians, being His children, we are commanded to act like it even in the midst of any storm. We should never act like there is no hope (1 Thessalonians 4:13). Nor should we act like we are alone in our troubles, because it's more than a continual theme throughout the Bible; it's a promise that He will never leave us or abandon us (Deuteronomy 31:6; 1 Chronicles 28:20; Hebrews 13:5). Furthermore, He will fight for you (Exodus 14:14; Deuteronomy 1:30).

When we become afraid, we can run to Him for our place of safety and in our need for help, because He loves us and He cares for us. Then don't just tell Him about our troubles, fears, and anxieties, give them to Him. If you are still fearful when you stop talking with Him, then it means you haven't given Him your fears yet. You need to trust Him because He has proven His love for us and promised that He will always be with us. I like what I heard more than one preacher say. Only one of us needs to stay awake over our problems, and if I am, He won't, and if He is, I won't need to. Remember He is God over this storm, over this disaster or trauma, over this coronavirus pandemic, and over every situation we will ever face in our lives. Also the way we trust Him during our time of crisis will be a big help and encouragement, let alone a powerful testimony to the people around us.

> *A father's tears and fears are unseen, his love is unexpressed, but his care and protection remain as a pillar of strength throughout our lives.* (Ama H. Vanniarachchy)

> *I am here to love you, to hold you in my arms, to protect you.* (Nicholas Sparks)

> *If by my life or death I can protect you, I will.* (J. R. R. Tolkien)

> *The day you came into my life, I knew what my purpose in life was. It was to love and protect you with everything I am and everything I have.* (Unknown)

> *Have I not commanded you? Be strong and courageous. Do not be afraid; do not be discouraged,*

for the Lord your God will be with you wherever you go. **(Joshua 1:9)**

But the Lord can be trusted to make you strong and protect you from harm. **(2 Thessalonians 3:3 CEV)**

No harm will overtake you; no illness will come near your home. **(Psalm 91:10 NET)**

Wise choices will watch over you. Understanding will keep you safe. **(Proverbs 2:11 NLT)**

"Daddy's Don't Leave"
Artist: Luke Combs
Sung by Nikki Davis

Daddy, I'm afraid. Won't you stay a little while?
Keep me safe 'cause there's monsters right outside
Daddy, please don't go. I don't wanna be alone
'Cause the second that you're gone, they're gonna know
Before he went to bed, he grabbed my hand and said

Just 'cause I'm leavin'
It don't mean that I won't be right by your side
When you need me
And you can't see me in the middle of the night
Just close your eyes and say a prayer
It's okay, I know you're scared when I'm not here
But I'll always be right there
Even though I'm leavin', I ain't goin' nowhere

Dad, we'll be late, and Uncle Sam don't like to wait
He's got a big old plane that's gonna take me far away
I know I act tough, but there's a churnin' in my gut
'Cause I just can't call you up when things get…
Before I left, he hugged my neck and said

Just 'cause you're leavin'
It don't mean that I won't be right by your side
When you need me
And you can't see me in the middle of the night
Just close your eyes and say a prayer

It's okay, I know you're scared, I might be here
But I'll always be right there
Even though you're leavin', I ain't goin' nowhere

Daddy, I'm afraid. Won't you stay a little while?
I never thought I'd see the day I had to say goodbye
Daddy, please don't go. I can't do this on my own
There's no way that I can walk this road alone
Well, Daddy grabbed my hand and said

Just 'cause I'm leavin'
It don't mean that I won't be right by your side
When you need me
And you can't see me in the middle of the night
Just close your eyes and say a prayer
It's okay, girl, I ain't scared
I won't be here, but I'll always be right there
Even though I'm leavin', I ain't goin' nowhere
I ain't goin' nowhere

You Are on a Journey

to change the world

There will be times when you feel like you're not going anywhere in this life or if you are that it's taking you places you don't want to go. No matter how you feel right now or where you are in life, I want you to know "you are on a journey" and you need to know that life is full of twists and turns that we can't always see around the next corner. However, we need to accept what comes our way and find the good in it or in spite of it. One of my favorite quotes is by the character Anne Shirley from the book *Anne of Green Gables*. When life has taken an unexpected turn for her, she says, "When I left Queen's my future seemed to stretch out before me like a straight road. I thought I could see along it for many a milestone. Now there is a bend in it. I don't know what lies around the bend, but I'm going to believe that the best does."

You might not think you are making a difference or you're changing anything big or small, let alone the world. In big ways and small, we have an ability to change the world. Do your best, and look for opportunities to make a difference in everywhere you go and with everyone you come into contact with. You never know what will make the difference or change someone's life or destination. A simple act of kindness, a kind word, or a friendly gesture. Truly the best thing we could ever do for anyone would be to tell them about Jesus and to pray with them. You never know where they are on their journey and what this might be the time they accept Christ and change their life.

No matter what the future holds or where this journey takes us, remember I'll be there with you for most of your journey, but if I ever happen not to be, remember that God still will and He will never leave you. I will just be waiting for you just a little beyond the finish line until you get there.

Life is a journey. It's not where you end up, but it's how you got there. (Unknown)

Life is a journey. Travel it well. (Unknown)

A journey is best measured in friends rather than miles. (Tim Cahill)

No act of kindness no matter how small is ever wasted. (Aesop)

Life is a journey to be experienced, not a problem to be solved. (Winnie the Pooh)

If you desire to make a difference in the world, you must be different from the world. (Elaine S. Dalton)

Throughout all their journeys, whenever the cloud was taken up from over the tabernacle, the people of Israel would set out. **(Exodus 40:36)**

And the priest said to them, "Go in peace. The journey on which you go is under the eye of the Lord." **(Judges 18:6)**

For He will command His angels concerning you to guard you in all your ways. **(Psalm 91:11)**

I Enjoy My Work and What I Do, but I Love My Family Most

Although, as you were growing up, there were many times when work was not going very well and I had to work a lot of longer grueling hours. There were too many of those times when I normally would have been at home and playing with you and your siblings but I was still at work. I hope you know that it wasn't because I put you or the family last. It was just that at the time I needed to do more to be able to pay the bills, to keep our family secure, or to not have to do without. I've always put my family first even when others thought differently.

I would have liked to have been able to have communicated my love and commitment to my family in a way that would have been more readily accepted and understood. I'm sure there were better ways than I knew how to express it. I know that more time communicates love better than less. Yet I also know that working hard to care for my family is a much higher demonstration of love than one who is willing to sacrifice their families' safety or security for fun or selfish endeavors. I know there must be a way to balance between the two, love shown through time and love shown through self-sacrifice and hard work.

To me, loving my family meant more about making sure that there was food, clothing, and shelter for my family. Although, if I was to live my life again, I would find more ways to be with my family more. I never pursued wealth as an end but only as a means. I have sacrificed much time, health, pleasure, and money for my family and don't regret that. Although, I would hope if I was able to redo my life, not only would I spend more time with my family, but I might be able to avoid many of the dangerous accidents, mishaps, and close calls the second time around too.

Find a way to speak your love to your family and the ones you love clearly and concisely not just in the language or way that we are the most skilled in or what comes easiest to us but in every way, and be willing to learn more ways to skillfully express your love. Then not only will your words and actions be able to communicate your love clearly, but your life will also be filled with the love you share. Learn to speak love fluently in many ways and languages.

What can you do to promote world peace? Go home and love your family. (Mother Teresa)

Hard work beats talent when talent doesn't work hard. (Tim Notke)

There is no substitute for hard work. (Thomas A. Edison)

Without hard work, nothing grows but weeds. (Gordon B. Hinckley)

Your work is going to fill a large part of your life, and the only way to be truly satisfied is to do what you believe is great work. And the only way to do great work is to love what you do. If you haven't found it yet, keep looking. Don't settle. As with all matters of the heart, you'll know when you find it. (Steve Jobs)

And whatever you do, in word or deed, do everything in the name of the Lord Jesus, giving thanks to God the Father through Him. **(Colossians 3:17)**

Work willingly at whatever you do, as though you were working for the Lord rather than for people. Remember that the Lord will give you an inheritance as your reward, and that the Master you are serving is Christ. **(Colossians 3:23–24)**

Whether therefore ye eat, or drink, or whatsoever ye do, do all to the glory of God. **(1 Corinthians 10:31)**

Never be lazy, but work hard and serve the Lord enthusiastically. Rejoice in our confident hope. Be patient in trouble, and keep on praying. **(Romans 12:11–12)**

And hardworking farmers should be the first to enjoy the fruit of their labor. Think about what I am saying. The Lord will help you understand all these things. **(2 Timothy 2:6–7)**

Love in Any Language

Artists: John Mays and Jon Mohr
Sung by Sandi Patty

Je t'aime
Te amo
Aishiteru
Ani ohevet othka, I love you
The sounds are all as different
As the lands from which they came
And though our words are all unique
Our hearts are still the same

We teach the young our differences
Yet look how we're the same
We love to laugh, to dream our dreams
We know the sting of pain

From Leningrad to Lexington
The farmer loves his land
And daddies all get misty-eyed
To give their daughter's hand
Oh, maybe when we realize
How much there is to share
We'll find too much in
    common
To pretend it isn't there

Though the rhetoric of government
May keep us worlds apart
There's no misinterpreting
The language of the heart

Love in any language, straight from the heart
Pulls us all together, never apart

And once we learn to speak it, all the world will hear
Love in any language, fluently spoken here
Love in any language, fluently spoken here
Love in any language, fluently spoken here

A Safe Haven Called Home

Here is a Safe Haven, a Place of Peace
Whenever You Need One.
Wherever I am, there is a welcome place of peace, hope,
safety, and encouragement for you to come home to.

I might not approve of every friend you will ever have or every decision you will ever make or everything you will ever do. I might not approve of every boyfriend you will ever fall for or every place you will ever go or every job you will ever have. Even so and no matter what, because I love you, I will always be here to support you, encourage you, love you, protect you, keep you safe, share my opinion with, and tell you the truth.

I'll fight for you or even die for you if necessary. No matter your decisions, passions, or place in life, no matter what the future may hold or where it may take us, I will always be here for you, because **I love you.**

No one in this world can love a girl more
than her father. (Michael Ratnadeepak)

Home is where love resides, memories are
created, friends always belong, and laughter
never ends. (Unknown)

What I love most about my home is those
who I share it with. (Unknown)

In this home...
We do second chances.
We do real.
We do mistakes.
We do I'm sorrys.
We do loud really well.

We do hugs.
We do together best of all. (Unknown)

> *My people will live in peaceful dwelling places, in secure homes, in undisturbed places of rest.* **(Isaiah 32:18)**

> *And thus you shall greet him: "Peace be to you, and peace be to your house, and peace be to all that you have."* **(1 Samuel 25:6)**

> *Whenever you enter a home, first say, "May God's peace be on this home!"* **(Luke 10:5)**

> *The L*ORD *curses the house of the wicked, but He blesses the home of the upright.* **(Proverbs 3:33 NLT)**

In this home…
We do second chances.
We do real.
We do mistakes.
We do I'm sorrys.
We do forgiveness.
We do loud really well.
We do hugs.
We do together best of all. (Unknown)

Love Isn't Just a Word or a Feeling

> love is an unselfish decision or commitment that is focused on the good and well-being of someone else.

If you go through life looking for a feeling that overwhelms you and causes you to feel elated or euphoric about another person, you might or might not ever find that. If you do find it, you will learn that those feelings will leave you as quickly as they came.

Your mother and I didn't base our marriage on how we feel, because many times we didn't feel happy with each other, we didn't feel "in love," we didn't feel married, we didn't feel we wanted to stay together, but we did. We didn't base our relationship, let alone our marriage, on a good feeling but commitment; and I'm so glad we did. It might be a bit of an old-fashioned, outdated idea, but if you haven't noticed, so is longevity marriages, and not too many are finding them.

If you have commitment as the basis of your relationships, it might not stop the storms from coming or the tears from falling, but it will mean you won't go through those times alone. It will also mean that you will have many of the good times, even great times that you can build on and outnumber the difficult ones. It even means that once you have gone down the road a ways and look back on the years, you will notice that even the difficult times will have had a value for you and have been worth the time and hardship of going through them.

> I am committed to love you forever.
> Nothing you can ever do could make me love you more.
> Nothing you could ever do could make me love you less.
> Just remember, I will always love you the most!
> I love you to the moon and back again.

Love is a commitment. Love is a verb, a constant effort. What it is not is an emotion. You don't feel love. You do it. (Unknown)

Love is a commitment that will be tested in the most vulnerable areas of spirituality, a commitment that will force you to make some very difficult choices. It is a commitment that demands that you deal with your lust, your greed, your pride, your power, your desire to control, your temper, your patience, and every area of temptation that the Bible clearly talks about. It demands the quality of commitment that Jesus demonstrates in His relationship to us. (Unknown)

Love is a combination of care, commitment, knowledge, responsibility, respect, and trust. (Bell Hooks)

Love is an unconditional commitment to an imperfect person. To love somebody isn't just a strong feeling. It is a decision, a judgment, and a promise. (Paulo Coelho)

In a far-off land the Lord *will manifest Himself to them. He will say to them, "I have loved you with an everlasting love. That is why I have continued to be faithful to you."* **(Jeremiah 31:3 NET)**

Above all, love each other deeply, because love covers over a multitude of sins. **(1 Peter 4:8)**

A new commandment I give to you, that you love one another: just as I have loved you, you also are to love one another. By this all people will know that you are My disciples, if you have love for one another. **(John 13:34–35)**

I Am on Your Side!

I don't care what anyone else says or thinks about you.

I remember when I was in school, I had a cousin who was in my grade and in many of my classes with me. He was shy and got picked on a lot at school, and I would always stand up for him. I would always let anyone who was picking on him know that they were picking on me, too, and if they wanted to fight him, they were going to have to fight me too. It wasn't just talk, and it cost me a lot. I got my butt kicked bad one time, but I didn't back down or fail to stand with my cousin then or after. (Shortly after that, I started into my martial arts training.)

We all face some time in our life when we just need to know that someone is on our side, someone will stand with us and stand up for us whenever we need them. Often if we just have one person we know is on our side, we can make it through whatever we are going through. (And it sure doesn't hurt if they are big and strong and know how to fight too.)

Just know I am here for you in your corner and by your side. You're not alone!

> *Daughter, I have created you for a unique and awesome purpose. Run forward in my love and approval. I am on your side…and I will never leave you or forsake you—NEVER!—God.* (Emily Toler, saved to Family, Faith, and the Future)

> *I am on your side, when times get rough, and friends just can't be found, like a bridge over troubled water, I will lay me down.* (Paul Simon, "Bridge over Troubled Water")

> *To the people I love: Please know I would never intentionally hurt or disappoint you. I may do both*

at times, but I'll always try to make it right. If you take time to share your feelings and needs, I am on your side. I am your friend and supporter. I may not be perfect, but I try, I care, and I will always be there. I will always be there for you. (Robert van M)

God will give us the strength to be able to handle things. I mean, you can try to do it on your own, and sometimes you can pull off some stuff, but in the long run, it's much easier with Him by our side. (Bethany Hamilton)

When you feel like no one loves you, remember that I love you. When you feel like no one is there to help you through things, remember that I am there, I am at your side. (Patience W. Smith)

I am on your side, and I will make sure that your land is plowed again and crops are planted on it. **(Ezekiel 36:9 GNT)**

*The L*ORD *is on my side, and I am not afraid of what others can do to me.* **(Psalm 118:6 CEV)**

Then my enemies will retreat on the day I cry for help. By this I will know that God is on my side. **(Psalm 56:9)**

I want you to realize that I continue to work as hard as I know how for you, and also for the Christians over at Laodicea. Not many of you have met me face-to-face, but that doesn't make any difference. Know that I'm on your side, right alongside you. You're not in this alone. **(Colossians 2:1 MSG)**

Live Your Life with Honesty and Integrity

And with as few regrets as possible.

Our life is an accumulation of all our thoughts, feelings, learning, things we have done as well as those we left undone, words we said and those we didn't say, and all experienced by the people we have touched and those who have touched us. That is who we are, and for the most part, we don't keep track of it. Only God does and knows. However, we can be careful with our daily actions, thoughts, feelings, and words we say. We need to be careful with how we impact and influence others as well as the opportunities we have to make sure we live this day honestly, truthfully, with integrity, and with kindness. If we do, we will have no regrets or things we will be held accountable for, and then we will have lived a good life today and can be proud of our actions.

> If anything matters then everything matters. Because you are important, everything you do is important. Every time you forgive, the universe changes; every time you reach out and touch a heart or a life, the world changes; with every kindness and service, seen or unseen, My purposes are accomplished and nothing will be the same again. (William Paul Young, *The Shack*)

I will always celebrate your successes and be there to encourage you through your failures.

I will be a good listener when you need to talk through something or someone who cares.

I will be a source of feedback or suggestions when you feel you've run out of options.

I will be with you and stand up for you whenever there is a line to be drawn.

I will always remind you of who you are and what you're capable of.
I will always try to guide you back whenever you've lost your way.
I will always remind you of God's love and plan for your life.
I will always pray for you and hope for the best for you.
I will always be there when you feel so all alone.
I will always care and want the best for you.
I will always try to protect and save you.
I will always defend you to the end.
I will always be a shield for you.
I will always be there for you.
I will always stand by you because
I will always love you.
I will love you
Always

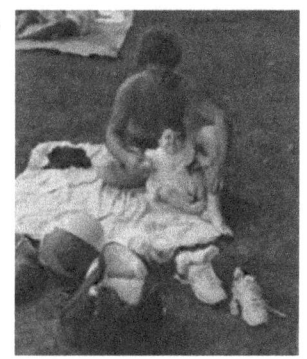

> *People of integrity and honesty not only practice what they preach, they are what they preach.* (David A. Bednar)

> *When you are able to maintain your own highest standards of integrity—regardless of what others may do—you are destined for greatness.* (Napoleon Hill)

> *A life lived with integrity—even if it lacks the trappings of fame and fortune is a shining star in whose light others may follow in the years to come.* (Denis Waitley)

> *Have the courage to say no. Have the courage to face the truth. Do the right thing because it is right. These are the magic keys to living your life with integrity.* (W. Clement Stone)

> *The Lord your God is in your midst, a mighty one who will save; He will rejoice over you with*

gladness; He will quiet you by His love; He will exult over you with loud singing. **(Zephaniah 3:17)**

It is God's will that you should be sanctified: that you should avoid sexual immorality; that each of you should learn to control your own body in a way that is holy and honorable, not in passionate lust like the pagans, who do not know God. **(1 Thessalonians 4:3–5)**

You Are More than Capable

I know that sometimes, my dear, you often doubt your ability to finish or accomplish something that I know you are able to do. There are times when the challenges and frustrations we face can get the better of us. Remember when you were trying to learn to write your cursive letters like the lower case *k*'s, and you would say, "I just can't do it!" It was definitely one of the times that it was hard on me not to just do it for you or excuse you because it seemed to frustrate you so much and made you struggle with it. But I want you to know "you are more than capable," you got this, and you can do it! I still remember your face when you finally mastered that cursive *s*.

> *God is able to do far more than we could ever ask for or imagine. He does everything by His power that is working in us. (Ephesians 3:20)*

> *I can do all things through Christ who strengthens me. (Philippians 4:13)*

> *No, in all these things we are more than conquerors through Him who loved us. (Romans 8:37 NIV)*

There Is Only One You!

You are special, and God made you unique and unlike anyone else who has ever lived or will ever live.

Your value is intrinsic. Your worth is eternal. No matter what struggles you have getting to where you are going, you will always be awesome to me.

There is only one you in all time. (Martha Graham)

What sets you apart can sometimes feel like a burden and it's not. And a lot of the time, it's what makes you great. (Emma Stone)

In order to be irreplaceable one must always be different. (Coco Chanel)

Always be a first-rate version of yourself, instead of a second-rate version of somebody else. (Judy Garland)

You are the light of the world. A city on a hill cannot be hidden. **(Matthew 5:14)**

You made me; You created me. Now give me the sense to follow Your commands. May all who fear You find in me a cause for joy, for I have put my hope in Your word. **(Psalm 119:73–74)**

For we are His workmanship, created in Christ Jesus for good works, which God prepared before-

hand, that we should walk in them. **(Ephesians 2:10 ESV)**

I praise You, for I am fearfully and wonderfully made. Wonderful are Your works; my soul knows it very well. **(Psalm 139:14 ESV)**

A Woman of Character

Strive to be a woman of character in all you do and say.

Reputation is who you are or what you do when others are watching. Character, on the other hand, is who you are and what you do when no one is looking.

> *Character is doing the right thing when nobody's looking. There are too many people who think that the only thing that's right is to get by; and the only thing that's wrong is to get caught.* (Unknown)

> *Nothing is more beautiful than a woman who is brave, strong, and emboldened because of who Christ is in her.* (Unknown)

> *Truthfulness is the main element of character.* (Unknown)

> *Character is what you are in the dark.* (Unknown)

> *Live such good lives among the pagans that, though they accuse you of doing wrong, they may see your good deeds and glorify God on the day He visits us.* **(1 Peter 2:12)**

> *And now, my daughter, don't be afraid. I will do for you all you ask. All the people of my town know that you are a woman of noble character.* **(Ruth 3:11 NIV)**

> *A wife of noble character who can find? She is worth far more than rubies.* **(Proverbs 31:10)**

And I want women to be modest in their appearance. They should wear decent and appropriate clothing and not draw attention to themselves by the way they fix their hair or by wearing gold or pearls or expensive clothes. **(1 Timothy 2:9 NLT)**

Always Hold Yourself to a Higher Standard

I know you were raised with the standard that all drug (except for doctor prescribed) and alcohol use is wrong. I know that the legal criteria of what is right and wrong seems to be changing and some politicians are trying to lower the legal age of drinking and make all drugs legal. I also know there is a lot of debate on this and a lot of people even feel it's okay for use recreationally. There are even many Christians and churches that have that belief or base their opinion on what the government currently says is legal or acceptable.

There are several reasons we took a strong prohibition against it:

First is that we wanted to keep you and your siblings safe from the influence of it.

To keep you guys safe from the effects of it.

To keep you guys safe from the fallout from it

Second, we wanted you to know that you don't have to lose your mind to have fun or to party.

Third, we didn't want you to think that you were more cool, popular, desirable when you are high than who you really are when you are completely in your right mind.

Fourth, I also knew that kids statistically will do twice the bad and half the good that they see their parents do. So I was really wanting to set you up for success.

If you hang around people who have a similar mind-set, it will help keep you and your family safer.

The feeling of getting high that is achieved from using drugs and alcohol is from the electrical system in your brain sparking and shorting out as brain cells are being killed as the drugs hit different brain cells while they are pumped through your blood and on into your brain. The strange thing is that you never know which brain cell will be affected or what the lasting effect will be after the high is gone. It could be cells from the part of the 80 percent of your brain that you are not currently using, or it could be the cells that keep you from drooling or from wetting yourself. I for one don't want to risk it, and I don't have any extra brain cells that I want to risk or give up.

Have you ever seen an old person who has used drugs or alcohol and compared them to someone the same age who didn't? The difference in their looks is very noticeable. Also, it weakens one's ability to use wisdom, reason to make the best choices, or be able to say "no". That's why every occult service/meeting always involves some kind of drugs and/or alcohol use. If that's not enough, the negative by far outweighs any good from using.

You are smart, beautiful, and fun just as you are.

I don't smoke, I don't drink, I don't use drugs. That may be boring for some people, but that's just me. That's how I live my life. (C. M. Punk)

The reason I don't drink is that the drinking lifestyle robs me of my musical intensity and sharpness. I live a super-healthy lifestyle not because it's sensible or that I'm contrite, but because I need to keep my focus on the music I'm making. To do that, I need to be wide awake. (Johnny Marr)

We don't do drugs, drink or use profanity. Instead, we instill morals and values in my boys by raising them with a love of God and a love and respect for themselves and all people. I believe they will have a chance. (Anita Baker)

My parents taught me a long time ago that you win in life with people, and that's important, because if you hang with winners, you stand a great chance of being a winner. (Pat Summitt)

Wine is a mocker and beer a brawler; whoever is led astray by them is not wise. **(Proverbs 20:1)**

Leaders can't afford to make fools of themselves, gulping wine and drinking beer, lest, hung over, they don't know right from wrong, and the people who depend on them will get hurt. **(Proverbs 31:4–5)**

It is better not to eat meat or drink wine or to do anything else that will cause your brother or sister to fall. **(Romans 14:21)**

"I have the right to do anything," you say—but not everything is beneficial. "I have the right to do anything"—but not everything is constructive. No one should seek their own good, but the good of others. **(1 Corinthians 10:23–24)**

Whatever You Are Going Through

Or no matter how bad it gets, just remember that this situation didn't catch God off guard and He has a plan for you that doesn't stop here.

Just hold on.
Don't quit.
And Never Give Up!
You're not alone.
Always remember, **I believe in you.**

There are times when, through no fault of your own, life really pulls the rug out from under your feet and it's just tough to know what to do or where to go. You're not alone in this. Others have been where you are and made it through it, so I know you can too. Sometimes, you just have to take it one day at a time, or even one moment at a time, and that's okay. Just don't give up. Keep going forward. Do your best and trust God with the rest. If you are following Him, He will lead you through whatever this situation is you are going through. I promise!

And if you need me, I'll be there. Because I love you.

I remember once I was working on building two stories up, everything was going good. It was a good day, and we were moving along quite well on the job. When all of a sudden, the next thing I knew, I was watching the building leave me, and I was looking up at where I was just previously standing. Then all of a sudden, there was an abrupt stop as I slammed into the ground flat on my back. The impact drove every bit of air from my lungs, and I felt every vertebrae of my back crack. My head was ringing, my vision went blurry, and I couldn't move. As I was almost on the ground, I felt the edge of the equipment trailer brush my short hair on one side of my head and a twelve-inch-tall steel form stake brush my hair on the other side of my head. I just lay there not knowing if I was alive or dead and if I was going to breathe or not, but I was, and I did. Although your grandfather and uncles and other employees I had working for me at the time all came running over to me to help me up, I just wanted to lie there until I could sit, then stand, and then slowly get back with my normal activity. By God's grace and little by little, I got back to doing what I needed to do.

Sometimes, life will drop you flat on your back and leave you gasping for air, but trust God, and take your time, and you'll be back up and running in no time. (Me)

I'm sorry and I believe in you and I'll always be near you, protecting you, and I will never leave you. I'll be curled around your heart for the rest of your life. (Jennifer Egan)

Promise me you'll always remember: You're braver than you believe, and stronger than you seem, and smarter than you think. (A. A. Milne)

I don't even think you know how great you really are. I believe in you. (Dick Vermeil)

I believe in you, I trust you, I know you can handle this, You are listened to, You are cared for, You are very important to me. (Barbara Coloroso)

God told you, "I will never abandon or forsaken you." **(Deuteronomy 31:6; Hebrews 13:5)**

I will never give you more than you can handle. **(1 Corinthians 10:13)**

You will always have a way through every problem. **(Isaiah 43:16–19)**

*Do not gloat over me, my enemies! For though I fall, I will rise again. Though I sit in darkness, the L*ORD *will be my light.* **(Micah 7:8 NLT)**

For though the righteous fall seven times, they will rise again. **(Proverbs 24:16 NIV)**

Sometimes the Best Things in Life Come in Threes

Three things in life that never come back when gone:
* Time
* Words
* Opportunity

Three things in life that should never be lost:
* Peace
* Hope
* Honesty

Three things in life that are most valuable:
* Our love
* Our faith
* Our health

Three things that can destroy a person:
* Lust
* Pride
* Anger

Three things in life that are constant:
* Change
* Death
* God

Three things that make a person:
* Hard work
* Sincerity
* Commitment

Three things I asked God for you:
* To bless you
* To guide you
* To ALWAYS protect you

Three things I want God to do for you:
* To save you
* To fill you with the Holy Spirit
* To use you mightily

Three who will always be there for you:
* Your God
* Your parents
* Your family

Three things you can't live without:
* Brain waves
* Heartbeat
* Breath

Three who love you and who will never leave you alone:
* The Father
* The Son
* The Holy Spirit

Three things everyone has:
* A past
* A present
* A Future

Three things everyone wants:
* Love
* Forgiveness
* Acceptance

Three words everyone wants to hear:
* I love you
* I forgive you
* Time to eat

There are three things that amaze me—no, four things that I don't understand... There are three things that make the earth tremble—no, four it cannot endure... There are four things on earth that are small but unusually wise... There are three things that walk with stately stride—no, four that strut about. (**Proverbs 30:18, 21, 24, 29**)

(Curious? Find out what they are. Read Proverbs 30:18–31.)

You Are Never Alone

From now to forever, I will always be with you, watching you, and cheering you on. You are not alone!

Sometimes, we get lost, confused, or even stressed out to the point that the world seems like a big, bad, deep, dark woods; and we feel all alone with no light, no hope, and no help. It could be a relationship gone bad, a financial crisis, a health problem, or a legal issue that seems to rock our world and leave us feeling hopelessly alone and afraid. Whatever the situation, life doesn't always play fair or nice and has a way to catch us off guard and leave us feeling hopeless.

It's not an indictment against you to feel this way or to be in these kinds of situations. Everyone will go through it at least once in their lifetime, most will go through times like that more than once, and some will many times. Sometimes, we can rightly avoid these falls, but what I've noticed is that the more we work with people, the more we will have to expect to go through some tough times.

Whenever you feel too afraid to walk alone, remember you are the center of God's attention, He's watching you, and He's with you always. His Holy Spirit will talk with you, guide you, and comfort you. God has set His angels around about you to protect you and keep you safe. All day, every day, everywhere, 24-7, 365; and if that's not enough, I'll always love you and be there for you too! (Smile.)

I will always be your greatest fan and be here to encourage and help you. Whenever you need me, I'll be here for you. You are never alone!

You've always had people who care about you. Always. Don't pretend like you have to go through this alone. (Emory R. Frie)

What lies behind us and what lies before us are tiny matters compared to what lies within us. (Ralph Waldo Emerson)

Loneliness is my least favorite thing about life. The thing that I'm most worried about is just being alone without anybody to care for or someone who will care for me. (Anne Hathaway)

I may not always be there with you, but I will always be there for you. (Unknown)

For Jesus is coming soon… Therefore encourage one another with these words. **(1 Thessalonians 4:16–18)**

Therefore encourage one another and build each other up, just as in fact you are doing. **(1 Thessalonians 5:11)**

And let us consider one another to provoke unto love and to good works: **(Hebrews 10:24–25)**

Even after I'm gone, I still will be watching, cheering you on, waiting to be with you again. *Such a large crowd of witnesses is all around us! So we must get rid of everything that slows us down, especially the sin that just won't let go. And we must be determined to run the race that is ahead of us.* **(Hebrews 12:1 CEV)**

I'm Already There

Artists: Richie McDonald, Frank Myers, and Gary Baker
Sung by Lonestar

I'm already there
Don't make a sound
I'm the beat in your heart
I'm the moonlight shining down
I'm the whisper in the wind
And I'll be there until the end
Can you feel the love that we share?
Oh, I'm already there

We may be a thousand miles apart
But I'll be with you wherever you are

I'm already there
Take a look around
I'm the sunshine in your hair
I'm the shadow on the ground
I'm the whisper in the wind
And I'll be there until the end
Can you feel the love that we share?
Oh, I'm already there
Oh, I'm already there

You Are Imperfect (and That's Okay)

Because I'm not perfect either, yet as you know, I can tend to be a recovering perfectionist. I'm not sure how that works, being an imperfect perfectionist that is, but I know there are an awful lot of us imperfect people who are trying to be perfect. I don't know how everyone else does it, but for me, I know I can sometimes blur the lines between high standards that I set for myself and expecting perfection in everything else. And I need to confess that those lines can get blurred even with the expectations I have for my family too.

You see enough "fake" perfection everywhere today, on highway billboards, magazines, Hollywood movies, store ads. Society is always telling us what they expect us to be, act, and look like; yet it's an impossible expectation that they themselves cannot achieve. I want you to know that you're not perfect, and I don't expect you to be, and that's okay. We had one perfect person in the world (Jesus), and He was perfect for us, and that's enough so you and I don't have to be. Thank God!

> *For everyone has sinned; we all fall short of God's glorious standard. Yet God, in His grace, freely makes us right in His sight. He did this through Christ Jesus.* **(Romans 3:9–24 NLT)**

> *Each time He said, "My grace is all you need. My power works best in weakness." So now I am glad to boast about my weaknesses, so that the power of Christ can work through me. That's why I take pleasure in my weaknesses, and in the insults, hardships, persecutions, and troubles that I suffer for Christ. For when I am weak, then I am strong.* **(2 Corinthians 12:9–10 NLT)**

Better to do something imperfectly than to do nothing flawlessly. (Unknown)

I'm not perfect in my walk, but I want to do the right thing. (Kirk Cameron)

If you're not perfect, don't expect the other guys to be perfect. (Kolo Toure)

You can learn a lot from your mistakes when you aren't busy denying them. (Unknown)

Rights, Wrongs, and Reasons

> Easy is Seldom Right, and Choosing
> What is Right is Never Wrong!

Always choose the best, the high road, the right way whenever there is a choice.

Especially when it's the hardest choice, because that's when it counts the most.

Best isn't the best because it's the easiest or the quickest or the most popular. It's Best because it's the most right thing we can do or answer we can give.

Right is always right, and wrong is always wrong, no matter the reason.

A lot of people look at a problem in different ways. Some always look for the easiest way to correct it or fix it or make it right. Some look for a way that would be the cheapest way to fix it. Others look for a way that would get them the most attention or praise. However, when the situation is done the right or best way, sometimes it is the cheapest, easiest way, or sometimes people do notice, but that can't be the reason for the decision. Whatever is the right or best way to make this decision is the correct answer for this problem.

Then, too, not every problem or decision has a right or wrong answer. On those, just do your best. But whenever there is a situation or problem that you are struggling to know how to handle, always take time to pray about it, and ask God what He would want you to do with it. Then do it the way that He impresses on you to do it. He will give you help whenever you ask Him, and He will lead you in the right way. And if ever I can be of help, I am here for you, Because I Love you.

> *Life is too short to try and please everyone. Take charge and do what's right—not what's popular.* (Farshad Asl)

Integrity is doing the right thing, even when no one is watching. (C. S. Lewis)

The time is always right to do what is right. (Martin Luther King Jr.)

The truth of the matter is that you always know the right thing to do. The hard part is doing it. (Robert H. Schuller)

The power of one man or one woman doing the right thing for the right reason, and at the right time, is the greatest influence in our society. (Jack Kemp)

And let us not grow weary of doing good, for in due season we will reap, if we do not give up. **(Galatians 6:9)**

See that no one repays anyone evil for evil, but always seek to do good to one another and to everyone. **(1 Thessalonians 5:15)**

So whoever knows the right thing to do and fails to do it, for Him it is sin. **(James 4:17)**

Decide Wisely

Wisdom compels us to look to wisdom to make wise decisions.

We, too, need wisdom in our lives to make the best decisions.

Talent is both learned and natural ability, and skill is needed to accomplish anything.

Knowledge is both formal and informally learned facts.

And, of course, experience is the things you have done yourself.

However, wisdom is knowing how to use the knowledge, experience, and even talents you have to make the best choices and know how to do what is right for that time, place, and situation.

To make good choices about things in our life or world, we need to have a general knowledge of how things work and why. If I am going to work on my car and keep it going, I need to know basically how it works and what the different groups or systems do and the purpose of the parts and how they work together. The same is true about my life or the world around me. I need to know basically how it works, why it's here, the purpose of each part, and how everything is supposed to work together. I can look at it from the world's point of view that everything just happened for no reason or purpose and our life is just a blurb on the evolutionary process to something better… No point, no purpose, no hope, no reason…

The other choice or perspective I can go from is, I can look at it from God's point of view that everything has a reason for being here—there is a grand plan and a purpose that involves you, me, and everything around us. That you were specially made with purpose and He promised you great things that He has planned out for you. That God has everything working intricately together from the farthest solar system to the smallest molecule. Therefore, all we have to do in every situation is to talk with Him and see what His plan is and what He wants us to do. If we know His plan and follow it, we can be confident in what is the right way and that it will always work out the way it is supposed to work out.

If ever you need help finding the right way to go, just ask, and I'll be glad to help.

If you ever need an excuse to do the right thing, you can always blame me; I don't mind.

> *Wisdom is knowing the right path to take. Integrity is taking it.* (Anonymous)

> *Wisdom is knowledge that is guided by understanding; we have to have the wisdom and the knowledge to understand why certain things happen in our lives and trust that God will lead us over any obstacles that comes in our way.* (Anonymous)

> *More than any other time in history, mankind faces a crossroads. One path leads to despair and utter hopelessness. The other, to total extinction. Let us pray we have the wisdom to choose correctly.* (Woody Allen)

> *The older you get, the more quiet you become. Life humbles you so deeply as you age. You realize how much nonsense you've wasted time on.* (Anonymous)

Get wisdom; develop good judgment.
Don't forget My words or turn away from them.
Don't turn your back on wisdom, for she will protect you.
Love her, and she will guard you.
Getting wisdom is the wisest thing you can do!
And whatever else you do, develop good judgment.
If you prize wisdom, she will make you great.
Embrace her, and she will honor you.
She will place a lovely wreath on your head;

she will present you with a beautiful crown. **(Proverbs 4:5–9 NLT)**

If any of you need wisdom, you should ask God, and it will be given to you. God is generous and won't correct you for asking. **(James 1:5 CEV)**

What Does Politics Have to Do with Anything?

My political standing

As you know, I am not soft-spoken or timid about what I believe about politics.

I'm sorry if it offends you or anyone else; but I am by no means a Democrat, a Liberal, or anything on the left. Even our founding fathers of this nation wanted to keep this nation from becoming a democracy because they believed that if it did, it would soon become nothing but a nation run by "Mob Rule," and our freedoms and morality would be lost. That's why the national pledge of allegiance reminds us we are a Republic. "And to the republic for which it stands..." Although, it might surprise you that I can't say that I have never voted for a Democrat before. I can't remember who it was, but it seems I remember a time that I might have back in the early 1980s. I can't say that the Democrat Party has always been the cesspool of morality and against everything I believe in or stand for, that it is today. If you look back in history, they were a lot further to the right than many of the Republicans of today.

On January 20, 1961, John F. Kennedy said, "Ask not what your country can do for you. Ask what you can do for your country," in an address to motivate people to civil and charitable action. In contrast, today's Democrats are fat cats getting filthy rich while supposedly "serving" the people of this nation. Most of the founding fathers lost all their wealth and lives in service to this country and did it knowing that would more than likely be their outcome. However, these politicians today have brainwashed the people to think that they are owed everything they want and for free—health care, college education, food, housing, and a monthly check to boot. Nowadays, they serve in Washington so they can get rich with the side deals and special interest groups that line their pockets.

The Dems have even made some feel they are owed everything, more yet because of their skin color or what happened to their grandparents five to ten generations back. So they should have the right to kill their babies. They have a right to have "A's" for their grades no matter how hard they work or not. They have a right to have everything given to them and get a monthly allowance to boot. They also have a right to disrespect our leaders, soldiers, flag, and country; and no matter what they do, they should get a free pass out of jail. This isn't just a statement of American delinquency; it's the lifestyle the modern-day Democrats are pushing on our country. It's bad, it's wrong, and it's poisoning our nation.

If that isn't enough, the Dems have formally Removed God from everything and have been becoming more and more hostile against God and the things of God, as well as the people of God and anything they would do or say. They promote abortion for any reason and for all nine months, and some are even pushing for an open-ended time for a legal abortion. Some have even said they want to make it legal for abortion to be performed even after natural birth. They have been for euthanasia rights (for now for terminally ill patients, whatever time line that might mean; but following other countries, it will soon be for anyone who want to kill themselves and for any reason). They have been promoting drug use and decriminalizing all drug use. They have also been promoting and trying to legalize, all types of immoral sex deviation and promiscuity and trying to make it all become socially acceptable behavior. Then they are defunding the police, getting rid of the military, and outlawing legal citizens from having any guns (in the news today, they were talking about outlawing kids from having water guns, BB guns, and other toy guns too). Then they open the borders to the country with no qualifying, stopping, or checking at the border at all, even for our enemies. They also want to get rid of our Constitution so they can change this nation into a socialist nation and then submit us under the authority of the other countries. This isn't everything that I can't stand about the Democrat Party. Their heroes are people like Karl Marx (under Marxism, more than one hundred million people have died, either from being murdered or from starvation) and Mao

Zedong (who, some reports say, is responsible for killing as many as sixty-five million of his own Chinese citizens to gain power and control). I could have just simply said that everything I believe in, they are against, and everything I am against, they are for. It's easy to read their entire platform online and find out for yourself what they believe and want.

*****

I am also against the Libertarian Party because they tend to be against any government control, police, laws, and the military. They tend to favor socialism, anarchy, privatization of the road system, the complete legalization of all drug use, and the worst thing is, they are for no restrictions on abortions. You can go to their parties' website, and see for yourself.

*****

I am very much against the Socialist Party although they say they are for equality and fairness they always put the value of the individual under that of the state or elite. They say they are against the classes of people and will make everyone equal; but they always produce two classes, the elite and the poor. They oppose or outlaw the church. The state is the final say and holds total authority, and the people have little value. Every socialist country has fallen and destroyed their wealth, their nation, and their people. There is nothing good or lasting that Socialist society has ever done; and they have all ended in death, destruction, poverty, and starvation. They totally subjugate the people and destroy the nation.

*****

The Natural Law Party is mostly just a joke party based on transcendental meditation and new age mumbo jumbo, but they're a for real political party in our country.

*****

I am totally against the Green Party. They are another socialist party, social justice, equality, worship the earth, and willing to sacrifice people for the earth. They are basically the same as the Democrats just to differing degrees on the same stupid radical beliefs.

*****

It might surprise you that I do not even consider myself a Republican, and I try not to ever vote straight ticket Republican, although they are the ones I most closely follow. For a while, the Republican Party was continually going further and further left. As a matter of fact, the Republican Party had left the right so far that they began to look like the Liberal Democrats did forty years ago. They came close to changing their party's political platform, moving away from their stance on opposing abortion, supporting military, church, and God among a lot of other stupid decisions. This was before President Trump took office in 2016. I was close to giving up on them. Then he brought the party back to a new high and "Made America Great Again" and renewed my confidence in the party. However, I will still watch them closely and be quick to vote quite a few of those jokers out of office if someone good would run against them.

*****

I do believe in the Constitution party or at least what they stand for. They are a total right-wing Christian-based party that wants to bring the country all the way back to its original Constitution roots as the founding fathers originally intended it to be. They also believe in the Christian principles that form the bases of this country from its beginnings. The only problem is I don't know if they will ever be a real challenge to the main runners in any race or vote, but if they ever could be, I would definitely be there with them.

*****

As far as my political views and what I do, first of all, politics are very important and something we need to not only talk about but be involved with. I believe we must pray for our president and leaders. Paul wrote, *"I urge, then, first of all, that petitions, prayers, intercession and thanksgiving be made for all people—for kings and all those in authority, that we may live peaceful and quiet lives in all godliness and holiness"* (1 Timothy 2:1–4). I believe we need to show proper respect to our leaders and the office they hold. *"Show proper respect to everyone, love the family of believers, fear God, honor the emperor"* (1 Peter 2:17). However, we can and we must keep our politicians accountable by contacting them regularly and reminding them of what they need to be doing—reminding them that they work for the people and if they can't do their job, we'll vote them out and find someone who will. Anyone I believe in and feel led to, I will support and help them in any way I can. I'll even work in their campaign if they need my help. I truly believe we need to be praying for whoever is in office, for God to lead, guide, protect, save, correct, or even remove them if necessary.

I will always try my best not to throw away a vote on a dead-horse candidate, especially if it might help put a much worse person in office if I do. Even if I like one candidate better but I know he is an impossible win, I would rather have my second favorite person that I hope can do the job than someone I know would be a terrible one to get into office.

I believe that when we are picking a leader especially, we need to try to pick someone as close to a true-blue real man (or woman) of God as possible. But follow God's leading because God can have something planned that just might surprise you. Romans 13:1 says that God establishes the leaders and those in authority, so we need to seek to choose the leaders whom God chooses for us (even if it's someone that you wouldn't necessarily choose). That's how it was the presidential election of 2016 with specifically now President Trump. There were other men I would have much rather have had on the ballot. However, after the primaries were over, I saw the only two real candidates who had a chance of winning were Hillary Clinton and Donald J Trump. I knew that Hillary Clinton was the farthest thing from anything right, good, or honest, let alone godly. I knew I had to vote for Trump, if only to vote against Hillary. There were others who ran on the Liberal ticket and Green ticket that almost split the vote enough that Hillary could have won the vote, but thank God she didn't.

There were many Christians who were upset about Trump just being a rich businessman and his millionaire playboy lifestyle that he was reported to be living and that he had been married three times, and so they refused to back him and tried to get others to turn from him. Problem is it almost got us Hillary as our president instead, and then still after the election was over, they did their best to make it harder for him to do all the good stuff he was trying to do. It also might have been one of the things that ended up costing us the 2020 election and given us the direction/future we now have. God, help us and forgive us.

*****

Let me interrupt this right now and say that, however long we have left here in this old world or until Jesus comes, whatever is to come, I believe the biggest changes for the future have started here and now. I want to say that I am truly sorry for what we (mine and the previous generations) have done to everything and now the condition it's all in as we hand it down to you. The world you have inherited is messed up exactly as the Bible warned us would happen if we walked away from Him… and we are sorry. We are praying for you, even now with what you have to work with and the time that is left. Seek God, His blessing, and His guidance for this country and what you do from here on until the end.

*****

God Has High Standards and Rules and Great Penalty for **Parents**.

Deuteronomy 7:14 and Psalm 127:3–5 say they must realize that children are a **blessing** from God.

Deuteronomy 6:6–9, 4:40, and Proverbs 27:11 say they must **teach** their children the Word of God.

Proverbs 1:8–9 says they must **instruct** and teach them what is right and true.

Proverbs 22:6 says they must **train** them to what is right for their future.

First Samuel 3:13 says they need to **confront** their children about any **evil** they know of them doing.

Joel 1:3 says they must **tell** their children **the stories** of what God has done.

Ephesians 6:4 says they must **not be cruel or mean** in their discipline and training.

Colossians 3:21 says they must **not allow** their children to become **discouraged**.

Proverbs 13:24, 19:18, 22:15, 23:13–14, and 29:15–17 say all speak of the importance of using **appropriate punishment,** including corporal punishment.

Malachi 4:6 says they must truly **Love** their children.

First Timothy 5:8 and Second Corinthians 12:18 say they must **Provide for** and take care of their family.

First Timothy 3:4 says they must **take care** of and teach their children respect.

First Timothy 3:5 says they must **manage** their house and family.

Luke 11:11–13 says they must **do good for** their children and take care of their needs.

Exodus 20:5 says they must realize that a parent's sin can bring a **curse** upon their children.

First Samuel 3:13 says they must realize that it's a **sin not to discipline** their children for their wrongdoings that they know of.

There are a lot of rules, regulations, and expectations placed on **Parents** to nurture, care for, provide for, teach God's word to, guide, correct, and discipline their children. There are also great consequences for those who don't or won't.

*****

God Has an Even Higher Standards and Rules and Greater Penalty for **Teachers**.

Deuteronomy 11:18–21 says to **teach the Word** of God all the time and in every way possible so the children will grow up and be blessed.

> *"Show yourself in all respects to be a **model of good works**, and in your teaching show **integrity**, **dignity**, and sound speech that cannot be condemned, so that an opponent may be put to shame, having nothing evil to say about us"* (**Titus 2:7–8**).

> *"Don't aim at adding to the number of teachers, my brothers, I beg you! Remember that we who are **teachers will be judged** by a much higher standard"* (**James 3:12 Phillips**).

Peter 2:1–2 says teachers who don't teach the truth will "*bringing upon themselves **swift destruction**.*"

There are a lot of rules, regulations, and expectations placed on **Teachers** and especially those who teach the Word of God, teach God's word. They should be a good example, watch what they say, have integrity, and have dignity. There are also great consequences for those who don't or won't.

God Has an Even Higher Standards and Rules and Greater Penalty for **Preachers**.

Jeremiah 3:15 says he must be a man of **wisdom, knowledge, and understanding**.

Ephesians 4:12 says he must **enable his people to serve** God.

First Timothy 3:2, Acts 20:28, and 1 Peter 5:2 say he must **shepherd** and **teach** those in his care.

First Timothy 3:2 and Titus 1:6 say he must be **male** and faithfully **married** to one wife.

First Timothy 3:5 states he must be able "to **manage his** own **household**."

First Timothy 3:12 says he "must **manage his children** and his household well."

First Timothy 5:17–18 says he should be **compensated** for his labor.

Second Timothy 4:2 says he must always be **ready to preach**, **correct**, **rebuke**, or **encourage** with patience.

James 1:19 says he must be "**slow to anger**" or not quick-tempered.

First Peter 5:2–3 says he must **not think that he is better** than those under his care.

He must not be concerned for **personal gain** or **profit**.

He must **be an example** to those watching him.

He must fulfill his calling **joyfully, not begrudgingly**.

Titus 1:6–9 says an elder must be **blameless**, faithful to his **wife**, a man whose **children** believe and are not open to the charge of being wild and disobedient. Since an overseer manages God's household, he must be **blameless**—not **overbearing**, not **quick-tempered**, not given to **drunkenness**, not **violent**, not pursuing **dishonest** gain. Rather, he must be **hospitable**, one who **loves** what is good, who is **self-controlled, upright, holy,** and **disciplined**. He must hold firmly to the trustworthy **message** as it has been taught so that he can **encourage** others by sound doctrine and **refute** those who oppose it.

Ezekiel 34:3 says he needs to be **concerned** for the people. He must not be in it for **personal gain**. He must **take care of** the flock. He must **strengthen** the weak, **heal** the sick, and bind up the injured. He must be **concerned** for the strays and the lost and **try to win them** back. He must lead with **kindness** and **compassion**. He must **watch over them** and try to protect and keep them from wandering off. He must **listen to** the voice of **God**. He must **care for** those under his care. He will be **punished** for not caring for those under his care. He will be **removed** from his position.

Second Peter 2:1, 3, 11, 12, and 17 say if he is a false shepherd, swift **destruction** will suddenly come upon them. If he is a false shepherd, he will be **condemned** to hell. The shepherds will be **judged**. The false shepherds will **suffer** and be **destroyed**. The **worst part of hell** is reserved for the false shepherds.

There are a lot of rules, regulations, and expectations placed on Church leaders and especially **Pastors** to nurture, teach God's word, and represent Jesus to those in their care. There are also a lot of severe consequences for those who don't or won't.

To the leaders in a church, *"Wherefore, brethren, look ye out among you seven men of **honest** report, **full of the Holy Ghost** and **wisdom**, whom we may appoint over this business"* **(Acts 6:3)**.

God Has High Standards and Rules and Great Penalty for Any **Leader** from Those of Small Groups to Large Groups.

To the leaders in the community, *"But select from all the people some **capable**, **honest** men who **fear God** and **hate bribes**. Appoint them as leaders over groups of one thousand, one hundred, fifty, and ten"* **(Exodus 18:21–25)**.

There are several rules, regulations, and expectations placed on **Community leaders** to have Skill or Ability, be Honest, Born Again, and not accept any Bribes. There are also consequences for those who don't or won't.

*****

God Also Has Standards for **Kings** or **Presidents**, That Must Be Considered for **Choosing a National Leader**. For Rulers of Nations They Are to consider the following:

Deuteronomy 17:14–15 says he must be the one whom **God has chosen**.

Deuteronomy 17:14–15 says he must be a **natural-born citizen** from among your people.

Deuteronomy 17:16 says he must **not work to collect** treasure or wealth for himself.

Deuteronomy 17:16 says he must **not make personal alliances** with your enemies.

Deuteronomy 17:17 says he must **not have many wives**.

Deuteronomy 17:17 says he must **not be allowed to gain a lot of wealth** while in office.

Deuteronomy 17:18–19 says he **must value**, read, and keep a copy of **the law** for himself.

> *"Then he will **not exalt himself** above his fellow citizens or **turn from the commandments** to the right or left, and he and his descendants will enjoy many years ruling over his kingdom in Israel"* (Deuteronomy 17:20 NET).

Psalm 2:10 says he must "*show* (good) ***discernment***" and **fear God**.

Psalm 16:12 says he must **do what is right** and not evil.

Proverbs 20:28 says he must be **committed to his nation** and do what is right.

Proverbs 29:4 says he must **do what is right** and **not accept bribes**.

Proverbs 11:14 says if he doesn't use wisdom or take good counsel, **the nation will fall**.

Job 12:23–25 says depending on the way the nation is led, **God will bless or destroy** it.

There are a lot of rules, regulations, and expectations placed on Kings or **Presidents** such as to, first and foremost, must be the one whom God has chosen. Beyond that, he must be a citizen of the country he is to serve, not be in there for personal gain or profit, not think he is better than the people, have good wisdom or understanding, know the law, be committed to his nation and its people, do what is right, not accept bribes, and be a Christian. There are also great consequences for those who don't or won't.

Everybody Needs Somebody Sometime

We all need someone on whom we can depend who won't let us down, someone to be our Jesus with skin on…and I hope I can be yours.

There once was a little boy who was scared of thunder and lightning. Of course, it was night, and he was supposed to be in bed but would wake up at each flash and crash and cry for his daddy. His dad would go to him talk to him and pray with him. Then before he would leave, he would tell him, "And remember, Jesus is here with you." Then the next flash and crash, and the whole process would start all over again. Finally, in desperation, his father said, "Don't you remember that Jesus is here with you?" And his son replied, "Yes, but sometimes, I just need Jesus with skin on."

I don't know about jumping tall buildings and flying through the air with the greatest of ease, but nothing can stop me from loving or helping you. I'll be your Jesus with skin on if ever you need one.

If you ever need me, I'll be there, <u>for I am</u> **Dad**!

> *My Father's two greatest superpowers was his ability to believe in me, and be there for me.*

> *When you're young, you think your dad is Superman. However, you grow up, and you realize he's just a regular guy who wears a cape. Then when you get old and look back, you find out he really was, and you wish he was still around.* (Unknown)

Of all the titles I've been privileged to have, "Dad" has always been the best. (Ken Norton)

Every dad, if he takes time out of his busy life to reflect upon his fatherhood, can learn ways to become an even better dad. (Jack Baker)

To her, the name of father was another name for love. (Fanny Fern)

So be strong and courageous! Do not be afraid and do not panic before them. For the Lord your God will personally go ahead of you. He will neither fail you nor abandon you. **(Deuteronomy 31:6 NLT)**

God assured us, "I'll never let you down, never walk off and leave you," we can boldly quote, God is there, ready to help; I'm fearless no matter what. Who or what can get to me? **(Hebrews 13:5 MSG)**

In My Daughter's Eyes
Artist: Martina McBride

In my daughter's eyes
I am a hero
I am strong and wise
And I know no fear
But the truth is plain to see
She was sent to rescue me
I see who I want to be
In my daughter's eyes

In my daughter's eyes
Everyone is equal
Darkness turns to light
And the world is at peace
This miracle God gave to me
Gives me strength when I am weak
I find reason to believe
In my daughter's eyes

And when she wraps her hand around my finger
How it puts a smile in my heart
Everything becomes a little clearer
I realize what life is all about
It's hanging on when your heart is had enough
It's giving more when you feel like giving up
I've seen the…

A Kiss Good Night

*It's not just children who need someone
to tuck them in at night.*

A piggyback ride, a bounce on the bed, a story, a tickle, a bedtime prayer, a kiss good night. Then a tickle, a tuck tight in bed, pulling the covers too high and then under your chin. Grins and giggles and one more kiss good night and then lights out door shut and one last "I love you the most." Then as soon as I sit down, a little voice calls with a desperate plea, a glass of water, a promise, and one secret to tell. Then lights out, but all is not done, because little girls like glasses of water and secrets, to sing songs and getting up one more time to go potty. But after a promise, a threat, a stern talking to, one more glass of water, a tickle, a prayer, and a kiss good night, finally the house goes dark, and to beds, we all go, and just as night gets quiet, we hear, "Good night, Jim-Bob. Good night, Maryellen. Good night, Johnboy." On it goes until your mom would say, "Now that's enough. Go to sleep." Then once again, just as night gets quiet and dark and sleep starts to come and all of the day seems done, the sound of little feet is followed by a little one climbing over me, and as my pillow is taken and I'm crowded half out of bed, I know all is well and my family is safe. Oh, how I just wish this could have gone on forever. What I wouldn't give to be able to do that all again tonight.

We tuck a small child in at night so they know that all is well and safe and they can relax and know that they are protected and loved…but I want you to know that as you lay your head on your pillow at night that I am bowing my head in prayer for you. I am thanking God for my daughter and asking for His Love and blessing to overwhelm you. As you close your eyes, I am placing a kiss upon your forehead. So sleep soundly tonight, my dear daughter, knowing all is well because you are forever loved and protected.

A daughter is a treasure and a cause of sleeplessness. (Ben Sirach)

Always kiss your children goodnight, even if they're already asleep. (H. Jackson Brown Jr.)

Now I lay her down to sleep, I know her love will not come cheap, her dreams and goals I forever will try, to keep her walking by the Savior's side. Help me, Lord, for I know not how to be the father she needs right now, but as we walk this path together, please, Lord, keep us both now and forever. (Me)

And the angels of the Lord shall pitch their tents round about them that fear Him. **(Psalm 91:11)**

I will lie down and sleep in peace, for You alone, O Lord make me dwell in safety. **(Psalm 4:8)**

For He gives to His beloved sleep. **(Psalm 127:2)**

When you lie down, you will not be afraid, when you lie down, your sleep will be sweet. **(Proverbs 3:24)**

Good Night, My Little Girl, I Love You the Most

I wish we could stay at the time when you still needed me, to read stories to you before you could settle down to sleep. Then you wanted me to get you a glass of water because you were sooo thirsty and had to have a glass of water before you could go sleep. Then there were the secrets you had to tell me and didn't want anyone to hear. Then just when we thought we finally had won and you were ready to go to sleep, you would want to ask me a very important question that you were thinking about. Then by the time we got through all of that, your mother would be upset that I was letting you waste too much time before getting you to bed… **Good times!** Where has time gone? It only seems like yesterday you would be calling out, "Daddy, Daddy, I need you."

I would like to think that you still do need me even if it's just for a distraction for what you otherwise should be doing or to help you settle down. The two greatest things any father has ever heard is, "Daddy, I love you!" and "Daddy, I need you!"

> *Always end the day with a positive thought. No matter how hard things were, tomorrow's a fresh opportunity to make it better.* (Unknown)

> *Before you go to sleep, don't forget to thank God for every good thing that has happened to you in the last twenty-four hours. For me, I am thanking God for you right now.* (Me)

I think the best way to get a good night's sleep is to work hard throughout the day. If you work hard and, of course, work out. (William H. McRaven)

Before you go to sleep remember, it's okay to not be okay. We all have our struggles. But God loves you too much to leave you that way. (John Reese)

When you lie down, you will not be afraid, when you lie down, your sleep will be sweet. **(Proverbs 3:24)**

For He gives to His beloved sleep. **(Psalm 127:2)**

I will lie down and sleep in peace, for You alone, O Lord make me dwell in safety. **(Psalm 4:8)**

Come to Me and I will give you rest—all of you who work so hard beneath a heavy yoke. Wear My yoke—for it fits perfectly—and let Me teach you; for I am gentle and humble, and you shall find rest for your souls; for I give you only light burdens. **(Matthew 11:28 TLB)**

Your Own Special Song

Each of you kids all had your own special song we made up to sing to you when you were little. Your mom or I would often sing your song to you starting when you were a baby until you were a few years old and started complaining about hearing it. We would often sing it when you were fussy, and we would try to get you to settle down and go to sleep.

"Annamarink-a-dink-a-dink"
Sung to the tune of "Skidamarink"

Annaamarink a dink a dink
Annaamarink a doo,
I love you.
Annamarink a dink a dink,
Annamarink a doo,
I love you.

I love you in the morning
And in the afternoon,
I love you in the evening
And underneath the moon;
Oh, Annamarink a dink a dink
Annamarink a doo,
I love you!

Little RuthyKate

Little RuthyKate, Little RuthyKate
Sitting so pretty by the gate
Little RuthyKate, Little RuthyKate
She's my little gal
Little RuthyKate, Little RuthyKate
With big blue eyes and a great big smile

Little RuthyKate, Little RuthyKate
She's my sugar gal.
Little RuthyKate, Little RuthyKate
She runs and plays all the livelong day
Little RuthyKate, Little RuthyKate
She's my little gal

TaylorRebecca

TaylorRebecca, TaylorRebecca
She's my little girl
TaylorRebecca, TaylorRebecca
She's my little girl
TaylorRebecca, TaylorRebecca
She's my little girl
TaylorRebecca, TaylorRebecca
She's the prettiest girl in the world

Sara Sara Baby
Sung to the tune of "Sherry Baby" by Frankie Valli & The Four Seasons

Sara, Sara Baby
Sara, Sara baby
My Sara, baby girl
Sara, Sara baby (My baby baby) Sara, Sara baby
Sara baby girl, can you come out to play?
(Come, come, come out to play)
Sara, Sara baby (My Sara baby girl)
Sara baby can you come out today?
Sara, Sara baby (My baby baby) Sara, Sara baby
Because you're your dad's little girl and
You're the cutest little girl in the world, and
So, my Sara baby, can you come out to play?

Mike's Song

Here Fishy Fishy, Here Fishy Fishy
way down in the sea
Here Fishy Fishy, Here Fishy Fishy
come right here to me
Here Fishy Fishy, Here Fishy Fishy
come and take a look
Here Fishy Fishy, Here Fishy Fishy
Come and bite my hook
Because you make me so happily
when I pull you in the boat
Because you will make me so happily
when I'm eating you wearing my coat.

"The Father's Song"
Artist: Matt Redman

Heaven's perfect melody
The Creator's symphony
You are singing over me
The Father's song

Heaven's perfect mystery
The King of Love has sent for me
Now You're singing over me
The Father's song

Listened to a thousand tongues
But there is one that sounds above them all (sounds above them all)
The Father's song, the Father's love
You sung it over me
And for eternity it's written on my heart

Heaven's perfect melody
The Creator's symphony
You are singing over me
The Father's song

The Father's song
The Father's love
You've sung it over me
And for eternity, it's written on my
    heart
I have heard so many songs

>...*He will rejoice over you with gladness. He will be quiet in His love. He will delight in you with singing.* (Zephaniah 3:17 CSB)

>...*As a bridegroom rejoices over a bride, so your God will rejoice over you.* (Isaiah 62:5 NET)

| 169

"Singing Over You"
(The Father's song to His children)
Artist: Winston Davenport

Just try and enter into rest
Hear the whisper, feel His breath
He could never love you more
You are who His heart beats for

Now let go of your cares and fears
Know that when you cry, He hears
He will wipe away your tears
Stay in His presence, stay right here

"Sing Over Me"
Artist: Bethany Dillon and Nichole Nordeman

You are mighty, You will save
Rejoice over me with singing
You will quiet by Your love
Glory over me with singing

You are mighty, You will save
Rejoice over me with singing
You will quiet by Your love
Glory over me with singing

Because I Love You So Much

I promise I will not always agree with you.

I might have seemed a little paranoid at times. "It's not fair" and "My friends' parents let them" are some of the things I often heard. Although you didn't understand it and it often made you mad, I would always pick keeping you safe over making you happy any day, even if it would break my heart to do it.

I know I have made and will make many mistakes, but if I am going to err, I would much rather err on the side of keeping you overly safe versus putting you in danger.

I know over the years you have been upset at many of my decisions about people we approved of or disprove of or would let you see or hang out with. I can honestly say that it was always because of my love and concern for you. I always took my responsibility to keep you safe and raise you to know God seriously and tried my best not to just do it but to also live it.

I know I may have missed the mark more times than I realize, but I'm sure there were many disasters we may have been spared because of the fact that I took it so seriously. I hope it will be an encouragement to you to always try your best to fail on the side of being too safe versus putting yourself, your family, or others in danger.

That's something that the world needs to learn today: that you can disagree and still be friends. (Jerry Falwell Jr.)

There is a way to disagree with someone, but it doesn't have to be threatening. (Iskra Lawrence)

You can have a great, deep connection with somebody and still disagree with their actions. (Merle Dandridge)

I think that if you make a strong statement of principle, even if the folks disagree with you, people will respect you for it. (Joe Klein)

It's a very important thing to learn to talk to people you disagree with. (Pete Seeger)

If you disagree with the way a colleague did something, call him up, invite him out for a coffee, talk about it. But don't do it publicly. (Antoine Fuqua)

You can disagree without being disagreeable. (Ruth Bader Ginsburg)

The people to fear are not those who disagree with you, but those who disagree with you and are too cowardly to let you know. (Napoleon Bonaparte)

If your brother sins, go and show him his fault in private; if he listens to you, you have won your brother. But if he does not listen to you, take one or two more with you, so that BY THE MOUTH OF TWO OR THREE WITNESSES EVERY FACT MAY BE CONFIRMED. If he refuses to listen to them, tell it to the church; and if he refuses to listen even to the church, let him be to you as a Gentile and a tax collector. **(Matthew 18:15–17)**

My friends, if someone is caught in any kind of wrongdoing, those of you who are spiritual should set him right; but you must do it in a gentle way. And keep an eye on yourselves, so that you will not be tempted, too. **(Galatians 6:1 GNT)**

Yet do not regard him as an enemy, but admonish him as a brother. **(2 Thessalonians 3:15)**

My brothers, if one of you should wander from the truth someone should bring him back. **(James 5:19)**

You Are Loved Just as You Are

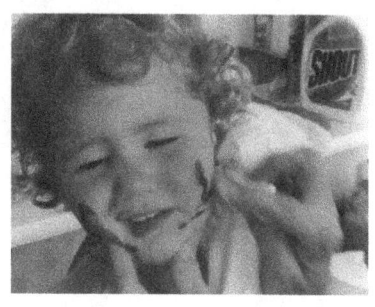

I know that we can, and sometimes have over the years, driven each other crazy, mostly with how different/similar we are! Your way to clean your room (or in my view, the lack thereof) could have been the thing that set me off into a lengthy lecture because you were doing it differently than I would. Then there were things I care about that you just didn't find important or worth your time. There were also things that were important to you that I just didn't understand. I wish I could have known or realized that what I was actually doing was expecting you to be a smaller (perfect-er?) version of me. Which you knew wasn't possible, and I know was wrong of me to do, but I just didn't realize that that is what I was doing, and so I'm sorry.

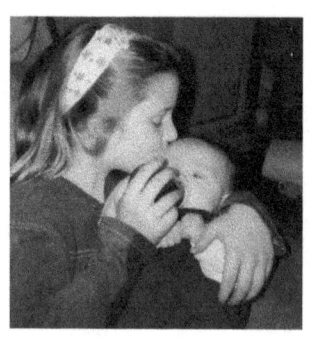

I just want to now remind you that you are loved for exactly who you are, no strings attached and no change required. You don't have to be like me or anyone else to earn my love or get more of my love. That doesn't mean there's no room for any of us to improve or grow, because we all can and should always be doing that. However, my love and affection for you are not dependent on the things you do or don't do. This also is exactly how Jesus loves you too.

There's a saying I often use:

> *Jesus loves us just as we are, but He loves us too much to let us just stay as we are.*

Always be a first-rate version of yourself, instead of a second-rate version of somebody else. (Judy Garland)

You must be the change you want to see in the world. (Gandhi)

Don't just be satisfied being different when you can be better. (Me)

It's not about being different for the sake of being different. It's about being different in a way that makes a difference. (Toni Newman)

We love because God first loved us. **(1 John 4:19 GNT)**

I have loved you, My people, with an everlasting love. With unfailing love, I have drawn you to myself. **(Jeremiah 31:3)**

Use your freedom to serve one another in love. For the whole law can be summed up in this one command: "Love your neighbor as yourself." **(Galatians 5:13–14 NIV)**

But God put His love on the line for us by offering His Son in sacrificial death while we were of no use whatever to Him. **(Romans 5:8 MSG)**

I Believe in You!

I believe you can do whatever you put your mind to doing.

I don't want you to take needless or unnecessary risks or put yourself in danger needlessly. However, to make any progress in anything, there is always some aspect of risk involved. To attempt to succeed, failure is the risk. To try to win, defeat is a possibility. No step forward is ever achieved without the risk of falling in the process. So don't avoid all risk; just evaluate what you are wanting to do, and make sure you can afford what it is that you're risking and that it's worth the risk.

I know that I had missed out on several great opportunities just because I didn't think I could pull it off or do it well enough. One was before the craze of storage units were ever thought of. Your grandpa Jackson tried to get me to buy some property we were looking at and start to build a couple of storage units. Yet for many reasons that I thought was good at the time, I just didn't. Now, many years later, there are storage units everywhere, and that same property I turned down has many huge storage units on it, and someone is making a lot of money.

Don't let apprehension or fear intimidate you from your potential or opportunities that God brings your way. Whenever there is an apparent opportunity or idea you have, pray about it, and when you have a sense of peace or confirmation, go for it. Don't waste potential because of fear, laziness, or intimidation. You can do it! I believe in you!

Don't live with a lot of "If I'd only" regrets.

If your real desire is to be good (or do something good), there is no need to wait for the money before you do it; you can do it now, this very moment, and just where you are. (James Allen)

You can do what you have to do, and sometimes you can do it even better than you think you can. (Jimmy Carter)

Everyone has a part to play. We have the power. You can do it. (Maxine Waters)

Do your job. Do it the best you can. Do it right, because somebody, sometimes your best friend, is waiting for you to screw up so she can take your place. (Abby Lee Miller)

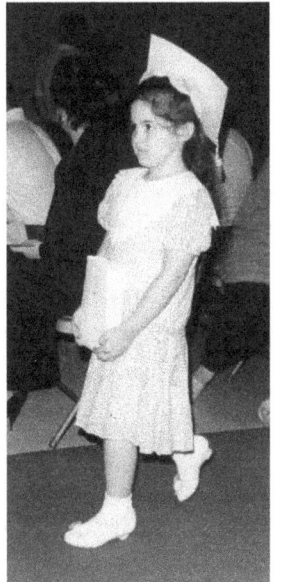

Jesus looked at them and said, "With man this is impossible, but not with God; all things are possible with God." **(Mark 10:27)**

Being confident of this, that He who began a good work in you will carry it on to completion until the day of Christ Jesus. **(Philippians 1:6)**

For we live by faith, not by sight. **(2 Corinthians 5:7)**

See, I care about you, and I will pay attention to you. Your ground will be plowed and your crops planted. **(Ezekiel 36:9 CJB)**

Judge with Wisdom

Is it right to judge people? Or should we just be accepting of everyone and everything?

One of the things I hear a lot of people saying is the "You can't Judge me"; or if they know you are a Christian, they say, "The Bible says, 'Judge not.'" However, the Bible verse really states, "*Judge not lest you be judged*" (Matthew 7:1–3), and it's not telling us not to judge but how to judge. The rest of the verse that they don't say says, "Lest you be judged," which means "other than the way that you will be judged or those additional rules you use will then be used to judge you too."

This was really focused at the church leaders of His day who were continually inventing rules that had nothing to do with what God said they had to do or follow. They were making additional rules adding to God's rule of "one day to focus on Him and rest." However, they were adding to that by saying how many steps a person could walk or how many pounds they could carry, or even what they could cook to eat. In fact, they took God's ten basic laws for living our lives in the right relationship with Him and others, and they added thousands of their own invented laws just to make themselves seem so important or holy. The funny thing was that Jesus said they weren't even following their laws themselves. Hypocrites!

We need to know when to judge, how to judge, and what standards to use when we judge. Judging is part of life. We have to judge people and situations just to be safe, to know which way to go, who to trust, or what to buy. We have to constantly make judgment calls all the time in our everyday life.

I want you to learn to be very good at judging people and situations to keep yourself safe. Always pray about every situation you are in (1 Thessalonians 5:17), and listen to the Holy Spirit's leading on what to do or where to go for every situation (Isiah 30:21). If you do that and really listen, He will tell you and lead you and help you in every situation. It really is amazing. Try it.

I never want you to feel you need to trust anyone or any situation that you feel uneasy about or feel is wrong. It doesn't matter if you might hurt someone's feelings or someone might be upset with you. Listen to your instinct, listen to the Holy Spirit, always do what is right, and always be safe. (Please do this for me.)

However, be careful to use the wisdom that God has given you, because we often judge people for their actions, but we want others to judge us by our intentions. The Bible tells us that if we judge ourselves by God's truth first and foremost, then we won't have a need for anyone to judge us. Try to always judge others by truth and character. Let people prove themselves and earn your respect.

It takes a lifetime to build your reputation, character, and earn respect; but it only takes a moment to ruin it.

> *Only with love and kindness can a person rightly judge another justly, and be able to make allowances for the complexity of their situation and uniqueness of their weaknesses.* (Me)

> *A kind eye, while recognizing defects, sees beyond them.* (Lawrence G. Lovasik)

> *I judge people based on their capability, honesty, and merit.* (President Donald Trump)

> *Never judge a stranger by his clothes.* (Zachary Taylor)

> *Children begin by loving their parents; after a time they judge them; rarely, if ever, do they forgive them.* (Oscar Wilde)

> *When you judge another, you do not define them, you define yourself.* (Wayne Dyer)

No accurate thinker will judge another person by that which the other person's enemies say about him. (Napoleon Hill)

Do not mind anything that anyone tells you about anyone else. Judge everyone and everything for yourself. (Henry James)

I can usually judge a fellow by what he laughs at. (Wilson Mizner)

You've got to judge people, ultimately, by their actions rather than their words. (Jacob Rees-Mogg)

People who are guided by the Spirit can make all kinds of judgments, but they cannot be judged by others. **(1 Corinthians 2:15 CEV)**

The one who is spiritual discerns (judges) all things, yet he himself is understood by no one. **(1 Corinthians 2:15 NET)**

Give your servant therefore an understanding heart to judge Your people, that I may discern (judge) between good and evil; for who is able to judge this Your great people? **(1 Kings 3:9 NIV)**

But solid food belongs to those who are mature, for those who through practice have powers of discernment (to judge) that are trained to distinguish (judge) good from evil. **(Hebrews 5:14 MEV)**

Stop judging by mere appearances, but instead judge correctly. **(John 7:24 NIV)**

Be Careful Where You Get Your Information

There was once a couple of goofy kids who were hired to roof an old barn. Well, they got everything going good and worked hard at it all day, and before they knew it, it was getting dark, and they were still on the roof of the barn. Then to make matters worse, they didn't notice that the ladder had fallen down.

Well, the kid said to the other, "What are we going to do? We have to get down, and no one is around."

The other one said, "It's okay. Before we came up here, I noticed that they had just cleaned out the pens in the barn and it was right at the end."

The first kid replied while looking over the edge, "Are you sure? I can hardly see it as dark as it is."

The other kid answered, "Yes, I'm sure, and just to be sure, I'll go first."

Then all of a sudden, he jumped, and in a moment, he said, "It's okay. Don't worry. It's a soft manure pile."

The first kid hollered back, "How deep is it?"

The other kid hollered back, "Knee deep."

So the first kid jumped…and landed neck deep in a big pile of manure. After the shock wore off, he said, "I thought you said it was only knee deep!"

The other kid answered, "Yes, it was. But I jumped headfirst."

Moral of the story is always know who you are following.

Respect Has to Be Earned

*Give respect to whom respect is due and
honor to whom honor is due.*

Respect is the feeling evoked from holding someone in high esteem or regard because of their position, qualities, achievements, or abilities. Due regard for the feelings, wishes, rights, or traditions of others, i.e. children, respect your parents.

Sometimes, in this crazy world, it's difficult to remember that everyone has intrinsic value and is worthy of love; but our actions and our character are how we earn our respect. Respect is not cheap, nor is it free, but we must give it to those who have earned it. Everyone deserves human decency, dignity, and respect. It's just that some people have earned more than others.

There Are Three Kinds of Earned Respect:

1. First is **respect by office** (for example of a judge, police officer, president, parent, or preacher).
2. Second is **respect by accomplishment** (such as a college graduate, an inventor, a scientist, a hero, or someone who spends their life helping others).
3. Lastly is **respect by character**, which is someone who is honest, true, and trustworthy (someone you can trust to do the right thing no matter the situation).

The best respect is earned by someone in all three categories.

Those who don't respect themselves tend to treat others badly. People who don't think anyone deserves their respect are selfish and tend to be rude and inconsiderate. They treat others like they are worthless or less important than themselves. No one enjoys being around people who treat others like that, and if you remove this kind of people from your life, you will see how your attitude and life will improve.

I Love everyone and some I even like.

Everyone deserves the right to be loved, just some deserve the right to be beat up too.

The respect you show to others (or lack thereof) is an immediate reflection of your own self-respect. (Alex Elle)

Knowledge will give you power, but character respect. (Bruce Lee)

We will not agree with everyone, but we should most definitely respect one another. (Brooke Griffin)

A child who is allowed to be disrespectful to his parents will not have true respect for anyone. (Billy Graham)

My friends, we ask you to be thoughtful of your leaders who work hard and tell you how to live for the Lord. Show them great respect and love because of their work. Try to get along with each other. **(1 Thessalonians 5:12–13 CEV)**

Pay all that you owe, whether it is taxes and fees or respect and honor. **(Romans 13:7 CEV)**

Show respect to the aged; honor the presence of an elder; fear your God. I am God. **(Leviticus 19:32 MSG)**

Be kind and honest and you will live a long life; (then) others will respect you and (they will) treat you fairly. **(Proverbs 21:21)**

You Are Forgiven

This is really important to know and understand, because we all mess up. Your mom does; your grandparents do; your aunts, uncles, and cousins all do; all your siblings do; you do; and I do too. Everyone has and still does mess up and blow it once in a while. We say things we don't mean, give looks we shouldn't give, and throw the occasional fit (and we do in one way or another too). So I just want to say that I have forgiven you from anything you have done or think you have done. Whether or not you think you deserve it, I forgive you.

Every once in a while, I think of some dumb or thoughtless thing that I had done, and I realize that I must have hurt your grandpa, or your great-grandparents; and I wish I could tell them I'm sorry and ask for their forgiveness, but I can't. It's too late. Oh, I can just speak it out and feel that at least I'm admitting it and that might help some. I can pray and ask God for His forgiveness for it and even ask Him to tell Grandpa I remember and now realize what I did, and I'm sorry… and that might help even more, but not as much as if I could have done it in person, when they were still here. Now as time goes on, I more so than ever regret ever doing or saying those things, but now it's too late to correct or make amends for it, let alone let them know how sorry I am for hurting them.

So because I am just as much, if not more, in need of forgiveness, there is no way I would want to hold you to more of a burden of needing forgiveness than I can bear myself. Jesus's loves you so much that even He offers you complete forgiveness from everything. I, too, hope that you also forgive me for all my many blunders and royal mess ups as a father over the years and probably still will occasionally make in the future.

Not forgiving is like drinking rat poison and then waiting for the rat to die. (Anne Lamott)

Forgiveness does not change the past, but it does enlarge the future. (Paul Boose)

How do I say the words, "I'm sorry," when I know that words are not enough? And how can I ask you to forgive me when I know I can't forgive myself? (Unknown)

Mistakes are always forgivable if one has the courage to admit them. (Bruce Lee)

Though your sins are like scarlet, they shall be white as snow. **(Isaiah 1:18)**

If we confess our sins, He is faithful and just to forgive us our sins and to cleanse us from all unrighteousness. **(1 John 1:9)**

He has not punished us as we deserve for all our sins, for His mercy toward those who fear and honor Him is as great as the height of the heavens above the earth. **(Psalm 103:10–14)**

Bearing with one another and, if one has a complaint against another, forgiving each other; as the Lord has forgiven you, so you also must forgive. **(Colossians 3:13)**

(From the Lord's Prayer) And forgive us our debts, as we also have forgiven our debtors. **(Matthew 6:12)**

Instead, be kind to each other, tenderhearted, forgiving one another, just as God through Christ has forgiven you. **(Ephesians 4:32 NLT)**

To Err Is Human, to Forgive Is Divine

"All people commit sins and make mistakes. God forgives them, and people are acting in a godlike (divine) way when they forgive" *(Alexander Pope from "An Essay on Criticism")*.

It's not a question of "if" a person will do something to hurt or offend you; it's *(really a matter of)* "when" and "how often" they will *(hurt you)*. When you have any relationship with anyone, you will have to be able to forgive them at some time or another. You really haven't developed a relationship with anyone or know them very well unless you found at least one thing you need to forgive them for. As a matter of fact, the longer you live, the more likely it will be that you'll have to forgive even the same people again and again. You will often find that you will need to forgive them repeatedly for the same thing. Sometimes, even the best people mess up once in a while and need to be forgiven more than once, and the longer you know them, the more you will have to forgive them.

When a deep injury is done to us, we never heal until we forgive. (Nelson Mandela)

Blame keeps wounds open. Only forgiveness heals. (Thomas S. Manson)

When you forgive, you in no way change the past—but you sure do change the future. (Bernard Meltzer)

Forgiveness is not an occasional act; it is a permanent attitude. (Martin Luther King Jr.)

Bear with each other and forgive one another if any of you has a grievance against someone. Forgive as the Lord forgave you. **(Colossians 3:13)**

For if you forgive other people when they sin against you, your heavenly Father will also forgive you. But if you do not forgive others their sins, your Father will not forgive your sins. **(Matthew 6:14–15)**

And when you stand praying, if you hold anything against anyone, forgive them, so that your Father in heaven may forgive you your sins. **(Mark 11:25)**

Stubbornness vs. Determination

There is a difference between being stubborn and being determined.

In your resolve to what is right and true, be as determined as a stone but open-minded to everything else. Only the Bible is 100 percent true and right; everything and everyone else might be wrong or mistaken.

There are many times that we believe we are right and want others to agree with us, but I wonder, to what cost are we willing to be right? If the situation is crucial and important—like a matter of national security or saving a business thousands of dollars, for a grade at school, or maybe even for a game—then, yes, it's best to state your case clearly and concisely and show off your superior intelligence. But when it comes to things that are of no consequence or make no real difference, showing off or proving that you know better may only hurt people, cause them to feel inferior or shamed, or could even compromise or irreparably damage your relationship. You can have great knowledge and value, more than others might realize. However, don't hurt or make others feel less than you just to show that you are smart. I know you are smart. You are awesome to me, and if you want to teach someone who can appreciate how smart you are, pick me. I love you.

Most people fail because they do not have determination and perseverance. Extraordinary people are determined and persevere that is what makes them extraordinary. (Catherine Pulsifer)

You get a much better return by giving people a bit of your heart rather than a piece of your mind. (Unknown)

True humility is being able to accept criticisms as graciously as we accept compliments. (Sabrina Newby)

Determination sets you steadfast to your goal but flexible to your method. Stubbornness sets you immovable in your method and causes you to lose sight of your goal. (Unknown)

Self-will—a stubborn, unteachable spirit; an arguing, talkative spirit; harsh, sarcastic expression; an unyielding, headstrong disposition; a driving, commanding spirit; a disposition to criticize and pick flaws when set aside and unnoticed; a peevish, fretful spirit; a disposition that loves to be coaxed and humored? (Unknown)

Do nothing out of selfish ambition or vain conceit, but in humility consider others better than yourselves. **(Philippians 2:3)**

But test everything; hold fast what is good. **(1 Thessalonians 5:21 ESV)**

Why do you pass judgment on your brother? Or you, why do you despise your brother? For we will all stand before the judgment seat of God. **(Romans 14:10 ESV)**

A prudent man conceals knowledge, But the heart of fools proclaims folly. **(Proverbs 12:23)**

Do not give what is holy to dogs, and do not throw your pearls before swine, or they will trample them under their feet, and turn and tear you to pieces. **(Matthew 7:6)**

Never Let Your Words Demean Your Character

Something that we all have trouble with, and I am including myself with this, too, and that is with our words.

We need to be careful with how we express ourselves to others. Not so much when we are happy, but even then, we can say things that hurt others in jest. However, more when we are upset, mad, or frustrated, we can tend to speak without weighing our words first. Try as much as possible to think how the words you are saying could be received, the impact they could make, and how they might even be misunderstood. Our Character won't be known, remembered, or judged by our situation or intent but by the outcome of our actions and words.

When you are hot and bothered about something and want badly to say something in response, think of your words before you say them. Think about how many ways it could be interpreted. Think of how it might be remembered a year or so later and the impact it will make. Then determine if that's really the best thing to say, way to communicate it, or best timing to say it.

There is also a peripheral damage that you need to consider. This is something I regret the most, what I have unwittingly caused others and even put you and your siblings through. I believe, at times, I have allowed things to be seen and heard that shouldn't have been communicated in the way I communicated them, and especially shouldn't have done, so you kids had to see and/or hear it in the way it was communicated. I am very sorry for that, and I really wish I could somehow take those words and actions back. Please forgive me, and learn from my mistakes. Always think twice and speak once. Always be Careful with your responses, and try to not over react over any situation. Think if there is any way that what you are wanting to communicate could be misinterpreted or taken in a way other than what you are meaning it. Also consider who else is listening and how it could be affecting them. When all is said and done, what will those around you think you meant by your words and actions? Also what will they remember from what was said and done?

> *Words are like toothpaste. Once it's out there, you can never put it back.* (Unknown)

> *Freely airing your words is like opening a feather pillow to a strong wind and scattering the contents. When you're done, some of the feathers may be able to be accounted for, but you will never be able to know how far they have traveled, and to collect them all would be impossible. So we never will know their total effect or how far our words may go, though we use them in only one place.* (Me)

> *Yes, a person can accept your apology and forgive you for what you've said, but they will never forget how you made them feel at that very moment.* (Unknown)

> *Live without pretending. Love without depending. Listen without defending. Speak without offending.* (Unknown)

> *He who guards his mouth and his tongue, Guards his soul from troubles.* **(Proverbs 21:23)**

> *I said, "I will guard my ways That I may not sin with my tongue; I will guard my mouth as with a muzzle While the wicked are in my presence."* **(Psalm 39:1)**

> *So also the tongue is a small part of the body, and yet it boasts of great things See how great a forest is set aflame by such a small fire! And the tongue is a fire, the very world of iniquity; the tongue is set*

among our members as that which defiles the entire body, and sets on fire the course of our life, and is set on fire by hell. For every species of beasts and birds, of reptiles and creatures of the sea, is tamed and has been tamed by the human race. **(James 3:5–8)**

"Words"

By Kenneth D. Jackson (March 31, 1933–December 10, 2013)
(Grandpa Jackson wrote it when he was in high school, approximately 1948)

Forgive me, Lord, for careless words
When hungry souls are near.
Words…not of faith and love,
Heavy with care and fear.

Forgive me, Lord, for words withheld
For some…they <u>might</u> have won,
A soul from darkened paths of sin,
To follow thy dear Son.

Words <u>are</u> such <u>mighty</u> things, dear Lord,
May I so yielded be,
That Christ…who spoke as mere man,
May <u>always</u> speak through me.

Be Careful to Not Allow Anger to Characterize You

This is something that a lot of people struggle with, and I will be quick to admit that I have struggled with at times myself. I am very thankful for God's grace and mercy, and for the mellowing of time and age, I have had more trouble with this in the past than what I have today.

Another problem I know I have is that I don't smile nearly as much as I think I am. I know that, at times, when I am serious or intently focused on something, my expressions might look like I'm mad. It might look like it, but that is not real anger, though I still need to work on it. I know many a times people have made the statement that I must be mad about something, or they'll ask me what I am upset about, yet I don't think I am. I don't feel mad about anything. At those times, I'm probably just deep in thought, serious about a situation. Maybe I'm feeling frustrated or having some difficulty dealing with something or someone. Yet all the more during our times of frustration, we need to make a conscious effort to control our outward appearance and avoid, to the best of our ability, looking angry. We should all try to make a conscious effort to have a smile on our face a lot more often than a scowl.

However, sometimes, I do find myself at my complete wits' end, trying to get others to understand or get some help, and then before I know it, all I feel is anger. Maybe you remember seeing me in times like that. Furthermore, I bet you've also felt that way yourself at times. If we were to admit it, every one of us at times feel this way. Some people are so even keel that I don't think they ever get upset, and I really don't understand people like that or like them much. (No, I'm just kidding. But I would just like to see what it would take to make them upset. LOL.) Jacob became very angry with his in-laws (Genesis 31:36). Moses got mad when the people were upset about the food and had a calf party without him (or God) (Numbers 16:15; Exodus 32:19). Nehemiah got mad when the people were walking away from the things of God (Nehemiah 13:25). Samson was angry when his wife cheated on him (Judges 14:1–20). Peter got mad when they came for Jesus (John 18:10). Even Jesus experienced anger when He had to deal with the pious, religious crowd, and especially when He saw what they were doing with His Father's House all made Him angry (Matthew 21:12–13.)

Anger, real anger that shows up regularly or too often, can get to be like a deep pit you fall into and can't climb out of. It can get to be habitual and even become detrimental to your health (mentally and physically), and most of the time, it will be damaging to any relationships it encounters. Some of my health issues are in direct relationship to the stress I am feeling at the time, mainly things like my fibromyalgia, migraines, blood pressure, and even reflux disease.

All anger is not bad, and it is impossible and very impractical to try to avoid it all together. There are things that should anger us, and as a matter of fact, if they didn't anger us, that in itself would be a sign that there was something seriously wrong with us. Just face it—there are times we need to get angry. If someone was hurting, threatening, or endangering you, believe me, I would be angry and ready for action in a heartbeat. Even so, we need to be able to keep our head in spite of being angry and still be able to think clearly so we can react appropriately. We also need to be able to, within a reasonable time, unplug from that situation and change our attitude and emotions, as well as being able to keep in focus who or what is the cause of our anger and not let it be transferred or broadcast on others undeservingly.

Like so many others, this, I have to admit, has been hard for me too. But anger is no excuse for being mean, bullying, being mouthy, or just demonstrating bad behavior. Many people have done some horrible things to others, regrettably, while angry and then live to regret later. Mean, nasty, hateful things, and not just to those they would say deserve it but to anyone often to innocent and easy targets. The worst thing is that family and friends are the ones who often get hurt by our anger. We are still responsible for our actions and words, and even our thoughts just as much when we are angry as when we are happy. Our emotions don't change our responsibility in the sight of the law, let alone in God's sight.

If there has ever been a time when you felt like you've been hurt or caught in the crossfire of my unrestrained anger, maybe while you were young or anytime, I am sorry. Fortunately, I have learned a lot over the years, but unfortunately, it's taken a lot of years to learn it. The problem is that the damage has already been done. It would have been avoidable had someone taught me what I am trying to teach you now. Don't let your anger cause you regrets or characterize who you are.

I shall allow no man to belittle my soul by making me hate him. (Booker T. Washington)

Anybody can become angry—that is easy, but to be angry with the right person and to the right degree and at the right time and for the right purpose, and in the right way—that is not within everybody's power and is not easy. (Aristotle)

Anger is an acid that can do more harm to the vessel in which it is stored than to anything on which it is poured. (Mark Twain)

Anger is one letter short of danger. (Eleanor Roosevelt)

And "don't sin by letting anger control you." Don't let the sun go down while you are still angry. **(Ephesians 4:26 NLT)**

Stop being bitter and angry and mad at others. Don't yell at one another or curse each other or ever be rude. **(Ephesians 4:31 CEV)**

Do not be quickly provoked in your spirit, for anger resides in the lap of fools. **(Ecclesiastes 7:9)**

Be angry, yet do not sin; on your bed, search your heart and be still. Selah. **(Psalm 4:4)**

If you are angry, you cannot do any of the good things God wants done. **(James 1:20 CEV)**

Whatever You Face, Just Remember "I Believe in You!"

My dear daughter,

I know you have already gone through things in your life that, at the time, you thought were very difficult and almost impossible; and when you are facing those situations, they truly seem impossible. Yet you did it! I wish I could say that you will never have to face something so difficult as that again; but more than likely you will, again and again, and even harder and more difficult situations too. The mountains we have to cross while we travel this life prepare us for the ones we will have to cross later on in our journeys. I know they're tough, and I know you will think you can't get through it, but you can. I know you can because you did the last one, and that one was bigger than you thought you could handle. However, this one is just one step bigger, one jump higher, one leap wider than the last one. So I know you can do it. When you get to your end, reach out to God, and trust Jesus to help and guide you through. If you call out to Him, He will toss you a rope, hold the ladder, show you the stairway, or just carry you in His arms. However, He does it. He will make sure you won't be overwhelmed and you will make it through.

I'm here for you if you need me. I love you no matter what you're going through.

I believe in you!

Dad

When troubles, trials, and tribulation come your way, when you feel there is no hope and all is lost, when you feel like your last friend has left you and you stand all alone, turn around because I will still be there for you. Cheering you on!

We're never alone.
There will be a way through every hardship, every difficulty, every dark and lonely place.
Remember, there will be a light at the end of every tunnel, and His name is Jesus
As long as you have breath, there is still a plan and a purpose for your life.
No matter how bad it gets, keep your head up and keep on going.
You are a winner, and you're gonna make it through this too.
When all is said and done, the Bible says we will win.
When you are following Jesus, He will work it out.
Every trap will have a way you can Escape.
His Light will shine through Darkness.
Darkness lasts only until morning.
Truth will triumph over all lies.
Just Keep on Keeping on.
Always Trust in God.
So never give up.
Do your best.
Never quit.
Don't stop.
Remember what Dory would say, "Just keep swimming! Just keep swimming!"

I will love the light for it shows me the way, yet I will endure the darkness because it shows me the stars. (Og Mandino)

Stay with God! Take heart. Don't quit. I'll say it again: Stay with God. (**Psalm 27:14 MSG**)

Live cheerfully expectant. Don't quit in hard times; (just) pray all the harder. (**Romans 12:12 MSG**)

You Are the Center of My World

I don't care what anyone else ever thinks of you,
because to me, You're not just a big part of my world,
But you will always be the center of my world

    I prayed for you to be you, before you were even you. I was so excited when I was told you were coming and counted down the days until you arrived. I was there and was the first person to see you, to care for you, to help you, to hold you. From the very first time you reached for my finger, you have had a hold of my heart. You are my reason for praise. You are my most precious possession. You are the apple of my eye. I thank God for you!

> *I want to thank you for the profound joy I've had in the thought of you.* (**Rosie Alison, *The Very Thought of You*)**

> *Every time I think of you, I thank my God.* (**Philippians 1:3 CEV**)

> *After a period of glory, the L*ORD *of Heaven's Armies sent me against the nations who plundered you. For He said, "Anyone who harms you harms My most precious possession. I will raise My fist to crush them, and their own slaves will plunder them." Then you will know that the Lord of Heaven's Armies sent me.* (**Zechariah 2:8–9 NLT**)

> *Keep me as the apple of Your eye; hide me in the shadow of Your wings.* (**Psalm 17:8**)

My Little Girl song
Artist: Tim McGraw

Gotta hold on easy as I let you go
Going to tell you how much I love
    you
Though you think you already know
I remember I thought you looked like
    an angel
Wrapped in pink, so soft and warm
You've had me wrapped around your
    finger
Since the day you were born

You're beautiful baby, from the outside in
Chase your dreams but always know
The road that will lead you home again
Go on, take on this old world but to me
You know you'll always be my little girl…

Put Your Past in Your Past...

Take the best of your past to build the best for your future.

You never have to stay down because of your past. For one reason is that you have both good and bad in your past, so just focus on the good and build on that. Another reason is that you can always look at the bad you have done and gone through and learn from it and be determined to go a better way and not allow that to happen again. So both ways you are building on your past and making your future better. Never just say that you have a bad past and you don't like what you went through and just do nothing to change it. To wish things would be different but do nothing about it or different is really to want things to continue the same way they've been.

Who you are today is a combination of your past experiences and choices, in addition to where your parents and grandparents have brought you with their life's choices and successes; but what you do with it and where you go from here are totally up to you.

Good or bad, history is to learn from, grow from, and build upon.

If all I've said and done are deemed inconsequential, thought to be of no value, or someday forgotten, I hope that future generations will at least know that I loved God and I loved my family with all of my heart and my number one desire was to see all my family in heaven someday.

We all carry, inside us, people who came before us. (Liam Callanan)

If I have seen further than others, it is by standing upon the shoulders of giants. (Isaac Newton)

A generation which ignores history has no past and no future. (Robert A. Heinlein)

It's a shame to be given such a grand foundation from the best of previous generations and not do our part to build on it a beautiful edifice for future generations to benefit from. (Me)

The former things are gone and God does a new thing in us. **(Isaiah 43:8)**

And I will shake all nations, so that the treasures of all nations shall come in, and I will fill this house with glory, says the Lord of hosts. The silver is mine, and the gold is mine, declares the Lord of hosts. The latter glory of this house shall be greater than the former, says the Lord of hosts. And in this place I will give peace, declares the Lord of hosts. **(Haggai 2:7–9 ESV)**

In the past, things went well with you. But in days to come, things will get even better. **(Job 8:7 NIRV)**

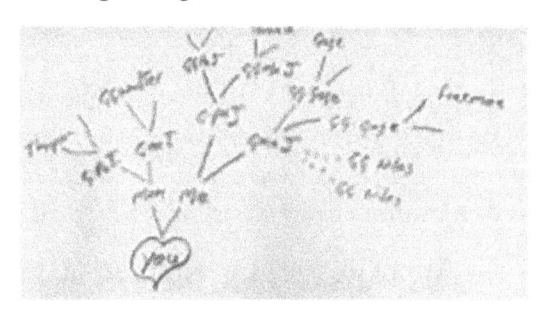

Be a Woman of Integrity, Purity, and Honor

As unpopular as they are today, and even though the movie stars and media all say they're old-fashioned, impractical, and not even possible today; however, Integrity, Purity, and Honor (*Sexual Purity and Morality have a lot to do with Abstinence until marriage and then only with the One to whom you are married for life*) are not only possible and important but are also crucial character traits. It's not just the best choice; it's the only choice for not just a Christian but someone wanting to protect themselves, their marriage, and their family, as well as avoid a lot of hurt in every area of life.

You is kind.
You is smart.
You is important.
(Kathryn Stockett)

When I was a kid, there were only a couple of different STDs that were really known about. Nowadays, there are hundreds, and some professionals say even thousands because of the mutations of each of the viruses. Doctors who work with this tell me that although most of the STDs only scar and mutilate you, many of them will also kill you. To make it worse, the worst STDs have no noticeable symptoms either until it's too late.

Not only is the statistics proven many times over about the health and longevity of a marriage that is between two Christians who are active in their church; there is also a lot of research on children raised in that kind of environment. Children raised in Christian homes have better grades; have higher achievements; have a better sense of who they are; are more well balanced; have a higher IQ; have less trouble going through their teenage years; a higher percentage of them graduate not just from high school but also college; and are more successful in their future careers, marriages, and parenting. The statistics are, of course, just the opposite of those parents who don't live their lives with Integrity, Purity, Honor, and Fidelity. It's not just good biblical values that I'm talking about. God requires them, and He requires them because they give us a better life here.

Like any Christian value, principle, and commandment, if we haven't been doing it, the best time to turn it around and start reaping the benefits from it is now. Just ask for God's forgiveness. Tell Him you didn't know or hadn't accepted it and want Him to help you change that area of your life from now on, and He will. It's never too late to start over and get your life on the right track.

I believe in you and know you can do it right, even if it's hard at first to make all the changes. I know you can do it. Because you are awesome.

> *You is kind. You is smart. You is important.* (Kathryn Stockett, from the movie *The Help*)

> *Being faithful is the best way to prove your love for someone. Not words. Not gifts or flowers. Not Sex. But good old-fashioned Fidelity.* (Kisstopher707, Reddit)

> *Faithfulness and truth are the most sacred excellences and endowments of the human mind.* (Vince Lombardi)

> *Fidelity in love requires abstinence, but only through it one can know the hidden beauty of love.* (Rabindrnaath Tagore)

> *Fidelity, enforced and unto death, is the price you pay for the kind of love you never want to give up, for someone you want to hold forever, tighter and tighter, whether he's close or far away, someone who becomes dearer to you the more you've sacrificed for his sake.* (Marguerite Duras)

> *Among you there must not be even a hint of sexual immorality, or of any kind of impurity, or*

of greed, because these are improper for God's holy people. **(Ephesians 5:3)**

However, each one of you also must love his wife as he loves himself, and the wife must respect her husband. **(Ephesians 5:33)**

It is obvious what kind of life develops out of trying to get your own way all the time: repetitive, loveless, cheap sex; a stinking accumulation of mental and emotional garbage; frenzied and joyless grabs for happiness; trinket gods; magic-show religion; paranoid loneliness; cutthroat competition; all-consuming-yet-never-satisfied wants; a brutal temper; an impotence to love or be loved; divided homes and divided lives; small-minded and lopsided pursuits; the vicious habit of depersonalizing everyone into a rival; uncontrolled and uncontrollable addictions; ugly parodies of community. I could go on.
This isn't the first time I have warned you, you know. If you use your freedom this way, you will not inherit God's kingdom. **(Galatians 5:19–21 MSG)**

Marriage should be honored by all, and the marriage bed kept pure, for God will judge the adulterer and all the sexually immoral. **(Hebrews 13:4)**

Flee from sexual immorality. All other sins a person commits are outside the body, but whoever sins sexually, sins against their own body. **(1 Corinthians 6:18)**

What I Want in a Son-in-Law

He doesn't have to be perfect, although that would help.

1. He needs to know and have a growing personal relationship with Jesus (2 Peter 3:18).
2. He must put others first to serve and be willing to sacrifice himself (Ephesians 5:25).
3. He must be a man of good character, of good reputation, and worthy of honor (1 Timothy 3:7).
4. He must be hardworking and willing to learn and able to provide for you (Ephesians 5:29).
5. He must be one who loves my daughter based on a commitment and determination and not just feelings of affection, happiness, or pleasure (Ephesians 5:31).
6. He must be an understanding person (1 Peter 3:7).
7. He must be willing to show honor to you (1 Peter 3:7).

"Husbands, love your wives, and do not be harsh with them" **(Colossians 3:19 ESV)**.

"Husbands, love your wives, as Christ loved the church and gave Himself up for her" **(Ephesians 5:25 ESV)**.

"In the same way husbands should love their wives as their own bodies. He who loves his wife loves himself" **(Ephesians 5:28 ESV)**.

"Therefore a man shall leave his father and mother and hold fast to his wife, and the two shall become one flesh" **(Ephesians 5:31 ESV)**.

We Are Not an Island

We are not an Island to live our lives unto ourselves, but We are Responsible for Others and for all the ways our lives affect and interact with everyone around us.

If you were to throw a rock into the middle of still lake or pond, there would be a big splash where the rock went in. Then the immediate result would be a wave of water that then lessens in size. The ripples would continue going out from there until they touched the shores around and then start rippling back to the center again to where you tossed the rock in.

Nothing we do affects us only. Really nothing we do stops with what we do or where we do it but only starts there, and then in one way or another, it continues out from there. Everything we do in one way or another affects many. Anything you do good or bad will always affect your family and friends and anyone else who is watching you rather quickly.

Statistics say that each person has approximately ten people who are watching us and are directly influenced by what we do. Then each one of those people has ten people who are indirectly affected by your actions, and then a group of ten from each of those is also to a lesser extent affected by our action. They actually say that within ten circles (some say six) of acquaintances from us, we have touched the entire world. When you think of it that way, what you do is very important. So be careful at what kind of an influence you are having on others.

We are responsible for the things we do, and we are also responsible for how it affects the people around us. We are responsible for their emotions if what we did caused them emotional harm. We are even more responsible if we by our actions cause someone else to think it's okay to do something wrong or bad. Romans 14:13–23 tells us even if what we want to do is not wrong or bad, if it leads or causes someone else to do something wrong, then it's wrong for us to do it.

We shouldn't only try to avoid doing anything negative that would hurt, harm, or in some way adversely affect those around us. We should try to do good. We need to continually look for opportunities to help those nearest to us first (family, friends, church…) and then those further away next who need our help or in whose lives we have an ability to make a difference. Once we see a need that we can do something about a problem, then we are responsible to do it. Find a way to Help them. Make a difference in the lives of as many as you can.

See a need Fill a need. (Bigweld, *Robots*)

Do all the good you can, by all the means you can, in all the ways you can, in all the places you can, at all the times you can, to all the people you can, as long as ever you can. (John Wesley)

The life I touch for good or ill will touch another life, and that in turn another, until who knows where the trembling stops or in what far place my touch will be felt. (Frederick Buechner)

You are never alone. You are eternally connected with everyone. (Amit Ray)

Whatever you do to help someone you're really helping Jesus. **(Matthew 25:35–40)**

These little ones believe in Me. It would be best for the person who causes one of them [harm or] to lose faith to be thrown into the sea with a large stone hung around his neck. **(Mark 9:42 GWT)**

God does both the making and saving. He creates each of us by Christ Jesus to join Him in the work He does, the good work He has gotten ready for us to do, work we had better be doing. **(Ephesians 2:10 MSG)**

Do Your Best to Become a Proverbs 31 Woman.

A Proverbs 31 kind of woman is a woman who is responsible, respectful, caring, compassionate, helpful, hardworking, encouraging, and ingenious. Basically, she is one who works hard to help anyone in need and make a difference wherever she goes.

> *But whoever has the world's possessions and sees his fellow Christian in need and shuts off his compassion against him, how can the love of God reside in such a person?* **(1 John 3:17 NB)**

> *If you know someone who doesn't have any clothes or food, you shouldn't just say, "I hope all goes well for you. I hope you will be warm and have plenty to eat." What good is it to say this, unless you do something to help?* **(James 2:14–26 CEV)**

Integrity and Character Forever

You are never on vacation from your integrity and character.

The right thing to do…
It's not always the most popular.
It's not always the easiest thing to do.
It's not always the most fun thing to do.
It's not always the thing we "want" to do.
It's not always the thing that will help us win.
It's not always the most convenient thing to do.
It's not always the thing that will get us the most money.
It's not always the thing that will get us the most friends,
It's not always the thing that will help us get the best grade.
It's not always the thing that others will tell us we should do.
But it will always be the Right thing to do, and therefore the best thing to do.
Always do your best to take the high road.
Do your best to make the best choice whenever there is a choice to be made.
Do the right thing when it's the hardest to do. That's when it counts the most.
What you do when others are watching builds your reputation, but what you do when no one is looking or will ever know shows your integrity and builds your character.
You will never be wrong if you stick to your integrity.
Surround yourself with people who you feel have at least as high or higher of moral standards and integrity as you have, and they will help you stay strong.

It's the action, not the fruit of the action, that's important. You have to do the right thing. It may not be in your power, may not be in your time, that there will be any fruit. But that doesn't mean you stop doing the right thing. You may never know what results come from your action. But if you do nothing, there will be no result. (Ghandi)

There's a difference between doing things right and doing the right thing. (Chris Fussell)

Sometimes it is better to lose and do the right thing than to win and do the wrong thing. (Tony Blair)

So whoever knows the right thing to do and fails to do it, for Him it is sin. **(James 4:17)**

He that walketh with wise men shall be wise: but a companion of fools shall be destroyed. **(Proverbs 13:20 KJV)**

Do not be deceived: "Evil company corrupts good habits." **(1 Corinthians 15:33 NKJV)**

You Are More Than You Know

> With God's help you can always do more
> good than you ever thought possible.

There is always hope.

If you always do your best, then the best result will ultimately happen. Then no matter what happens, you can always be proud that you gave it your best shot. I will be proud of you too.

No one can fault someone who always does their best.

If something is worth doing, it's worth going well.

When you always try to do your best, you will always have the best chance of having things turn out right.

Don't do things halfheartedly, sloppily, or in any way less than your best. In the Corp, we would always say "Don't be a slacker! Nobody like a slacker." Don't settle for an okay job when you can do a better job. Always do your best. It doesn't matter if it's someone else's best or not. It might not be as good as someone else can do it, but you can always be proud of your best effort. Just learn from it, or learn from those who can do it well. Then the next time you do it, your best will be even better yet. But whatever you do, if it's important to do, do it good. If you are concerned or apprehensive about something, don't forget to pray about it and ask God for His help, because not only is He all-knowing and Good, He also does all things good (Romans 8:28).

> *Whatever you do, work at it with all your heart, as working for the Lord, not for man.* **(Colossians 3:23)**

> *"Because you're not yet taking God seriously," said Jesus. "The simple truth is that if you had a mere kernel of faith, a poppy seed, say, you would tell this mountain, 'Move!' and it would move.*

> *There is nothing you wouldn't be able to tackle."*
> **(Matthew 17:20 MSG)**

> *Jesus said to him, "As far as possibilities go, everything is possible for the person who believes."*
> **(Mark 9:23 GWT)**

If You Need Me, I Will Be There for You

No matter how far you go, no matter what you do, no matter where you are, no matter whom you're with, no matter why it happened, no matter when you need me, I will be there for you.

"I Will Be There for You"
Artist: Unknown

When life turns upside down
I will be there for you
When things seem not to be working
I will be there for you

When you need me most
I'll be there for you
I will hold your hand
Until the end of time

No matter the distance
You are still close to me
You are always in my heart
You are always in my thoughts

Every step in life you make
I will be there for you
When the wind strongly blows
I will protect you
In times of happiness
I will be there for you

I will enjoy every moment I spend with you
As you are my daughter and I love you

*****

I love those who love Me, and those who seek Me find Me. (**Proverbs 8:17**)

I was in terrible trouble when I called out to You, but from Your temple You heard me and answered my prayer. **(Psalm 18:6 CEV)**

Then call on Me when you are in trouble, and I will rescue you, and you will give Me glory. **(Psalm 50:15 NLT)**

God did this so that they would seek Him and perhaps reach out for Him and find Him, though He is not far from any one of us. "For in Him we live and move and have our being." As some of your own poets have said, "We are His offspring." **(Acts 17:24–28)**

Let Patience Guide You

When you spend your life accumulating or building things, in the end, all you've accomplished will someday be torn down, faded away, or burned up; but when you spend your life helping people, that work will last forever.

Sometimes, Patience just happens, and we need to follow where it leads.

When you are running late and the car in front is going too slow but, as you pass them, you find out it was just a dear little old lady needing a little extra time, your kindness and patience would make all the difference in the world to her. Maybe she doesn't drive very often but needs to get her sick husband to his doctor's appointment. She is very nervous but needs to get him there and just praying there are no deer or dogs or mean drivers that she'll have to contend with. I always think that she is someone's grandmother, and I need to treat her like I hope someone will treat my grandmother in the same situation. I don't know how she is or what her situation is. I just know she needs my kindness and patience.

When you're on a flight sitting next to a woman and her two small kids who won't stop crying, she is all alone and needs help. The people around you are all making it known that they are frustrated with her noisy kids and are starting to complain to the stewardess. You were hoping to get some sleep but offer to hold the baby, and the mom apologies but quickly accepts. Then with a little attention, you find that you can make them happy, and everyone around you soon is happy again. I didn't know who they were or why they were traveling. I just knew they were a family who needed some patience and kindness and a little of my help. It turned out to be a little messy for me but a lot of fun too.

When you are at the store to quickly run in and pick up a couple of items on your way home from work. As always, you jump in the shortest line just to find and the old guy in front of you is searching through his pockets to try to find a couple more bucks to pay for his groceries or looking to see if he puts a couple of cans of soup back will that be enough so he can afford to pay for it… The people behind you are starting to make some sarcastic sounds of disgust at the delay, just as you realize just a few dollars could save his day. I don't know who he is or why he doesn't have enough money. All I know is that with a little patience and kindness, the whole situation is easily changed.

When you're hurrying back to your car after a busy day at work, and out of the corner of your eye, you just happened to see a kid trip and fall. You know he got hurt, maybe not seriously, but you do see a silent tears forming in his eyes, and even though you don't have time, you stop to help him, and you know just a moment of kindness and compassion will make it better. I don't know who he is or where he is going; all I know is a Kleenex and a couple of minutes of my time will make all the difference for him.

When you notice some old couple in the Walmart parking lot, struggling trying to get their bags in their car. Although they are a row away from your car and there are several other people around who could help them, you notice no one is. So you quickly put your bags in your car and go over there and offer to help them. I don't know who they are or why they let the cashier fill their bags so full, but I do know that with just a little help and just a few seconds of my time will make their day much better.

When there's that one who has been talking to you nonstop and bothering you without limit, yet you know that it's because they're secretly hurting. As much as you would rather talk with someone else or just have some quiet time, you know just a little time and understanding might help. I don't know why they are such talkers today or why they are wanting to talk to me, but I know with just a little patience and time, I might be able to make a difference and help them through whatever they're going through.

When your child has been a pain in the butt and you know they've had a hard day, so you take time to read with them or play a game. It's not convenient or really what you would prefer, but you know it would be something that would help them to feel special and make up for their difficult day. I don't know why the day was so difficult or really what got them down, but I do know that changing my time a little and spending it with them will mean something to them.

When your spouse has been hurting and you know the day has been tough, so you offer a backrub and a big glass of tea. It's a little thing, but because you noticed and took the time, it really makes a big difference.

We can decide to be patient, and that's good, but at that point, it's just words or good intentions. However, when it's put to the test is when it really counts, and when it costs us something is when it really matters. Sometimes, a little patience is all we need combined with a little time and or a little effort to make a big difference in someone's day or life.

I know it might seem a little funny coming from me, but like I've said before, some lessons take some of us a little longer to learn. This is one lesson I wish I could go back and redo the many times I should have done so much more but didn't. Too many times, I just wanted to get where I was going or get done with what I was doing. Yet now, looking back, I really don't know what was so urgent that I couldn't have waited just a moment longer to show someone some kindness or help. I wish I would have at times taken the time to be able to show you, your siblings, or your mother, or maybe even some stranger just a little more patience or consideration along the way. I know if nothing else, I would have at least been a better person because of it, and I would have had a few less regrets in life too.

> *Patience is not the ability to wait, but the ability to keep a good attitude while waiting.* (Anonymous)

> *God has perfect timing; never early, never late. It takes a little patience and it takes a lot of faith but it's worth the wait.* (Anonymous)

> *Patience is when you're supposed to get mad, but you choose to understand.* (Anonymous)

To lose patience is to lose the battle. (Mahatma Gandhi)

Be always humble, gentle, and patient. Show your love by being patient with one another. **(Ephesians 4:2)**

Hot tempers cause arguments, but patience brings peace. **(Proverbs 15:18)**

Let your hope keep you joyful, be patient in your troubles, and pray at all times. **(Romans 12:12)**

The end of something is better than its beginning. Patience is better than pride. **(Ecclesiastes 7:8)**

What Makes a Person Strong?

A person's strength is not the force of their hand or the loudness of their voice, but the kindness of one's heart.

By your wealth you can change the value of something. (In 1995, DJ Trump bought 40 Wall Street for $1 million and renovated it for $35 million. Today, it's worth over $500 million.)

By your skill, you can change the way something looks (Michelangelo took a discarded piece of marble and carved the Statue of David, estimated to be worth $200 million.)

By your influence you can change the way something is perceived. (There was a commercial that said, "When **E. F.** Hutton talks, people listen.")

By strength you can change where something is located. (The official world's record heaviest deadlift was by Oleksii Novikov who lifted 1,185 lb. in 2020.)

By loudness of your voice you can change how far something is heard. (It's said that some voices have been heard to travel 10.5 miles across the ocean on a still night.)

By the kindness of your heart you can begin to change the world. (During World War II, Lieutenant General Dwight David Eisenhower of the Allied Forces heading to an emergency meeting in France delayed his arrival just to help an unknown stranded elderly couple on the street. In doing so, he unknowingly foiled an assassination plot, Hitler intended to kill Eisenhower and everyone with him that night, which may have changed the outcome of the war and future of the USA.)

Take time to be kind

*****

I've always enjoyed doing acts of kindness for people whom I know or don't know. Sometimes, I've been taken for a ride by a con artist or two; but most of the time, there have been some whom I really believe I did make a difference by helping them or just letting them know that someone cares for them. When that happens, it makes a difference for them, but it also does something for me too. It lets me know that my life has a purpose bigger than myself and I really can make a difference in this world. I've also found out that even when I've been conned that because I was really trying to do everything in a way to honor Jesus, that I am still blessed for doing it, so it was still worth doing.

So try, as much as you can, as often as you can, in as many places as you can, and for as many people as you can to show all the kindness you can and change the world one kind deed at a time.

> *You can accomplish by kindness what you cannot by force.* (Publilius Syrus)

> *Kindness is the language which the deaf can hear and the blind can see.* (Mark Twain)

> *Love and kindness are never wasted. They always make a difference. They bless the one who receives them, and they bless you, the giver.* (Barbara de Angelis)

> *Wherever there is a human being, there is an opportunity for kindness.* (Lucius Annaeus Seneca)

> *Beginning today, treat everyone you meet as if they were going to be dead by midnight. Extend to them all the care, kindness and understanding you can muster, and do it with no thought of any reward. Your life will never be the same again.* (Og Mandino)

> *This woman was full of good works and kind acts that she was doing.* (**Acts 9:36b YLT**)

Whoever pursues righteousness and kindness will find life, righteousness, and honor. **(Proverbs 21:21)**

A man who is kind benefits himself, but a cruel man hurts himself. **(Proverbs 11:17)**

Be kind to one another, tenderhearted, forgiving one another, as God in Christ forgave you. **(Ephesians 4:32)**

Whoever despises his neighbor is a sinner, but blessed is he who is generous to the poor. **(Proverbs 14:21)**

Being Honest Is Being Best

Honesty is not just the best policy; it needs to be the only policy.

To be honest, to do what is right, to tell the truth is always the right thing to do. (Me)

When your actions contradict your words, your words don't mean anything. (Anonymous)

Honesty and integrity are two things that never go out of style. (Me)

Honesty is the fastest way to prevent a mistake from turning into a failure. (James Altucher)

Being honest may not get you a lot of friends, but it'll always get you the right ones. (John Lennon)

Speak with honesty, think with sincerity, and act with integrity. (Anonymous)

The foundation stones for a balanced success are honesty, character, integrity, faith, love, and loyalty. (Zig Ziglar)

Honesty is more than not lying. It is truth telling, truth speaking, truth living, and truth loving. (James E. Faust)

Each time you are honest and conduct yourself with honesty, a success force will drive you toward greater success. Each time you lie, even with a little

> *white lie, there are strong forces pushing you toward failure.* (Joseph Sugarman)

> *An honest man's word is as good as his bond.* (Anonymous)

> *My parents taught me about the importance of qualities like kindness, respect, and honesty, and I realize how central values like these have been throughout my life.* (Kate Middleton)

The definition of *honesty* is "the quality or fact of being honest, uprightness, and fairness."

The quality of the friends we have or the people we associate with is influenced by what people know and think about us. What people know and think about us is learned by observing the life we live. The life we live is defined by our character. Our character is controlled by our integrity. Our integrity is formed by our honesty. If we want to be known as someone who is honest, then we must tell the truth. So if you want to have a better quality of friends, always tell the truth, and then you will be known as an honest person. Then by being an honest person, your integrity will begin to shine. If you want to have better friends, make sure you become a woman of integrity in everything you do, and then your character will be easily seen. Next, if you want to have better friends, make sure you are a person of great character, and then the life you live will be seen and known as one of high quality. Finally, if you are wanting better friends and associates, live your life as a high-quality person of great character, full of integrity, who is completely honest and upright; and then people of the same character and integrity will want to be and be known as your friend too.

> *Make your light shine, so that others will see the good that you do and will praise your Father in heaven.* **(Matthew 5:16 CEV)**

The ways of right-living people glow with light; the longer they live, the brighter they shine. **(Proverbs 4:18–19 MSG)**

Then your light will shine like the dawning sun, and you will quickly be healed. Your honesty (and integrity) will protect you as you advance, and the glory of the Lord will defend you from behind. **(Isaiah 58:8 CEV)**

Live Life as a Faithful Steward

Live with open hands and a faithful heart
with everything your hands touch.

A Good Steward of People

In this life, we really don't control much of anything. It's more like we just use and care for everything we have and what is around us. When you look at it that way, it's really more **stewardship** that we are involved in than ownership when you stop and think of it. Everything from our money, resources, time, health, to even our friends and family we have for a moment in our lives and really have such limited control or ownership. So be a good **steward** of everything you have and especially the people in our lives for however long they are in our lives. *"Making the very most of your time [on earth, recognizing and taking advantage of each opportunity and using it with wisdom and diligence], because the days are [filled with] evil"* (Ephesians 5:16–26 Amplified Bible).

Everything in this life is just given on loan to us, for just a while and not for us to keep. Whether it be for a moment, a day, a while, a season, a year, a time, a decade, or a lifetime, however short or long that might be, nothing remains in our possession for long and, in many cases, not near long enough. No matter how hard we try to hang on to anything, it's only just a matter of time before it leaves us, they let go of us, or we leave them. Whichever the case, it's not that long, and then they soon are gone. Whether through time, deterioration, poverty, or death, everything in this life is fleeting at best. *"So teach us to consider our mortality, so that we might live wisely"* (Psalm 90:12 NET). Although our children we claim as our very own, and to prove it, as parents, we are willing to pay a very high price for them, their care, and their pleasure, even willing to pay the ultimate price for their safety and protection (if and when necessary). Yet even they are here for just a short time; and then they quickly grow up, go off to college, join the military, meet a special someone, and move away. Then we are left alone with only our dreams of yesterday when our hopes were high, and they still needed us. However, they are only ours for a season, for a brief moment in time, and then they are gone.

The same is true for the rest of our family and friends. Although our connection with them is different, still they are only in our lives for differing moments in time. Before you know it, a job changes, a move happens, and life itself can just pull the rug out from under us with a sickness or even death. Since our time with and responsibility for those around us varies and our time with them is unsure and fleeting, we need to be great **stewards** of those relationships for however long we have them in our lives and take our responsibility seriously.

We need to be careful with the example or influence we have on them, with the opportunities to make a difference in their lives (whenever possible,) and even being careful of the words we speak to them or around them. Then once we have done our best with them, we must hold them in (as it were) an open hand, knowing they belong to God and He has a wonderful plan specific and special for them. For they are only ours for a moment, a season at best before they are gone. Then all we are left with is the memories of our times together or regrets of what we missed or should have done while we had the opportunity.

It's been said that over the last hundred years or so, every evil leader had attended an American college or university at one time or another. The thing that I wonder about is what would be different in the world today if someone would have befriended Hitler, Stalin, Mussolini, Saddam Hussein, or some of the others and helped them to see some kindness or told them about Christ while they were here. Would history have been written a little different? Would the world be different today if someone would have been a better **steward** of the influence they might have had with maybe a strange foreign student.

God desires you to be a good **steward** of your family (1 Timothy 5:8).
God desires you to be a good **steward** of your church family (Galatians 6:6; 1 Timothy 5:17–18).
God desires you to be a good **steward** of your community (Acts 1:8; John 4:28–30, 38–42).
God desires you to be a good **steward** of those in need (Matthew 25:35–40).

God desires you to be a good **steward** of those who need to be saved (Acts 1:8; Colossians 4:5).

> *"Be wise in the way you act toward those who are not believers, making good use of every opportunity you have"* **(Colossians 4:5 GNT)**.

> *"But if anyone has the world's goods and sees his brother in need, yet closes his heart against him, how does God's love abide in him?"* **(1 John 3:17)**.

> *"I tell you that on the day of judgment, people will give an account for every worthless word they speak"* **(Matthew 12:36 NET)**.

> *"So then, whenever we have an opportunity, let us do good to all people, and especially to those who belong to the family of faith"* **(Galatians 6:10 NET)**.

Be careful of all the moments you have with the people God places around you. God has entrusted us to wisely interact with each one for a specific reason and outcome for which He has orchestrated our meeting and planned the amount of time we need to accomplish it. Even the mean, the frustrating, the obnoxious, or the cantankerous one that you might see once or you might see quite often (like a couple of my brothers or uncles in the past were). God has trusted you to maybe show a little kindness into their life or be a little Christlike to them, or even plant seeds that might lead them to the Lord and totally change their lives and future.

However, unless you and I live up to the expectation and responsibility God has placed on us and be good **stewards** of our relationships, we will more than likely miss the opportunities He has given us. *So make the most of all the time you have* (Ephesians 5:16). Some of the opportunities He has given us are for our personal growth, our learning, or our pleasure and entertainment. Other opportunities are for us to make a difference in the lives of the people around us, to be a lifeline, a help, an encouragement, to share a hope with, to lend a shoulder to cry on, to be a friend when all others have left, to be a source of energy, or to help carry a load of emotion that's been pent up for too long. We're just to be whatever Jesus would be or do in that particular situation. That's what being a good **steward** with the people and relationships around us is all about.

> *Kindness is the language which the deaf can hear and the blind can see.* (Mark Twain)

> *You can't live a perfect day without doing something for someone who will never be able to repay you.* (John Wooden)

> *He who plants kindness gathers love.* (Saint Basil)

> *No act of kindness, however small, is ever wasted.* (Aesop)

> *When your life is done, let it be seen as if looking back over a garden that can be enjoyed by all, by bountifully planting everyday a great variety seeds of kindness and compassion, and by weeding out the weeds of bitterness, discord, and hatred.* (Me)

A Good Steward of Your Work

If you have a job that you worked hard to get it and are able to care for and meet the needs of your family with it, then you are blessed and need to be very thankful for it. Most of us would recognize in this day and age that our jobs are a blessing, or some would say you are lucky if you have a good one (I don't believe in luck). So if having God give us a job is a blessing, then we also must recognize that ultimately the type, benefits, and the duration of the job then are also in the hands of the one who blessed us with it too. So we need to be good **stewards** of our work and the responsibilities we have entrusted to our care. (As I write this, most of the world has been shut down for as much as the last ten months because of the coronavirus and certain politicians in charge. So many millions of people have been struggling without jobs.)

We need to understand that work isn't a bad thing; as a matter of fact, it was given to us in the garden and was part of the perfect world before sin. *"Then the Lord God took the man and put him in the Garden of Eden to farm the land and to take care of it"* (Genesis 2:15 GW). Our work was one way He planned for us to enjoy the world He created. So then, right after we were created, God gave us a different responsibility which also showed our greater importance or position above everything else that He had created—(that being the plants, animals, fish, birds…and everything else He created) to manage it, organize it, work it, cultivate it, nurture it, protect it, categorize it, name it, care for it, and use it wisely for Him. This is called **stewardship**. We have the responsibility to work within His creation and to look after it.

Man was given the task to care for, manage, or **steward** his particular area of work or responsibility, not own it. *"To work it and take care of it"* (Genesis 2:15) or to be **steward** of it. By this, God made man a **Steward** of this world. He gave him the job of tending and taking care of it with Him or for Him. So then, we as head over all of His creation are then responsible as **stewards** to care for all of His creation that He left in our care. If you can think about how right now, God is watching over all the planets and stars, every day's weather, plants growing, and children being born... Then we get to work with Him and take care of the stuff we can handle—teaching at school, interpreting wherever I can help, preaching, farming, and especially doing the stuff that we can do to make a difference with other people. We are given the privilege of being able to do our part at working with God in all His great creation. So we must do our part to take care of this world and everything in it to the best of our ability and make a real effort to leave it a little better than when we arrived. Everywhere we go and whatever we do, we always need to do our best in whatever we do.

"*For we are God's fellow workers*" (1 Corinthians 3:9). Elsewhere, Paul mentions that we are "*working together with Him*" (2 Corinthians 6:1).

> **Making the World a Better Place**
>
> No matter where you are or what you are doing, however it was when you arrived, or no matter who gets the credit when it's done, always strive to leave it a little better than when you arrived.

Our jobs are to be a blessing to or caring for what we've been given and is a means of expressing our unique personality and creativity and a means of productive application of our time, demonstration of our talent, and increase our training. Even more importantly, they are also given to us to care for and always do our best with, for as long as they are in our care. Have you noticed that no one has a particular job or responsibility their entire life? It's actually required by God that our jobs are right for us and not be more than we can handle. Numbers 8:24–26 requires the older priests to exchange their more demanding jobs for ones that they can more easily handle. Work in itself, isn't anything that anyone would ever create (although some, especially kids, do cause a lot more work) no one would never make any work for themselves. We might find it, discover it, or we might even find a better way of doing it; but, however, it happened. Our work was ultimately given to us and, therefore, created by God especially for us. Even those who are great entrepreneurs and inventors are great at finding work that no one else has found, but they didn't create it. I might be nitpicking semantics with this, but I do feel the work, and even our right job was created by God especially for us, and therefore we need to seek God's direction and blessing to find the right job He has planned for us.

Work is given to us as a blessing since the very first day man was on the earth, and that for time and a season. It is not necessarily ours, and even if we work for ourselves, we must still realize that we have been blessed with our job, and we must do our work knowing we really are working for Jesus Himself (Colossians 3:23). Because we know that our job was given to us to do our best with and because we are really doing it all for Jesus Himself, then it is also being done as a means of worship to God in the way we do it and by being thankful for it. So not only do we need to do the kind of work that God would be glorified in, we need to do it in a way or how He desires so that He will be proud of what you are doing.

With that in mind, we need to be good **stewards** of our work. Not just our job but also the quality of our work and the influence of our work, knowing it, too, belongs to God; and so as Christians, what we do must always be done in such a way that He receives glory through it. Whatever our job is or even how much we like it, we only have it for a season in our lives.

> *Each of us must give an account to God for what we do.* **(Romans 14:12 CEV)**

> *Employers, treat your workers with equality and justice as you know that you also have a Lord and Master in heaven who is watching you.* **(Colossians 4:1 TPT)**

> *Honor God with everything you own; give Him the first and the best.* **(Proverbs 3:9 MSG)**

> *Your work is going to fill a large part of your life, and the only way to be truly satisfied is to do*

what you believe is great work. And the only way to do great work is to love what you do. (Steve Jobs)

Everyone has been made for some particular work, and the desire for that work has been put in every heart. (Rumi)

If it falls your lot to be a street sweeper, go out and sweep streets like Michelangelo painted pictures. Sweep streets like Handel and Beethoven composed music. Sweep streets like Shakespeare wrote poetry. Sweep streets so well that all the hosts of heaven and earth will have to pause and say, here lived a great street sweeper who swept his job well. (Martin Luther King Jr.)

A Good Steward of Your Possessions

We are also to be good **stewards** of our possessions and the resources we have or available to us. Be a good **steward** of the possessions and the resources we have been entrusted with.

Owners have rights, **stewards** have responsibilities.

In general, "to be a **steward**" means we are entrusted to manage something on someone's behalf. When a friend, family member, or employer asks you to watch or take care of something for them, then you're being a **steward** or manager of whatever they entrusted to your care. *"So Joseph found favor in his sight and attended him, and he made him overseer of his house and put him in charge of all that he had"* (Genesis 39:4). Joseph didn't own this home or anything in Potiphar's home; he only cared for it and watched over it. Many translations just say *"made him **steward** of his household"* because **stewardship** sums up everything that is implied with his new responsibilities. Nothing was his or was given to him; he just had to manage and care for it the best he could and however he thought was in the owner's best interest. That would be to make it shine the best, produce the best, earn the best return on the investment, or make others think highly of the owner because of the **steward's** work.

We are **stewards** of our homes, not owners of a house. God made us to be the manager of the house and the household affairs that we oversee—from making sure the home stays clean and maintained to managing the finances and perhaps the other workers (or servants). All that we do we are managing everything on behalf of the owner.

The beginning of all biblical principles comes from the basic doctrine that we as (Christians) are the **stewards** of all our possessions and that Christ Lord over all. Meaning that Christ owns everything (Job 41:11; 1 Timothy 4:3–5).

*And he called him and said to him, "What is this I hear about you? Give an account of your **stewardship**, for you can no longer be **steward**."* **(Luke 16:2 NSV)**

For by Him all things were created, in heaven and on earth...all things were created through Him and for Him. **(Colossians 1:15–16)**

Teach us to use wisely all the time we have. **(Psalm 90:12 CEV)**

Wealth is not what you have for yourself. Wealth is what you share with others. (J. R. Rim)

Do your little bit of good where you are; it's those little bits of good put together that overwhelm the world. (Desmond Tutu)

Don't judge each day by the harvest you reap, but by the seeds you plant. (Robert Louis Stevenson)

Think of giving not only as a duty but as a privilege. (John Rockefeller)

Be a Good Steward of Your Wealth

Be a good **steward** of your finances and the wealth you have been entrusted with.

We are to work faithfully and responsibly and do our best with whatever we do and so we will in time be rewarded for our good work. Although we might never become rich for our labor, we will be blessed financially proportionate to our efforts. We know the general principle is that the harder we work, the more blessed we will be financially. Therefore, the natural response to that is to feel, "It is mine because I worked hard for it!" and "So I can spend it however I please." However, the Bible lets us know that is totally a wrong perspective or deduction to have because it's totally forgetting, or leaving out, where it came from and why we received it. God gives us everything good not to accumulate or hoard but to be good **stewards** of even our finances. This not only means that it is a gift from God for our use, but also that it's not our possession. *"I am the one who gave her the grain, the wine, the olive oil, and all the silver and gold that she used"* (Hosea 2:8). Yes, it is in our care and almost in our complete control to do with as we see fit, but when we forget to honor God with our finances and our wealth and act like it's all ours, we are actually robbing God (Malachi 3:8–12).

When we realize all the parts of our life and the world around us that we are involved with, including our money and how much God is involved with, we would realize just how little our part really is. We are only to be responsible with what opportunity we are given; and God blesses us with all the other parts like opportunity for advancement, environment, our health, availability, transportation, help… That makes it all come together and work out for us. *"Instead, remember that the* Lord *your God gives you the strength to make a living. That's how He keeps the promise He made to your ancestors"* (Deuteronomy 8:18).

So the finances we have is only the portion of the finances that He has entrusted to our care, and because they are His, we need to be careful to be good **stewards** with the finances we've been given. Our work then with our finances, because it is for Him, is an act of service to Jesus, and therefore a type of worship to Him. So be thankful for everything He has given us, honor God with what we have, and don't forget to be generous in our tithes, our offering, and blessing others around us. When we do that faithfully, God knows He can trust us and then gives us more to take care of for Him; and if we do good with that, He will then give us even more. Each time we prove our trustworthiness, God then tests us with a little more. *"Whoever can be trusted with very little can also be trusted with much, and whoever is dishonest with very little will also be dishonest with much"* (**Luke 16:10**). So then we need to be good **stewards** with everything He gives us. Then as we do, we will be set up to receive more and more continual blessings from God and never run out of the good things He has for us.

One thing that I have always been proud of you for is that you are a generous person. When you see someone in need, you are sensitive to the Lord's leading and desire to help in some way. Whether it be in giving money to help or physically doing something to be helpful to them in their need. You are kindhearted and generous in nature. These are characteristics that God has given you, and it is your responsibility to continue to develop them in a way that continues to honor God. I love you and am proud of who you are and talk of you often to those I work with. Continue being the awesome caring person you are.

> *Then you ought to have invested my money with the bankers, and at my coming I should have received what was my own with interest.* (**Matthew 25:27 ESV**)

> *"The silver and gold will be mine," says the LORD who rules over all.* (**Haggai 2:8 NET**)

> *Honor the LORD with your wealth and with the first and best part of all your income.* (**Proverbs 3:9 GW**)

*We were created to take care of, **steward** the land. That is mankind's purpose on earth, to steward and take care of the land as it feeds off of it.* (Wes Studi)

The tithe is a wonderful goal but a terrible place to stop. (Bill Hybels)

Don't tell me you're trusting God until you trust Him with your pocketbook. (J. Vernon McGee)

*The surplus wealth we have gained to some extent at least belongs to our fellow beings; we are only the temporary custodians of our fortunes, and let us be careful that no just complaint can be made against our **stewardship**.* (Jacob Schiff)

You Are Blessed

If you woke up this morning with more health than illness,
you are more blessed than the million who will not survive the week.
If you have food in your refrigerator, clothes on your back, a roof over
your head and
a place to sleep, you are richer than 75 percent of the world's
population.
If you have money in the bank or in your wallet,
you are among the top 80 percent of the world's wealthiest people.
If you hold up your head with a smile on your face and are truly
thankful,
you are blessed because the majority can, but most do not. (Author unknown)

Never Compromise on What Is Right and True.

What's Right is always Right, and to compromise on what is right is always wrong. It's like making a good recipe with the best ingredients and then trading just one ingredient for a poisonous one. Even if there were ninety-nine really good and healthy ingredients and only one poisonous one, the dish would be poisonous. Anyone who knew what you did would not want any of it even if you said there are ninety-nine healthy ingredients in it and only one poisonous one. Still, no sane person would want to eat any of it. The same is true with our lives. When we compromise on what is right and true, no one who knows that will really want anything to do with us, or we, at least, will have soon ruined our reputation and our character to the point that no one will really trust us.

There is a difference when we are talking about things that really don't matter or things that are just a matter of preference or taste, in situations such as those compromising to keep peace or to make someone happy is a good thing. However, when we are talking about compromising what is right or true or when one's character is involved, then no compromise is ever acceptable or good. The Truth is always the Truth, and Right is always Right.

You got to know when to hold them, and know when to fold them, know when to walk away, and know when to run. (Kenny Rogers)

Be open to things you don't know, flexible with things you know that don't really matter, and stubborn with what you know is true and right.

What is good is a cheap substitute for what is right.
There is no compromise in truth and no glory in a lie. (Me)

I will never compromise the truth for the sake of getting along with people who can only get along if we agree. (Dr. Silva)

So whoever knows the right thing to do and fails to do it, for Him it is sin. **(James 4:17 ESV)**

Turn away from evil and do what is right! Strive for peace and promote it! **(Psalm 34:14)**

And let us not grow weary of doing good, for in due season we will reap a reward, if we do not give up. **(Galatians 6:12 ESV)**

Preferences and Convictions

There is a big difference between our preferences and convictions.

Each of us has to decide if we live by our preferences or convictions. Our preferences are always changing throughout our entire lifetime. I would prefer to have four to five crispy strips of bacon with some sort of eggs for at least five breakfasts a week. I would also prefer to eat some kind of fried foods at least four times a week for dinner. I guess the rest of the meals could be a mix of soups, salads, Chinese food, and sushi… I guess I would prefer praline pecan ice cream for dessert. I am also pretty sure I would prefer to spend my days out on the water instead of going to work every day. I would definitely prefer to drive a fancy new truck or some sporty convertible instead of living practical and within my budget. And I definitely would prefer to do something else other than fix up and take care of our house and farm… We all have preferences, some we can indulge in a little or in moderation. Some of our preferences we—for responsibility's, morality's, and integrity's sakes—must avoid altogether.

Preferences are things we like or enjoy. They are mostly on a sliding scale of our mood. You might say, "What am I in the mood for today?" They also are related to our particular taste. Not just with food but even simple things like style or color. They also have to do with our beliefs we currently hold. We like them. We believe them to be best, but we could be convinced to believe something else or try something else if it seems more beneficial to us.

Preferences are not foundational for our life or the way we live. They are always changing depending on our circumstances, current trends, or style. We can be convinced to try something that might be better or just different. If there is a better offer, we can easily be swayed to abandon our previously held preferences. Then if temptation is strong enough (and if the truth be told, most of the time, not much real temptation is needed), we can be pulled from a preference that we previously thought was right and true.

However, a conviction is immovable. It's a rock-solid belief that the truth you believe in is etched in stone and unchangeable, such as the Bible. Conviction is being completely convinced of a truth so much so that you are willing to hold to it or stand up for it no matter what the consequences of doing so would be. These are truths we live by and die with. They give us direction for our everyday lives and every decision we make along the way.

Convictions keep us focused on what's important, and they keep us focused on our goals in life. They also become a defense for us against distractions and temptations to change from what we know is right and true.

> *He who believes is strong; he who doubts is weak. Strong convictions precede great actions.* (Louisa May Alcott)

> *If you press me about how I feel about an issue, you're going to see my convictions.* (Kirk Cameron)

> *Never for the sake of peace and quiet deny your convictions.* (Dag Hammarskjold)

> *As you know so well from what you've seen and heard, this man Paul has persuaded many, many people.* **(Acts 19:26)**

> *But if you have doubts about whether or not you should eat something, you are sinning if you go ahead and do it. For you are not following your convictions. If you do anything you believe is not right, you are sinning.* **(Romans 14:28)**

Why Do We Compromise Our Convictions?

What motivates us to do wrong, even when we know what's right, and compromise our convictions?

> *"For I do not do what I want, but I do the very thing I hate… For I have the desire to do what is right, but not the ability to carry it out. For I do not do the good I want, but the evil I do not want is what I keep on doing"* **(Romans 7:15, 18b–19)**. WHY DO I KEEP DOING THAT!

There's a Cost to live by your Conviction. There's usually a cost to do what is right. Sometimes, it costs us our friends, like when they want to do something you know is wrong and so you won't go along with them or do what they want. It might cost you a promotion you've earned, or even your job, if you won't falsify records or do a cheaper job than what you know is safe or right. It could cost you financially if you have to buy something when it would be so easy to just take something that no one would miss, but you know it's wrong.

> *"Is there anyone here who, planning to build a new house, doesn't first sit down and figure the cost so you'll know if you can complete it? If you only get the foundation laid and then run out of money, you're going to look pretty foolish. Everyone passing by will poke fun at you: 'He started something he couldn't finish'"* **(Luke 14:28–30 MSG)**.

You might be Criticized for living by your Convictions. Today with social media, we are all so connected, and we all want everyone else to like us and what we are doing. Yet at the same time, everyone today seems so free and easy to criticize everyone else on

Facebook, Twitter, Snapchat, and many more I don't know about. Most people think that anything goes today and everything is acceptable unless, of course, it's something that's Right, Moral, or Biblical; then you might be mocked, belittled, criticized, and even told what to do with your convictions.

> *"Don't be like the people of this world, but let God change the way you think"* **(Romans 12:2 CEV)**.

You might be Rejected for living by your Convictions. Often when we live by our convictions especially biblical God-honoring convictions, we may experience rejection. It's kind of funny, most people don't really mind if you have "Religion" or even strong convictions as long as you don't live like it. However, if you live by your convictions of what is right or wrong or God honoring with your life, you are basically drawing a line in the sand, and some people will find themselves on the other side of that line.

> *"But I say, love your enemies! Pray for those who persecute you"* **(Matthew 5:44 NLT)**.

You might even end up Losing out on some Opportunities just because you are living by your Convictions. Nobody likes to be treated unfairly or miss out on things they have earned or been looking forward to. It's even worse when the reason is not for doing anything wrong but for doing things right. However, when we live by our convictions and do what we know is right, we might miss out on what some would call the good life, living in the fast lane, the fun party life, or hanging out with the old friends... Truth be known, we will probably lose some of our old friends just because we have a higher standard we are trying to live by. As Christians, we should live with the determination to please Christ in everything we do and say; then we won't have any regrets (or a lot fewer anyway) when we stand before Him on judgment day, having been faithful to Him and His Word.

"The fear of man brings a snare, But whoever trusts in the L<small>ORD</small> *shall be safe"* **(Proverbs 29:25).**

Think about the journey of your life this far. What kinds of temptations have you already compromised your beliefs or convictions with? We all have drawn our line in the sand at one time or another, but it's sad to say that most of us have also willingly stepped over that line too. Some have even disregarded their previously held convictions altogether or have drawn other easier lines further over to the left. However, if you build your life on something you know is rock-solid like the Lord Jesus Christ and the Word of God, you will know what you believe is true, and it will help you to be able to stand firm with your convictions. Open the Word of God, and discover the truth where you can not only draw your line on but also build your life on too. Living an uncommitted, wavering, compromising life is really a miserable life and no more enjoyable than a soggy bowl of old cereal.

> *But when you pray, you must believe and not doubt at all. Whoever doubts is like a wave in the sea that is driven and blown about by the wind.* **(James 1:6 GNT)**

> *So that we may no longer be children, tossed to and fro by the waves and carried about by every wind of doctrine, by human cunning, by craftiness in deceitful schemes.* **(Ephesians 4:14)**

> *But if you stand for nothing you will have nobody for you and nobody against you.* (John Madden)

> *If you don't stand for something, you'll fall for anything.* (Irene Dunne)

> *Joyful are people of integrity, who follow the instructions of the* L<small>ORD</small>. *Joyful are those who obey*

His laws and search for Him with all their hearts. They do not compromise with evil, and they walk only in His paths. You have charged us to keep Your commandments carefully. **(Psalm 119:1–4 NLT)**

We've been surrounded and battered by troubles, but we're not demoralized; we're not sure what to do, but we know that God knows what to do; we've been spiritually terrorized, but God hasn't left our side; we've been thrown down, but we haven't broken. **(2 Corinthians 4:8–9 MSG)**

When We Fall Down, We Get Back Up

When you fall off a horse, you have to immediately get back on it and try it again. If you don't, not only will you not learn how to ride, but you could develop a fear of riding; beyond that, the horse will feel it won and develop more bad habits of dislodging its rider.

> Failing to succeed is not the same as failure or defeat.
> Failing to succeed is just one step in the line of success.
> Failure or defeat is just a decision to quit trying or to give up.
> Never quit.
> Never give up.
> Never stop trying.
> Try it one more time.
> Take time to pray about it.
> One more step is one step closer.
> You will get there if you just keep going.
> Remember to seek advice from someone you trust.

Thomas Edison failed more than ten thousand times in his attempt to invent the light bulb. When asked about that, he just said he didn't fail—he just succeeded at finding ten thousand things that didn't work.

> *He is no fool who gives up what he cannot keep for that which he cannot lose.* (Jim Eliot)

> *Don't give up. Don't lose hope. Don't sell out.* (Christopher Reeve)

> *That's right. Because I, your God, have a firm grip on you and I'm not letting go. I'm telling you, "Don't panic. I'm right here to help you."* **(Isaiah 41:13 MSG)**

Without good direction, people lose their way; the more wise counsel you follow, the better your chances. **(Proverbs 11:14 MSG)**

Get all the advice you can, and you will succeed; without it you will fail. **(Proverbs 15:22 GNT)**

For with clever strategy you wage your war, and victory comes from having many advisers. **(Proverbs 24:6)**

"We Fall Down"
Artist: Bob Carlisle

'Cause if the priest who fell could find the grace of God to be enough
Then there must be some hope for the rest of us
There must be some hope left for us
We fall down, we get up
We fall down, we get up
We fall down, we get up
And the saints are just the sinners
Who fall down and get up

What I Remember I Never Forget

What I forget I have a hard time remembering.

I have a mind like a steel trap. Just that, lately I'm thinking I might have lost the key. I know there are a lot of things we have to try to remember throughout our life, and so many of them, I've forgotten. I've had to learn some Spanish and some German when I was young. I've taken formal Japanese and French and ASL classes; and the only one I can carry on a conversation with is ASL. I believe the old saying is true that if you don't use it, you lose it. So the things I want to remember I need to keep using, refreshing my memory, or learning again.

> I want you to always remember this;
> You got this. I know you do.
> You can do it. I know you can
> You are loved, and you are wanted.
> You are special. One of a kind
> You are a winner. Ahead of the rest
> You are made with a purpose. And there's more to be done
> You are an overcomer. No matter what the test
> You can make a difference. In everyone around and
> You have a dad who loves you, and cares for you,
> I believe in you, and will always be in your corner with you.

> *Blessed are those who can give without remembering and take without forgetting.* (Elizabeth Bibesco)

> *God is within her, she will not fall; God will help her at break of day.* **(Psalm 46:5)**

My child, never forget the things I have taught you. Store My commands in your heart. If you do this, you will live many years, and your life will be satisfying. **(Proverbs 3:1–2 NLT)**

You are holding firmly to the truth that you were given. But I am still going to remind you of these things. In fact, I think I should keep on reminding you until I leave this body. And our Lord Jesus Christ has already told me that I will soon leave it behind. That is why I am doing my best to make sure that each of you remembers all of this after I am gone. **(2 Peter 1:12–15 CEV)**

In everything I did, I showed you that by this kind of hard work we must help the weak, remembering the words the Lord Jesus Himself said: "It is more blessed to give than to receive." **(Acts 20:35)**

I Will Be There to Help You Keep Going

When You Feel You Can't go any further
Never just lie there when you still have the strength to sit
Never just sit when you still have the strength to stand
Never just stand when you still have strength to walk
Never just walk when you still have the strength to run
Never just run when you have the strength to fly (Isaiah 40:31)
Never just guess when you can find the answer
Never just do what is easiest when you know what is best
Never just compromise your values when you know what is right
Never just go with the flow when you know that they're going the wrong way
Never just do what they are doing if you know what they are doing is wrong
Never just Surrender when there was still something worth fighting for and
Never forget no matter what anyone else thinks, says, or does
If you did your best, I will always be proud of you

> *"I can do all things through Him who strengthens me"* (**Philippians 4:13**).

I Will Be Here for You

No matter where you go or how far life takes you away from me or what you will ever do, I will always be believing in you and praying for you. I'll be looking forward to the next time I will get to see you again. Until my last breath, I will always be here for you because I love you!

> *Is there anyplace I can go to avoid Your Spirit? To be out of Your sight? If I climb to the sky, you're there! If I go underground, You're there! If I flew on morning's wings to the far western horizon, You'd find me in a minute—You're already there waiting! Then I said to myself, "Oh, He even sees me in the dark! At night I'm immersed in the light!" It's a fact: darkness isn't dark to You; night and day, darkness and light, they're all the same to You.* **(Psalm 139:7–12 MSG)**

To Help You Find Your Way

I will be there when you want me to help you find your way.

I think one of the things I miss the most about my dad is just to be able to call him up and be able to ask for his advice or pass something by him to see what he thinks. I could always count on him for encouragement when I was feeling down. He would lift me up when I didn't have any strength to stand. When I was lost and felt like quitting, I always knew he would be there to help me find my way. I want to be there for you to give you guidance anytime you need it or want it. It's not that I think you can't do it, because I know you can. If there's an idea I have or a suggestion I could share or a hand I could give that would help you get through it, get over it, or make it happen, I'll be here for you anytime you need me.

When you are in trouble or searching for the right thing to do or which way to go, the first thing to always do is pray, and then you will find the answer to every situation, and your way will be clear and simple to find. Do everything you can to find what is right; and once you find what is right, work at it, do it, stick by it, don't give up, don't give in, and don't quit. And once you've done everything you can do, then trust God with the results.

Get action. Seize the moment. Man was never intended to become an oyster. (Theodore Roosevelt)

Be prepared. You're up against far more than you can handle on your own. Take all the help you can get, every weapon God has issued, so that when it's all over but the shouting you'll still be on your feet. Truth, righteousness, peace, faith, and salvation are more than words. Learn how to apply them. You'll need them throughout your life. God's Word is an indispensable weapon. In the same way, prayer is essential in this ongoing warfare. Pray hard and long. Pray for your brothers and sisters. Keep your eyes open. Keep each other's spirits up so that no one falls behind or drops out. **(Ephesians 6:13–18 MSG)**

I Will Be That Voice You Hear

To call you back when you've lost your way.

When it really doesn't matter, when it's a matter of preference or taste, I will try not to say too much about it. When it's important or dangerous, I will do all I can to keep you safe and help you change your direction when you've lost your way. Even if me doing so may upset you or make you mad at me, I would much rather have you be or stay safe than to think I am the coolest dad or even to like me if that is what my choices are. I will never sacrifice your safety for my comfort.

"If you wander off the road to the right or the left, you will hear His voice behind you saying, 'Here is the road. Follow it'" **(Isaiah 30:21 GNT).**

You Are the Moon That Shines in My Night Sky

It doesn't matter what anyone else says or believes about you. No one could think more highly of you or love you more than I do.

I am proud about everything good that I hear you do, or even when I hear you try to do or learn something new. Anytime I've heard you do something unselfish to help or make a difference in the life of someone in need, I about burst a button over it. I can't stop thinking about you. Can't stop talking about you. I can't stop bragging on you. Because I'm your dad and I Love You!

You are one of the greatest joys of my life.

I want you to know that I am so proud to be your dad.

> *Do everything readily and cheerfully—no bickering, no second-guessing allowed! Go out into the world uncorrupted, a breath of fresh air in this squalid and polluted society. Provide people with a glimpse of good living and of the living God. Carry the light-giving Message into the night so I'll have good cause to be proud of you on the day that Christ returns. You'll be living proof that I didn't go to all this work for nothing.* **(Philippians 2:14–16 MSG)**

Your Tears Wet My Eyes

When you are weak, I'll strengthen you
When you are sick, I will sit with you till you are well
When you are wounded, I will bind up your wounds
When you are sad, I will cheer you up
When you are hurt, I will comfort you
When you are lonely, I will be with you
When you are needing to talk, I will be a good listener
When you stumble, I will catch you
When you fall, I'll lift you up
When you cry, I'll cry with you
When you feel unloved, I will never stop loving you
I will always be there for you, because I believe in you.

> *You know that a good, long session of weeping can often make you feel better, even if your circumstances have not changed one bit.* (Lemony Snicket)

> *It opens the lungs, washes the countenance, exercises the eyes, and softens down the temper; so cry away.* (Charles Dickens)

> *The Christian life is not a constant high. I have my moments of deep discouragement. I have to go to God in prayer with tears in my eyes, and say, "O God, forgive me," or "Help me."* (Billy Graham)

> *If one day you feel like crying, call me I can't promise to make you laugh, but I am willing to cry with you.* (Unknown)

> *People have said, "Don't cry," to other people for years and years, and all it has ever meant is, "I'm too uncomfortable when you show your feelings.*

Don't cry." I'd rather have them say, "Go ahead and cry. I'm here to be with you." (Fred Rogers)

LORD, you know the hopes of the helpless. Surely You will hear their cries and comfort them. **(Psalm 10:17)**

He will wipe every tear from their eyes, and there will be no more death or sorrow or crying or pain. All these things are gone forever. **(Revelation 21:4)**

Whenever danger was near you my heart would race
Whenever someone threatened you my blood would boil
Whenever you was scared I would be quick to come
Whenever you were sad my heart would break
When you would laugh my world brightens
When you would say, "Daddy, I love you!" my life was worth living.

Why Do You Carry Me?

You once asked me, "Daddy, why do you have to carry me?"

I carried you for a while to keep up with us.
I carried you because you were so small
I carried you because you were to tired
I carried you because it helps you
I carried you because it comforts you.
I carried you because it keeps you safe.
I carried you because it makes you feel taller.
I carried you because it helps you to see better,
I carried you because I was trying to show you off.
I carried you because I was proud of you
I carried you because I was your daddy
I carried you mostly because I Love You
I carried you because you were mine!
If you ever need me to carry you to get you help, to make you safe, I would. However, let's say at this stage of my life, I will always walk with you if you need someone to walk with. I will sit with you if you ever want someone to sit with you.
I carried you for a while lying in my arms,
I carried you for a while wrapped in my arms
I carried you for a while sitting on my arm in front of me
I carried you for a while holding to your legs and you clinging to my back
I carried you for a while sitting on my shoulders but now
I will always and forever carry you in my heart,
because no matter where you are, in my heart is where you have always been.

Pile your troubles on God's shoulders—He'll carry your load, He'll help you out. He'll never let

good people topple into ruin. **(Psalm 55:22–23 MSG)**

Listen to Me, family of Jacob, everyone that's left of the family of Israel. I've been carrying you on My back from the day you were born, And I'll keep on carrying you when you're old. I'll be there, bearing you when you're old and gray. I've done it and will keep on doing it, carrying you on My back, saving you. **(Isaiah 46:3–4 MSG)**

Find Your Moral Compass

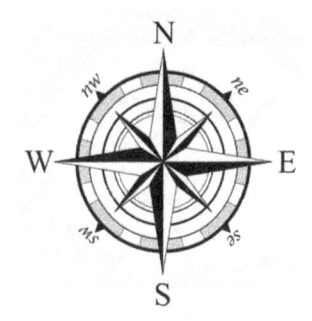

To get where you want to go, you need to know where you came from, where you are headed, and a plan of how to get there. Your grandpa Jackson would often say, "If you don't know where you are going, how will you know when you get there?" and "If you don't know where you are going, you won't like where you end up!"

I hope that the life I've lived will have established a path that is easy for you to follow, to help you find your way when you feel lost and can't find your way. I know I have failed with this many times and in many ways more than I even care to know. I know I have not been the dad that I should have been. It's just too bad that wisdom tends to come with age, and that only hindsight is 20/20. I hope and pray that I will have at least been able to lead you to the perfect example, to help you know what to do in most of the situations you will face.

I remember, as a young boy, being lost in a national forest; and it could have ended badly, but I did have a cheap compass and a decent head on my shoulders. I didn't give up or just stop trying. I didn't know as much as I should have, but I knew what my grandpa told me and followed it with my compass, and I eventually made it out safely on my own (with a lot of walking). My grandma was very upset, and the police were out with other search parties… It was a little embarrassing to say the least. I was cold, wet, and very tired; but I was safe because I remembered what I was taught and followed the path, used my compass, and found my way.

Please keep alert of what you are doing and your surroundings, watch the signs, know the right path, and follow your compass. Jesus is not just a great leader. He is also our perfect example. When you know Him, you will always know the way to go.

When you're going into an employment environment that looks pretty scary, it is easy to lose your moral compass, your decency, your sense of civility and your sense of community. (Henry Rollins)

Much of the world's moral compass is broken. The moral north reads south and the moral south reads north. (Dennis Prager)

Kids who evolve into creative adults tend to have a strong moral compass. (Adam Grant)

Sometimes, in order to follow our moral compass and/or our hearts, we have to make unpopular decisions or stand up for what we believe in. (Tabatha Coffey)

Follow my example, as I follow the example of Christ. **(1 Corinthians 11:1 NIV)**

Good leaders abhor wrongdoing of all kinds; sound leadership has a moral foundation. **(Proverbs 16:12)**

*Charm is deceitful and beauty is vain, But a woman who fears the L*ORD*, she shall be praised.* **(Proverbs 31:30)**

Jesus answered, "I am the way and the truth and the life. No one comes to the Father except through Me." **(John 14:6 NIV)**

You Can Make a Difference

You have much to offer this world.

You are more than you think you are, and you can be much more than you think you can become. I believe you are a teacher, a leader, and a person of influence, whether or not you ever do it professionally is up to you; but it doesn't change your ability or what you have the potential to offer.

What you say is important, and what you know is worth sharing. However, knowing when and how to share it, and knowing when it is not that important or worth the effort, is very important. How to communicate it is very important, and the saying "Timing is everything" is true in so many ways and areas of life. Sometimes, there is a good time to share your knowledge; but sometimes, the greater wisdom is in holding your tongue, at least until the time is right, anyway. There are people who will never listen to truth or wisdom, so don't waste it on them. However, if it is crucial or urgent information, don't quit trying to convey or convince them of it. If there was a fire, I would be very persistent and probably even violent by dragging the person from the fire. If there was someone's child in the road, I would try to convince the parent of the danger; but if the danger was imminent, I would just run and save the child myself. But if the problem is a bad investment and you are going to lose your shirt, I'll try to convince you with good reason and proof; but if you won't listen, then you will have to learn the hard way. Maybe I know the cheetah is the fastest land animal and the teacher thinks it's the rhino, and if for me to argue the point would appear to be making him look dumb, I wouldn't tell him during class. I might talk to him individually after class and tell him or write him a note later, if I think it's even that important.

To be one that is constantly correcting others on unimportant or unappreciated information or facts even though it's true makes you into a "know-it-all." It also cheapens your wisdom and knowledge. Use most of it where it makes a difference and is appreciated.

Things of low importance or significance really are not worth correcting anyone on most of the time. Yet things of high importance, especially if someone's life or safety is involved, then try your best. Then no matter what the outcome is, you will know you tried your best to do what is right and help them.

Knowledge, like sugar, is good but to be shared; however, it should be used in the proper way and with moderation for most people to appreciate it.

Wisdom, like guns, are important to know how to use them correctly and are crucial to have when you need them, and it's always best to have more than you think you'll ever need, but it's best not to share them with just anyone.

You can always impress me, and I enjoy listening to you.

> *Leadership is intelligence, honesty, and doing the right thing.* (Julie Zeilinger)

> *Be the change you wish to see in the world.* (Mahatma Gandhi)

> *There is nothing more beautiful than someone who goes out of their way to make life beautiful for others.* (Mandy Hale)

> *The purpose of life is not to be happy. It is to be useful, to be honorable, to be compassionate, to have it make some difference that you have lived and lived well.* (Ralph Waldo Emerson)

> *There is no exercise better for the heart than reaching down and lifting people up.* (John Holmes)

Ezekiel 33: 1–20 reminds us that we that know what is right and can help, must help those that don't know or need our help.

She opens her mouth with wisdom, and the teaching of kindness is on her tongue. **(Proverbs 31:26)**

Do not give what is holy to the dogs; nor cast your pearls before swine, lest they trample them under their feet, and turn and tear you in pieces. **(Matthew 7:6)**

And who knows but that you have come to your royal position for such a time as this? **(Esther 4:14)**

Evil people will keep on being evil, and everyone who is dirty-minded will still be dirty-minded. But good people will keep on doing right, and God's people will always be holy. **(Revelation 22:11 CEV)**

Stand on My Shoulders

I want my learning, understanding, knowledge, experiences, and wisdom to all be for you, to help you on your way. In that way, you'll be taking me with you on your life's journey as you strive for your future and reach for your stars.

"If I have ever done anything great, rose a little higher, or seen a little further than my fellow man, it's because I've been able to stand on the shoulders of giants" (Isaac Newton in 1675).

The Bible speaks about the value of two people walking together or working together (Ecclesiastes 4:9–10). It also speaks about valuing the counsel of others. There is a lot teaching in the Bible about being teachable and being a lifelong learner.

I have traveled a lot of miles in my many years on this earth. I have seen many strange and interesting things. I have been a greenskeeper, a door-to-door salesperson, a farmhand, landscaper, a pool maintenance and installation technician, an insulation installer, an asbestos abatement technician, a YFC leader, a US Marine, and I was hired as a state trooper, a salesman at a new cars dealership, a security guard, a fitness center trainer/coach, a general contractor/builder, a hobby farmer, an interpreter, a real estate inspector, an advocate, a counselor, a teacher, and a pastor. I received my first preacher's license in 1980 with the Wesleyan denomination. Then in 1984, I switched my license to the Assemblies of God denomination. I was an associate pastor with Trinity A/G for about fifteen years and then moved to Wisconsin and have been doing what I can to pastor out here. I started learning sign language in 1985 and soon after was pulled into being an interpreter ever since then. As an interpreter, I worked in personal family gatherings, clubs, organizations, and many different political and public meetings. I've interpreted in more schools, colleges, and universities than I can count. I've worked in jails, prisons, courts, hospitals, and dozens of other kinds of businesses. I've been on TV, interpreted for commercials, training webinars, and videos. I've even interpreted for a former president of the United States. I've also attended many different colleges and have three degrees earned from two of them. I currently work in the education field at a local public school district, preach every Sunday, and farm, and am trying to finish our house remodeling while building a home for your grandmother. (And that's just the bare highlights.)

They say with a car it's not so much a problem with the years that makes a car old; it's how many miles it's traveled. If that's true with a car, it's even more true about people. All my gray hair is one hundred percent earned, and much by being your dad (haha); and if the Bible says it's a sign of wisdom, then maybe I do have something to share.

The first and best resource for gaining wisdom is in gaining knowledge of the Bible (Exodus 35:31) and learning to fear God is where it all starts (Proverbs 9:10). But beyond that, I will always be honored if somehow my knowledge, experience, skills, wisdom, or opinion would be of some help or benefit to you.

> *If I have seen further than others, it is by standing upon the shoulders of giants.* (Isaac Newton)

> *Our chief want in life is someone who shall make us do what we can. This is the service of a friend. With him, we are easily great.* (Ralph Waldo Emerson)

> *Someone is sitting in the shade today because someone planted a tree a long time ago.* (Warren Buffett)

> *Life's too short to learn from your own mistakes. So learn from others.* (Unknown)

> *The Bible is the book of my life. It's the book I live with, the book I live by, the book I want to die by.* (N. T. Wright)

Whatever you have learned or received or heard from me, or seen in me (if there has been any good you've seen in me)—put it into practice. And the God of peace will be with you. **(Philippians 4:9)**

Listen with respect to the father who raised you, and when your mother grows old, don't neglect her. Buy truth—don't sell it for love or money; buy wisdom, buy education, buy insight. Parents rejoice when their children turn out well; wise children become proud parents. So make your father happy! Make your mother proud! **(Proverbs 23:22–25 MSG)**

People learn from one another, just as iron sharpens iron. **(Proverbs 27:17 GNT)**

Arrogant know-it-alls stir up discord, but wise men and women listen to each other's counsel. **(Proverbs 13:10 MSG)**

Wise words come from the lips of people with understanding, but those lacking sense will be beaten with a rod. **(Proverbs 10:13)**

Fools are headstrong and do what they like; wise people take advice. **(Proverbs 12:15 MSG)**

Look, Daddy, Look at Me!

*If I could have stopped and watched,
maybe you would have known.*

Life is busy, and we are always in a hurry, but if I could have stopped each time you wanted me to look, maybe you would have seen how much you really matter. When we were trying to get things done and there was soo much left to do, but somehow, if only I would have taken time to watch you when you wanted me to, maybe you would have known just how much I really cared. I know we were often running late trying to get where we needed to go, but if I would have watched just a minute longer when you wanted to show me something, you might have learned just how special you are to me. But life is busy and hurried and hectic, with all the important things we now can't remember. Yet the things that mattered most of all, the things we can still remember, are those things we thought we would have plenty of time to do later. However, now those days are gone, and those special bugs have long since crawled away. The special leaf or rock or flower has now been lost, and what you wanted me to see is past. If I could go back and change just one thing—it would have to be the one thing that I now regret the most—the one thing I would most wish that I could go back and change is I wish I would have spent more time with you while you were growing up.

I know now that if I could have just slowed down, it would have been more easily seen just how much that I love you. I know this is something I haven't done very well, especially when you were much younger. It doesn't mean that I thought of you any less or that you were not worth it to me. It was just the stress, my work, my life that seemed to steal my time and attention. So I apologize for not stopping whatever I was doing at the time and taking the time to focus more on you when you needed me to. We all still need that, and I do hope that I am doing a better job with that now.

Whatever you're doing, I want you to know I am watching, looking, and listening now.

One of the greatest things about daughters is how they adored you when they were little; how they rushed into your arms with electric delight and demanded that you watch everything they do and listen to everything they say. Those memories will help you through less joyous times when their adoration is replaced by embarrassment or annoyance and they don't want you to see what they are doing or hear what they are saying. And yet, you will adore your daughter every day of her life, hoping to be valued again, but realizing how fortunate you were even if you only get what you already got. (Michael Josephson)

Children will listen to you after they feel listened to. (Jane Nelsen)

In the eyes of a child you will see the world as it should be. (Unknown)

Seven things every child needs to hear: I love you, I'm proud of you, I'm sorry, I forgive you, I'm listening. This is your responsibility. You have what it takes to succeed. (Sherrie Campbell, PhD)

You may choose to look the other way but you can never say again that you did not know. (William Wilberforce)

Kiss his son, or he will be angry and your way will lead to your destruction, for his wrath can flare up in a moment. **(Psalm 2:12 NIV)**

Fathers, don't make your children resentful, or they will become discouraged. **(Colossians 3:21 GWT)**

Parents, don't come down too hard on your children or you'll crush their spirits. **(Colossians 3:21 MSG)**

The Value of a Hug

According to recent research, hugging has many health benefits.
It can help to calm the nervous system
It can help to reduce stress
It can help us to feel safer
It can help to reduce blood pressure
It can help to relieve anxiety
It can help to get a better night's Sleep
It can help to reduce depression
It can help to instill Hope after a disaster
It can help to encourage healing
It can help to give Encouragement
It can help us to feel Happier
It can help a child's brain to grow
It can trigger the release of a hormone called dopamine in the brain which makes us feel happy
It can even trigger the release of a hormone called oxytocin, which can lower stress levels
Some research even goes as far as to say that
"To just maintain our health, we need at least eight hugs a day.
"If we want to get stronger or more healthy, we need at least twelve hugs a day."
If you ever need a hug or someone to sit by or hang out with, I'm always available.
If you ever find yourself in an uncomfortable awkward or insecure situation and you need help, I'll be there.
If you ever need an excuse of why you have to do something or why you can't do something you can always blame me.
I'll be your Shield.
I'll be your protector.
I'll be your encouragement and greatest fan.
I'm here for you if ever you need me.

When I come home, my daughter will run to the door and give me a big hug, and everything that's happened that day just melts away. (Hugh Jackman)

"*When you come looking for Me, you'll find Me.*
    "*Yes, when you get serious about finding Me and want it more than anything else, I'll make sure you won't be disappointed." God's Decree.*
    "*I'll turn things around for you. I'll bring you back from all the countries into which I drove you"—God's Decree—"bring you home to the place from which I sent you off into exile. You can count on it.*" **(Jeremiah 29:13–14 MSG)**

What Hugging Can Do
By Dean Walley, *The Messenger*

It's wondrous what a hug can do.
A hug can cheer you when you're blue
A hug can say, "I love you so,"
Or, "I hate to see you go."

A hug is "Welcome back again."
And "Great to see you! Where 'er you been?"
A hug can soothe a small child's pain
And bring a rainbow after rain.

The hug, there's just no doubt about it—
We scarcely could survive without it!
A hug delights and warms and charms;
It must be why God gave us arms

Hugs are great for fathers and mothers,
Sweet for sisters, swell for brothers;
And chances are your favorite aunts
Love them more than potted plants.

Kittens crave them, puppies love them,
Heads of states are not above them.
A hug can break the language barrier
And make your travel so much merrier.

No need to fret about your store of 'em;
The more you give, the more there's more of 'em.
So stretch those arms without delay
And give someone a hug today!

*****

For God so loved the world that He gave His one and only Son, that whoever believes in Him shall not perish but have eternal life. **(John 3:16)**

But God demonstrates His own love for us in this: While we were still sinners, Christ died for us. **(Romans 5:8)**

For I am convinced that neither death nor life, neither angels nor demons, neither the present not the future, nor any powers, neither height nor depth, nor anything else in all creation, will be able to separate us from the love of God that is in Christ Jesus our Lord. **(Romans 8:38–39)**

See what great love the father has lavished on us, that we should be called children of God! And that is what we are! **(1 John 3:1a)**

"Butterfly Kisses"
Artist: Bob Carlisle

Sweet sixteen today
She's looking like her mama a little more everyday
One part woman, the other part girl.
To perfume and makeup from ribbons and curls
Trying her wings out in a great big world.
But I remember…

Butterfly kisses after bedtime prayer;
sticking little white flowers all up in her hair.
"You know how much I love you, Daddy,
"But if you don't mind I'm only gonna kiss you on the cheek this
    time."
Oh, with all that I've done wrong I must have done something right
to deserve her love every morning and butterfly kisses at night.

All the precious time
Like the wind, the years go by.
Precious butterfly.
Spread your wings and fly.

She'll change her name today.
She'll make a promise and I'll give her away.
Standing in the bride-room just staring at her.
She asked me what I'm thinking and I said
"I'm not sure—I just feel like I'm losing my baby girl."
She leaned over

Gave me butterfly kisses with her mama there,
Sticking little white flowers all up in her hair
"Walk me down the aisle, Daddy—it's just about time."
"Does my wedding gown look pretty, Daddy? Daddy, don't cry"

Oh, with all that I've done wrong I must have done something right.
To deserve her love every morning and butterfly kisses

I couldn't ask God for more, man this is what love is.
I know I gotta let her go, but I'll always remember
Every hug in the morning and butterfly kisses…

Home of the Wise and Free

Did you see enough wisdom and understanding growing up?

Looking back, I'm sorry to say that I don't think I did a good job with this for a number of reasons. I don't think I did as good of a job communicating this as I had hoped or even well enough to be understood. However, I always wanted you kids to grow up knowing you can talk to me about anything (love, hate, like, dislike…) even if it was about me or against me. The only criteria was that you needed to do it respectfully.

I wanted to teach you that your feelings were your own and they were neither right nor wrong, but there is a right and wrong way to express or deal with them. In the USMC, if I knew how to show the proper respect due, I could pretty much tell anyone anything. That's what I was trying to teach you when you were growing up. I'm sorry if I never got that across to you, but what you think and how you feel is very important to me.

Even still, I hope we can go on from here and have a more open communication between us.

> *If we do not express our disappointment, it will start to build up and transform into a more difficult emotion, such as anger, hurt, or even betrayal. It is best to share your disappointment in a non-critical way, rather than leaving it to build up inside you.* (Haemin Sunim)

> *Home is a place you grow up wanting to leave, and grow old wanting to get back to.* (Unknown)

> *A man travels the world over in search of what he needs, and returns home to find it.* (George Moore)

There is nothing more important than a good, safe, secure home. (Unknown)

Home is where everyone comes for respite and rest, but if a home environment does not provide the love that children need, then they will seek it elsewhere. (Nicoline Ambe, *Being Dad*)

The future of their child depends on how they were raised at home. Thus, the foundation they receive from us is the same criteria they know well to discipline and raise their own child in the future. (David Bishopson, *How to Discipline a Child*)

No matter our living circumstances, our living space is a place of ministry to family and friends. The attitude we have in keeping our home, in how we relate to our family and friends, and in caring for others reflects God's love to us. When we take care of our spiritual health and seek wisdom from God's Word in how to love others, that outpouring of love appears in our homes. (Kim Brenneman, *Home Management: Plain and Simple*)

Love the LORD *your God with all your heart and with all your soul and with all your strength. These commandments that I give you today are to be on your hearts. Impress them on your children. Talk about them when you sit at home and when you walk along the road, when you lie down and when you get up.* **(Deuteronomy 6:5–7)**

Come. Sit down. Let's argue this out. (Let's discuss this.)

This is God's Message:

*"If your sins are blood-red, they'll be snow-white.
If they're red like crimson, they'll be like wool.
If you'll willingly obey, you'll feast like kings.
But if you're willful and stubborn, you'll die like dogs."
That's right. God says so.* **(Isaiah 1:18–20 MSG)**

Plans go wrong for lack of advice; many advisers bring success. **(Proverbs 15:22 NLT)**

Listen to counsel and accept discipline, That you may be wise the rest of your days. Many plans are in a man's heart, But the counsel of the Lord *will stand.* **(Proverbs 19:20–21)**

Be Free

No truth no freedom, know truth and know freedom.
Real truth is from God no matter where it is found.
The Bible is the basis of all truth. Anything that disagrees with the Bible is not true. A person that walks with God walks in truth.

Honesty is a very expensive gift. Don't expect it from cheap people. (Warren Buffett)

The greatest advantage of speaking the truth is that you don't have to remember what you said. (Unknown)

To tell the truth doesn't cost you anything, but to tell a lie could cost you everything. (Unknown)

Never lie to someone that trusts you, and never trust someone that lies to you. (Unknown)

Jesus told the people who had faith in Him, "If you keep on obeying what I have said, you truly are My disciples. You will know the truth, and the truth will set you free." (**John 8:31–32 CEV**)

Jesus said to him, "I am the way, and the truth, and the life. No one comes to the Father except through Me." (**John 14:6 ESV**)

Seriously Silly

*It takes wisdom to know when to be
serious and when to be carefree.*

In my observation and years of living, as much as I wish it was different, I believe life is at least 80 percent serious and the rest is a mixture of normal mundane or everyday business to funny and even silly stuff. There are a lot of people I know who think life is all fun and games, and never take anything seriously, and there are others I know of who think everything is a serious drama and never smile or laugh at anything. We really need a variety, a good mix. However, it's important to know the difference, and yet we need to be careful that we don't take everything too seriously, nor should we ever think everything is just a big joke or not important. It's funny, if you take something too seriously that is not serious, that can be a serious problem; and yet if you don't take something serious enough, that is really a serious situation. That too can be a serious problem. No, really, I'm serious (haha).

Learn to laugh a lot when it's the right time to laugh, and make sure you find plenty of times to laugh. Yet learn to be serious when it is important to take the situation seriously, because sometimes you won't get a second chance.

As Kenny Rogers said, "you have to know when to hold them and know when to fold them." And I'm being serious about that. Well, not the part about Kenny Rogers, but with the rest of it, I was. Haha.

Develop a habit of regularly taking a very serious look at your life and your choices, and the conse-

quences of those choices, then make changes to your direction accordingly. (Unknown)

Always laugh when you can. It is cheap medicine. (Lord Byron)

Modern society will find no solution to the ecological problem unless it takes a serious look at its lifestyle." (Pope John Paul II)

I never would have made it if I could not have laughed. It lifted me momentarily out of this horrible situation, just enough to make it livable. (Viktor Frankl)

If you look over the course of a hundred years, I think the gradual erosion of the consensus that's held our country together is probably more serious than a few bearded terrorists who fly into buildings. (Pat Robertson)

You don't stop laughing when you grow old, you grow old when you stop laughing. (George Bernard Shaw)

Insincerity is always weakness; sincerity even in error is strength. (George Henry Lewes)

It pays to take life seriously; things work out when you trust in God. A wise person gets known for insight; gracious words add to one's reputation. **(Proverbs 16:20–30 MSG)**

Yes, if a man should live many years, let him rejoice in them all; yet let him [seriously] remember the days of darkness, for they will be many. All that comes is vanity (emptiness, falsity, vainglory, and futility)! **(Ecclesiastes 11:8)**

A right time to cry and another to laugh, A right time to lament and another to cheer. **(Ecclesiastes 3:1–8 MSG)**

In a similar way, urge the younger men to be self-restrained and to behave prudently [taking life seriously]. **(Titus 2:6)**

Even so must their wives be serious, not slanderers, sober, faithful in all things. **(1 Timothy 3:11)**

Live with a Proper Perspective

Your **perspective** is the way you see something. If you think that cell phones are bad and are destroying our young people and ultimately causing the downfall of America's, then from your **perspective**, a cell phone store is an evil place. *Perspective* has a Latin root meaning "look through" or "**perceive**," and all the meanings of *perspective* have something to do with "looking." So then **Perspective** has to do with the way that we look at things. It's also an artistic technique to give an allusion of depth or distance on a flat paper. An example of artistic **perspective** in a drawing is where the artist will draw the city street with its building shrinking off into the distance.

There are a lot of things that affect our **perspective** of things around us.

Our upbringing, training, or what we were taught when we were young.

What we observe going on around us or how we see others doing what they do,

Our friends and what they do, like, want, or believe,

Media and what they say advertise, push on us, or try to convince us to like, or do,

Culture and what we see or hear other people our age doing, or people in a given area

Influence of people we respect, think as heroes, or idolize and what they say or do,

Our experiences,

Our feelings,

What we have seen happen,

What we feel, or believe is right or wrong,

And what we believe that the Bible, our pastor, or God Himself says about it.

Then even our miss understands on any given subject, event, or thing,

Or what we thought we saw or heard happen.

All of these come together to determine our **perspective**.

When I was responsible to interpret a drama, I had to work with the stage lighting crew and usually was given a stage light with a colored gel (a colored plastic sheet) over the light. This was to dim the light so it wouldn't be too overpowering and cast distracting shadows across the stage. It also was to color the light so it would fit the mood or the tone of the stage. Then, too, after the director had his say of what they wanted, I hoped there was enough light so the deaf could clearly see my signs. Sometimes, I had to argue with the director about the amount of lighting I needed and might even have to compromise and use a darker-colored gel or even use white gloves to make my hands more visible. This was because not only the amount of light but also certain colors of light changed the mood or look of the scene or cast and could either add to or take away from the scary or sad or happy feeling they were trying to communicate in a particular scene. The way the audience felt about or **perceived** the scene could be greatly miscommunicated by just using the wrong filter (or gel) at the wrong time and could cause the feeling or **perception** of a scene to change, and the audience could lose the whole point of that scene. Even though all the words could be right, what was actually communicated or what the audience thought was said could be totally different.

That is just like life, because we often struggle to either have the right **perspective** of any given situation or react appropriately to the situation because of all the filters we are working with. It's just like with marriage. Many people have a squired **perspective** of marriage because they can't just see marriage as it is, and God created it to be, they can only see it through the many different filters they've collected along the way. They might think it's really not so important, because our culture is saying it's not important, "it's just a piece of paper." They laugh a lot at modern day comedies making fun of problem marriages and relational frustrations. Maybe their parents or their friends' parents got a divorce. Maybe they heard people bad-mouth their marriage partner or put their partner down, and they think the Bible says we "shouldn't get divorced," but they don't know where, and yet they are pretty sure that God wants them "happy." Then they might not have heard a preacher preach against divorce either; so with all those filters, they have a **perspective** that marriage is not that great, divorce is acceptable, and living together is actually the best idea. Little to no light (truth) is coming through all those filters.

There was one time your mother went to court to support a friend who was going through a tough situation. Well, the court was full, and she ended up sitting in the only place available which was on the opposite side of the court from her friend she went to be with, and she ended up having to sit next to the one her friend was opposing. Later she found out that her friend was very offended with her because from her **perspective** it looked like your mom was intentionally sitting next to this person and she thought that your mother had her arm around their shoulders consoling them. It wasn't true, and nothing like that had happened, but this person swore that it was, because to her and from her **perspective**, it looked like that is what was happening. Sad thing was she got mad and wouldn't be convinced otherwise and broke off the friendship with us, and we were only there as a friend and to be a support for her.

I have also seen people who would be quick to break off relationships with their family over misunderstandings of what they thought someone meant or said, and in their **perspective**, it was way worse than what anyone else thought it to be, even at times judging them not even by what they said or did but their interpretation (or perception) of why they did what they did. The worst thing is that they allowed their filters of past feelings, frustrations, maybe what their friends were saying, and who-knows-what-else-was-going-on determine the outcome; and they severed ties with their family, instead of just judging the current situation on its own merit or better yet give their family member the benefit of any doubt of ulterior motive.

There is an old saying that says, "Always use a magnifying glass to view your date, and always wear rose-colored glasses to view your spouse." It means don't give lots of grace, kindness, and understanding to strangers or even friends and yet at the same time pick apart family and especially one's spouse. It should always be the other way around. We should always value our family highest of all and always think the best of them. We should always try to keep the **perspective** that our spouse and our family are the best blessings from God we have. Furthermore, even if at the time our feelings might be hurt or misunderstanding may happen from time to time, I will always first of all believe that it was just a misunderstanding that can all be worked out in time; and our family is always worth working through whatever for…because I love you and I love our family!

> *As we look not to the things that are seen but to the things that are unseen. For the things that are seen are transient, but the things that are unseen are eternal.* **(2 Corinthians 4:18 ESV)**

> *Set your minds on things that are above, not on things that are on earth.* **(Colossians 3:2 ESV)**

> *Casting all your anxieties on Him, because He cares for you.* **(1 Peter 5:7 ESV)**

> *I can do all things through Him who strengthens me.* **(Philippians 4:13 ESV)**

> *For nothing will be impossible with God.* **(Luke 1:37 ESV)**

> *Gratitude is one of the strongest and most transformative states of being. It shifts your **perspective** from lack to abundance and allows you to focus on the good in your life, which in turn pulls more goodness into your reality.* (Jen Sincero)

> *The only thing you sometimes have control over is your **perspective**. You don't have control over your situation. But you have a choice about how you view it.* (Chris Pine)

I pray to start my day and finish it in prayer. I'm just thankful for everything, all the blessings in my life, trying to stay that way. I think that's the best way to start your day and finish your day. It keeps everything in **perspective**. (Tim Tebow)

Perspective *is the most important thing to have in life.* (Lauren Graham)

Is Fair Really Fair

Equality or sameness is not the same as fairness.
A person that is treated fair is a person that is given a lot of room for opportunity;
For those who want to work for it, they can be treated as exceptional.
For those who have unique skills or abilities, they can be treated as special.
For those who are very artistic, they can be treated as exceptional.
For those who are near and dear to us, they can be treated with love and affection.
For those who are hurt or disabled, they can be treated with extra care.
For those who are giving us needed help, they can be treated with much appreciation.
For those who are willing to sacrifice themselves for us, they can be treated with extra honor.
For those who are able to lead, they can be treated with due respect.
For those who are able to make us laugh, they can be treated with delight and joy.
For those who are able to make us happy, they will always be treated with a big welcome.

Life is rarely fair but as much as I can I want to treat everyone fairly. Fair does not mean the same because if everyone was treated the same no one could achieve more or be able to be treated special.

All of us have dreams for our future and what we want our lives to be. Yet, fair wouldn't be for all of us to have the same dream or life.

Life isn't fair when we've planned and worked and scrimped and saved, but financial disaster still hits.

Life isn't fair when we have friends and family whom we love and can't live without, but we lose by distance, broken relationships, sickness, and even death.

Life isn't fair when we've fallen in love and got married, then have children, yet even so, our family ends up still torn apart.

Life isn't fair when our Dreams are dashed and left shattered on the floor. Life isn't fair when we are left paralyzed with disappointment. Life isn't fair when it feels like our heart is ripped out of our chest and we are left not knowing what to do or which way to go. We might even find ourselves in times like these, shaking our fist at heaven and saying, "But God, WHY? THIS IS NOT FAIR!" Yet even when Life isn't fair, God is still good! All this stuff is just temporary at best.

As much as I wish I could make it so or I could promise it for you, God never promised that life would be fair, easy, or trouble-free. However, He does promise that even during our times of disappointment and frustration, God will be with us. Whatever trauma or crisis may arise, whose fault it was or wasn't, however unfair it seems, no matter what you are currently going through, just remember that I am here for you and God is on your side. Just turn to Him for comfort, guidance, and help to get through the times when life is unfair. He doesn't promise "Fair" in this life, but He does promise that He will lead you through it and on to better things ahead if you will just trust and follow Him. Most of all, remember, no matter what happens or what you are going through, I will always love you and be here for you.

Your talent is God's gift to you. What you do with it is your gift back to God. (Leo Buscaglia)

Believe in yourself! Have faith in your abilities! Without a humble but reasonable confidence in your own powers you cannot be successful or happy. (Norman Vincent Peale)

Though your experience may indicate that God has forgotten you or has left you alone, He is on your side. He is the God of grace, and He is actively working on your behalf. (John Townsend)

My argument against God was that the universe seemed so cruel and unjust. But how had I got this idea of just and unjust? A man does not call a line crooked unless he has some idea of a straight line. What was I comparing this universe with when I called it unjust? (C. S. Lewis, *Mere Christianity*)

Some would say that at times life is just a bunch of "crap," but that is the fertilizer from which flowers grow. So when you are going through some really bad stuff, you can start looking forward to some really good stuff in the future. (Me)

Whenever you feel forgotten, just remember God will help you if you let Him.

"God is always fair. He will remember how you helped His people in the past and how you are still helping them. You belong to God, and He won't forget the love you have shown His people" **(Hebrews 6:10 CEV).**

When you feel your faith is being tested, stay true, do what is right, and trust God because better days are coming if you just hold on.

"God will bless you if you don't give up when your faith is being tested. He will reward you with a glorious life, just as He rewards everyone who loves Him" **(James 1:12 CEV).**

No matter how much they bring against you, in the end, they will lose, and you will be proven righteous.

"'No weapon formed against you shall prosper, and every tongue which rises against you in judgment You shall condemn. This is the heritage of the servants of the Lord, and their righteousness is from Me,' says the Lord" **(Isaiah 54:17).**

I Want You to Learn to Be Strong

Turning the other cheek does not mean you become a big pushover or you allow yourself to be used, abused, or even to put yourself in danger.

I really wish you and your sibling would take martial arts classes to learn how to defend yourselves and kick anyone's butt that threatens you or your safety or puts you in danger.

Before you go anywhere especially that is unsure or dangerous, PRAY. Ask God for His protection and safety and to send His angels to keep guard around you. Then keep talking to Him as you go about your business.

Never date anyone who doesn't value you and treat you with dignity and respect. If they disrespect you or treat you inappropriately, make sure that very moment they at least have their ears start ringing and they start seeing stars (or at least when they regain consciousness). For guys, that helps their brain to start working better.

Never go anywhere alone if you can at all help it.

Never walk out into a parking lot and stop at your car door to do anything nonchalantly or unaware of your surroundings.

Have your keys out and ready before you leave the building or store and ready to get in your car. Have your keys in your fist and sticking out between your fingers as a weapon just in case you have the need to protect yourself.

Hold your purse or packages securely and children (when and if you have them).

Be careful with loose clothing, long strap purses, scarfs, or anything someone can get a hold of to pull you, hurt, or control you with.

Always keep track of your surroundings, everyone, and every sound.

Look for safe places and exits or places to hide on your way.

Look for things you can use as a weapon or for a defense.

Stay away from dark or poorly lit places, even if you have to walk further to do it, Do it.

Walk quickly and don't dawdle on your way to your car.

Don't look scared. Always look and act confident and tough.

Look in your backseat as you are walking up to your car and before you get in.

As soon as you get in your car, quickly shut and lock the doors and then leave the area.

Don't sit there adjusting your mirror, fixing your seat, or checking your packages.

Drive away without delay.

If you have someone approach you or threaten you or make you feel uncomfortable, fight! Hit your panic button on your key remote.

If you can kick a fancy or newer car, it will trip their car alarm too.

Fight like a crazy woman. Don't be nice! don't be kind!

Make a lot of noise.

Fight hard and make them hurt fast.

Always go for their eyes, nose, groin, kicking their knees backward hard.

Sink your thumbs into their eyes as hard and far as you can.

Look for anything you can find around you to hit them or stab them with.

Even a pen or pencil can make a great weapon.

Don't stop because they are sorry, hurting, or crying, until they are completely incapacitated. Even then, tie them up (use string, twine, a belt, shoelaces, duct tape...) then go for help. Remember, *I'd always rather go to court with you than to go to the morgue for you.*

Never go with them,

Never get into the car with them.

Always try to get away (and keep trying) and run no matter what they say, what they do, or what they have. If you are wearing

heels, carry them or get rid of them (although they can be good weapons too). You might get hurt escaping, but more than likely, you'll be alive, but if you go with them or don't escape, your chances are greatly diminished.
Always keep yourself and your family safe at all times. And God have mercy on anyone that would dare threaten you. I want you and your family to always be SAFE.

Even when my father didn't have my hand, he always had my back. (Linda Poindexter)

You who sit down in the High God's presence, spend the night in Shaddai's shadow, Say this: "God, You're my refuge. I trust in You and I'm safe!"
That's right—He rescues you from hidden traps, shields you from deadly hazards.
His huge outstretched arms protect you— under them you're perfectly safe; His arms fend off all harm.
Fear nothing—not wild wolves in the night, not flying arrows in the day,
Not disease that prowls through the darkness, not disaster that erupts at high noon.
Even though others succumb all around, drop like flies right and left, no harm will even graze you.
You'll stand untouched, watch it all from a distance, watch the wicked turn into corpses.
Yes, because God's your refuge, the High God your very own home,
Evil can't get close to you, harm can't get through the door.
He ordered His angels to guard you wherever you go.
If you stumble, they'll catch you; their job is to keep you from falling.

You'll walk unharmed among lions and snakes, and kick young lions and serpents from the path. **(Psalm 91:11–13 MSG)**

Therefore, my dear brothers and sisters, stand firm. Let nothing move you. **(1 Corinthians 15:58)**

So then, just as you received Christ Jesus as Lord, continue to live in Him, rooted and built up in Him, strengthened in the faith as you were taught, and overflowing with thankfulness. **(Colossians 2:6–7)**

Be Who I See You to Be

Always be the lady who rightly portrays
the lady I see you to be.

In this day and age, everyone seems to be confused over what they are or what bathroom they are supposed to use or who they are supposed to date or marry. In case there is ever any confusion or argument, I just want you to know that who you are is exactly who you are supposed to be, and that is the best you that you can be.

God made you perfect just the way you are.

Just work to be the best you that you can be.

You can't expect to ever have a gentleman for a husband if you don't first learn to act like a lady.

Be the person you would be proud to introduce to your family and friends, or be someone you would be proud to be seen with at a publicized event.

No matter what you want to be, always be your best.

A virtuous woman isn't ruled by her passions—she passionately pursues an incomparable God. (Darlene Schacht)

A virtuous woman isn't ruled by her passions, but she does passionately pursue her purpose. (Me)

A woman's heart should be so hidden in God that a man has to seek Him just to find her. (Max Lucado)

As a "Godly Woman in Progress" are you choosing to keep your heart with all vigilance, real-

izing that from it flows the springs of life? (Patricia Ennis)

Nothing is more beautiful than a woman who is brave, strong, and emboldened because of who Christ is in her. (Joni Lamb)

But by the grace of God I am what I am. **(1 Corinthians 15:10)**

And to put on the new self, created after the likeness of God in true righteousness and holiness. **(Ephesians 4:24)**

A kindhearted woman gains honor, but ruthless men gain only wealth. **(Proverbs 11:16)**

Make every effort to add to your faith goodness; and to goodness, knowledge; and to knowledge, self-control; and to self-control, perseverance; and to perseverance, godliness; and to godliness, brotherly kindness; and to brotherly kindness, love. **(2 Peter 1:5–7)**

Welcome Home

I hope our home will always be a welcome place
of faith, safety, love, and hope for you.

I want you to always know that at any time and for any reason, our door will always be open for you.

Something I always took comfort in knowing was that Grandma and Grandpa J's house was always open to me. They always wanted me to come visit. I never needed a reason. I never had to explain, but they were always there to comfort and encourage if I needed it. It was always a place I felt safe and cared for.

I hope that coming home will always be a Safe Haven, a sense of Peace, a feeling of Hope and Acceptance, a breath of fresh air…

We are always praying for you. Praying that God will do whatever it takes to keep you in His plan and living your life for His glory.

Remember that no matter how good or how bad this life may go, the time we are here on Earth is just a brief moment compared to Eternity. So live your life preparing for the next not overly worried about the temporary we have now. So no matter how bad it gets, we can always know for sure that "this too shall pass."

> *Do not let your hearts be troubled. You believe in God; believe also in Me. My Father's house has many rooms; if that were not so, would I have told you that I am going there to prepare a place for you?* **(John 14:1–2)**

> *For our present troubles are small and won't last very long. Yet they produce for us a glory that vastly outweighs them and will last forever. So we don't look at the troubles we can see now; rather, we fix our gaze on things that cannot be seen. For the things we see now will soon be gone, but the things we cannot see will last forever.* **(2 Corinthians 4: 17–18 NLT)**

"Welcome Back"

Artist: John Sebastian
Also known as the theme song for the 1970s
sitcom ***Welcome Back, Kotter***.

Welcome back, your dreams were your ticket out
Welcome back, to that same old place that you laughed about
Well, the names have all changed since you hung around
But those dreams have remained and they've turned around
Who'd have thought they'd lead ya
(Who'd have thought they'd lead ya)
Back here where we need ya
(Back here where we need ya)
Yeah, we tease him a lot 'cause we got him on the spot
Welcome back, welcome back, welcome back, welcome back
Welcome back, welcome back, welcome back
We always could spot a friend, welcome back
And I smile when I think how you must have been
And I know what a scene you were learning in
Was there something that made you come back again
And what could ever lead ya
(What could ever lead ya)
Back here where we need ya
(Back here where we need ya)
Yeah we tease him a lot 'cause we got him on the spot
Welcome back, welcome back, welcome back, welcome back
Welcome back, welcome back
Yeah, we tease him a lot, welcome back, welcome back
'Cause we got him on the spot, welcome back, welcome back
Yeah, we tease him a lot 'cause we got him on the spot
Welcome back, welcome back, welcome back, welcome back
Welcome back, welcome back, welcome back
Welcome back, welcome back, welcome back

Hands

Hands are very useful things that God has given, and although two are useful, so often three would be much better.
The things that our hands can do are endless, it's true.
I can grasp a glass to get a drink of water.
I can hold a screwdriver to fix a loose handle on a pan for your mother
I can open a door for a person that has their hands full.
I can carry a box of ornaments to the attic to wait for another year
I can carefully pull a painful sliver from my daughter's finger and make her happy again
I can clean a scraped knee and carefully place a Band-Aid there to protect it.
I can push the crazy hair from the face of a sad little girl.
I can help blow a nose and dry tears from sad eyes.
With my hands I can even lift a little girl to my shoulders and hold her safely.
I can hold her feet and throw her high in the sky so she can giggle and splash.
I can swim under the water and sneak up behind her and tickle her.
I can collect a treasure of rocks and shells and driftwood for her.
I can try to catch the little fish swimming around us.
I can dig a deep hole with her to see if we could trick mom to walk into it.
I can make sand sculptures with her on the beach, fish, mermaids, or muscle men…
I can help build the biggest sand castles complete with motes, draw bridges, and towers.
I can build a bonfire, help my little girl roast a marshmallow, or hotdog.
I can hold someone to keep them safe.
I can lift someone up to pick a special leaf or apple or pinecone.
I can lift someone up to see in a nest or put an ornament on the Christmas tree.

I can hold a hand while we take a walk.
With my hands I can help catch a frog.
I can steady a wobbly bike.
I can push someone to the moon on the highest swing in the world.
I can play Frisbee with my little girl.
I can catch a rabbit someone let out on accident again.
I can help carry a bouquet of the prettiest wildflowers we picked for mom.
I can hold a bunch of the prettiest rocks we could find.
I can help catch the little crab that moves so fast in the stream.
I can teach a little girl how to skip a rock across the water.
With my hands I can be there to help if ever you need me or
I can just walk hand in hand with my little girl if ever she wants to be with me.
Hands are truly wonderful things

*****

They can be used to help, to touch, to hold, to shake, to pat, to caress, to lift, to carry, to soothe, to ease, to feel, to stroke, to scratch, to itch, to wipe, to flick, to pick, to pinch, to squish, to poke, to slap, to knock, to hit, to punch, to push, to chop, to fight, to defend, to praise, to clap, to snap, to grasp, to clutch, to take, to crush, to move, to fling, to toss, to throw, to play, to work, to write, to text, to keyboard, to pluck, to strum, to drum, to point, to direct, to beckon, to show, to create, to paint, to dig, to sculpt, to fix, to wave, to wash, to tie, to button, to knit, to sow, to wraith, to gesture, to build, to putty, to peal, to yo-yo, to Sign, and to say ILU.

> *Let the beauty of the Lord our God be upon us, and establish the work of our hands among us; yes, establish the work of our hands.* **(Psalm 90:17 MEV)**

> *Give her the fruit of her hands; and let her works praise her in the gates.* **(Proverbs 31:31 LB)**

Aspire to live quietly, and to mind your own affairs, and to work with your hands. **(1 Thessalonians 4:11 ESV)**

"Daddy's Hands"
by Holly Dunn

I remember daddy's hands
Folded silently in prayer
And reaching out to hold me when I had a nightmare
You could read quite a story in the calluses and lines
Years of work and worry had left their mark behind

I remember daddy's hands
How they held my momma tight
And patted my back for something done right
There are things that I've forgotten that I loved about the man
But I'll always remember the love in daddy's hands

Daddy's hands
Were soft and kind when I was crying
Daddy's hands
Were hard as steel when I'd done wrong
Daddy's hands

Weren't always gentle but I've come to understand
There was always love in daddy's hands

I remember daddy's hands working til they bled
Sacrificed unselfishly just to keep us all fed
If I could do things over
I'd live my life again
And never take for granted the love in daddy's hands…

Find Someone to Help

*One of the greatest joys we can experience
in this life is found in serving others.
Living for self is awfully small but living
to bless others touches all.*

Always find ways to make a difference in the lives of others. You might not always have the time, money, or talent to do everything you want to do or take every opportunity that comes your way, or do even everything that everyone requests of you. However, you can always do something. You can always find someone to help, in big ways or small. When you reach out to help a person in a community, you do not just help that person but that whole community. When you lift up one person who has fallen, you in part have helped to change the world.

Find a way to make a difference in the lives of others. That is really the only way we can make life worth living.

I enjoy helping people, and really I don't even feel I've been worth my salt until I have in some way helped someone. I guess that's why on my favorite vacations, I am always working on something for someone or doing whatever I can to help someone in some way. I really enjoy making a difference in people's lives.

I had built several things for both sets of grandparents, built a barn for Uncle Rich. Done some remodeling for Uncle Tom. Done some plumbing and wiring stuff for Uncle Todd and Uncle Troy. Pretty

| 307

much I am always looking for a way to make a difference at anyplace I go. It doesn't just make them happy; it also makes me feel good. Being a blessing to others blesses me even more. I guess that's why my most enjoyable exotic vacations were the mission trips I went on.

Don't get me wrong. I do enjoy doing the fun stuff like everyone else. It's just that I think helping people is also a lot of fun. It does something that usually means more to the people it was done for, and the effect or result lasts longer too. It's my way of saying "I love you" without using words.

Whenever you help another you have helped Me. (Jesus)

You are not here merely to make a living. You are here in order to enable the world to live more amply, with greater vision, with a finer spirit of hope and achievement. You are here to enrich the world, and you impoverish yourself if you forget the errand. (Woodrow Wilson)

The first question which the priest and the Levite asked was: "If I stop to help this man, what will happen to me?" But…the good Samaritan reversed the question: "If I do not stop to help this man, what will happen to him?" (Martin Luther King Jr.)

So then, as we have opportunity, let us do good. **(Galatians 6:10)**

For we are God's masterpiece, created to do good works which God prepared in advance for us to do. **(Ephesians 2:10 NIV)**

The king will answer, "Whenever you did it for any of My people, no matter how unimportant they seemed, you did it for Me." ... *The king will say to them, "Whenever you failed to help any of My people, no matter how unimportant they seemed, you failed to do it for Me."* **(Matthew 25:40–45 CEV)**

Comfort in the Storms, and Share in the Stressed

Storms are always coming and going, and stress is something we all face. In my experience, stress never comes at us just one at a time but in multiples, sometimes one right after another, and at other times one on top of another.

Nighttime reminds us that we all at times face things that seem dark, dreary, and have a feeling of hopelessness. All of us feel lost and alone in the midst of the darkest nights. However, remember that just when the night seems to be at its darkest, the morning is beginning to break through.
Whenever you feel you can't go on any further just remember;
New Beginnings always follow our darkest moments.
Always do your best and trust God with the rest.
There is always a chance.
There is always hope.
There is always help.
There is a way.
It's just a little further.
You are almost there.
You can make it.
You can do it!
I believe in you!

What to Do When You're Feeling Stressed

- ☐ Count to 10
- ☐ Read a book
- ☐ Pray

- ☐ Read the Bible
- ☐ Work on an art or craft project
- ☐ Sing a song
- ☐ Paint a picture or a room
- ☐ Take a ride
- ☐ Go for a walk
- ☐ Do a road trip

- ☐ Write down your thoughts
- ☐ Exercise
- ☐ Attend a special church activity or service
- ☐ Binge watch some Bible stories
- ☐ Go to the park or zoo
- ☐ Write a poem or song
- ☐ Go for a swim or boat ride
- ☐ Go fishing
- ☐ Go for a run
- ☐ Come home for a while…

But whatever you do, find a way to appropriately deal with your stress.

The temptations in your life are no different from what others experience. And God is faithful. He will not allow the temptation to be more than you can stand. When you are tempted, He will show you a way out so that you can endure. **(1 Corinthians 10:13 NLT)**

And the God of all grace, who called you to His eternal glory in Christ, after you have suffered a little while, will Himself restore you and make you strong, firm and steadfast. **(1 Peter 5:10)**

Character and Integrity Are Everything

Character is what defines you. It's what people see in you. It's what people will say about you behind your back or when you're not around, or even after you pass away. Character is one of the most important things you have. Character is the value you put on yourself, and you can set it as high as you want. What is the price you are setting for yourself? How are you investing in yourself? Character is shown in how you deal with things. How would others describe your character when you're not there? Can people easily know what you value and believe in by watching what you do and how you live? Can people see your faith in the things you do? Your character is even reflected in how you serve Christ.

Remember that when you pass away, Jesus will either say, "Welcome, sister, job well done," or "I never knew you. Be gone!" It's what you do here and now that decides where your future is. True character is shown in how you act in any situation. Your actions do speak louder than your words. Character is those things that you hold fast to inside, those things that people can see inside of you from the outside. More importantly, it is something that God always sees in you. Take some time, and think about how you are living your life.

Your Reputation is what others believe about you.

Your Character is what you do when no one else is looking.

Character is the value you set for yourself.

I value you greatly, but only you can set your value by building your character.

> *A good name is more desirable than great riches; to be esteemed is better than silver or gold.* **(Proverbs 22:1 NIV)**

> *A wife of noble character who can find? She is worth far more than rubies.* **(Proverbs 31:10)**

A wife of noble character is her husband's crown, but a disgraceful wife is like decay in his bones. **(Proverbs 12:4 NIV)**

All the people of my town know that you [Ruth] are a woman of noble character. **(Ruth 3:11 NIV)**

Learn How Things Work

If you know how things work, you will
know how to keep them working.

If it's broken now and instead of just disposing of it or hiring someone else to fix it, you try to fix it yourself; but then even after trying, if you find out you can't fix it, you're really not out anything; it will still need to be fixed. Yet if you try to fix it, you just might learn how to, and it actually might not be as bad as you first thought. Just a hint: it doesn't mean you're smarter than the manufacturer if you put it together and find you have extra parts you didn't use (haha).

I know for most things you are smart enough to be able to do it, make it, or fix it; and if you don't know how, you can "YouTube" it and find out how. However, if that doesn't work, try duct tape and bailing twine. As they say, "If you can't fix it with duct tape or bailing twine, it can't be fixed!" (Haha.)

<u>*Trying to learn*</u> *what is pleasing to the Lord.* **(Ephesians 5:10)**

Try to show God that you are a good worker. Do nothing you would be ashamed of. Tell the true message in the right way. **(2 Timothy 2:14 WE)**

You Got This

As much as you can figure it out, fix it yourself.

You can look it up online and watch a few YouTube videos and learn how to fix just about anything. Your uncle Todd looked up how to fix his furnace and replaced the parts himself. If he could figure out how to do a job like that, then you can the same way.

You are very smart. You can do anything you put your mind to. But if you need help, just let me know. I'd be glad to help you with whatever, whenever, and wherever I can.

Asking for other's guidance helps you see what you may not be able to see. It's always important to check your ego and ask for help. (Ken Blanchard)

Keep on asking, and you will receive what you ask for. Keep on seeking, and you will find. Keep on knocking, and the door will be opened to you. For everyone who asks, receives. Everyone who seeks, finds. And to everyone who knocks, the door will be opened. **(Matthew 7:7–8 NLT)**

You Can Fix it

Things break, so just learn how to fix them for yourself.

Work at collecting a complete set of tools.

Make sure you get a ratcheting screwdriver with the one-fourth-inch replaceable driver bits (it should have a good selection in the handle or a separate case). Get at least a twenty-foot tape measure, a light trim hammer, not the baby hammer they have in women's tool kits. A good retractable carpenter's knife, crescent wrench, channel locks, vise grips, medium-size pliers, needle-nose pliers, and a set of one-fourth-inch or three-eighths-inch sockets. And a toolbox to store them in. This would be a good starter kit.

Then start collecting at least a dozen of all the different screws and nails you use.

Whatever you use, by a few extra, because if you needed them once, you will probably need the same kind again sometime later.

Buy a multidrawer organizer with the small drawers and put the nails and screws in it. If not that, then use some medicine bottles in a good shoebox will work too.

Next, get some duct tape (regular and extra-strength), masking tape, and shipping tape.

Also get white glue (regular paper glue), wood glue, and some crazy glue.

Get some string (bailing twine is best) and a few feet of wire (light fencing wire is best)

Then, with this stuff, you should be able to fix most anything that goes wrong yourself and save yourself a lot of money...

or I'll be able to do it for you when I come to visit.

My Love for You Is Unconditional

Just remember,
I love you the most!
Always have, always will.

> *God told them, "I've never quit loving you and never will. Expect love, love, and more love!* **(Jeremiah 31:3 TMB)**

> *We love because He first loved us.* **(1 John 4:19 HB)**

Always Love God First and Family Second

I love you! I love you! I love you! I love you! I love you! I love you! I love you!
We love a lot of people, but do we love everyone the same.

The Bible mainly uses three words for *love*:

1. *Philia*—friendship bond. "*By this all people will know that you are My disciples, if you have love for one another*" (John 13:35 ESV).
2. *Eros*—romantic love. "*As a lily among brambles, so is my love among the young women*" (Song of Solomon 2:2 ESV).
3. *Agape*—unconditional "God" love. "*This is how much God loved the world: He gave His Son, His one and only Son. And this is why: so that no one need be destroyed; by believing in Him, anyone can have a whole and lasting life*" (John 3:16 MSG).

The Greeks added one more word for love:

4. *Storge*—Family love, empathy bond. Like a parent to a young child. "*Be kindly affectioned one to another with brotherly love, in honour preferring one another*" (Romans 12:10 KJV).

Psychologists say that there are three more types:

5. *Ludus*—playful or uncommitted love. "*Little children, let us not love in word or talk but in deed and in truth*" (1 John 3:18).

6. *Pragma*—practical love founded on reason or duty and one's longer-term interests.
7. *Philautia*—self-love, which can be healthy or unhealthy. "*None of us ever hate our own bodies. Instead, we feed them, and take care of them, just as Christ does the church*" (Ephesians 5:29 GNT).

Our Love Needs to Be

1. God is always first.
2. Spouse (or your parents if you're not yet married)

After you're married, of course, it's your spouse.

You can pick your seat,
You can pick your friends,
You can even pick your nose,
But your family you are stuck with.

3. Family immediate family (first, your immediate family, then the extended family
4. Church (immediate church family first, then any brother or sister in Christ second)
5. Country (thanking God for, praying for, volunteering or serving and voting…)
6. Your vocation (find a job that you prayed about and felt God has called you to. Learn to do your best and then love what you do.)

Your family is your family whether you like it or not. They are yours, and you are stuck with them. The good, the bad, and the ugly are all yours and are to be valued and cherished. They are God's special gift for you. Even though you'll go through many friends, good and bad, over the course of a lifetime, your family will still be your family.

People who don't take care of their relatives, and especially their own families, have given up their faith. They are worse than someone who doesn't have any faith in the Lord. **(1 Timothy 5:8 CEV)**

Brothers and sisters, do not slander one another. Anyone who speaks against a brother or sister or judges them speaks against the law and judges it. When you judge the law, you are not keeping it, but sitting in judgment on it. **(James 4:11)**

> I smile because you are my daughter,
> But I laugh because there is nothing you can do about it.

Dear Father in Heaven
Grandma J wrote in the fall of 2019 and enjoys singing it whenever she is alone.

Dear Father in heaven, I love you,
    I love you, I love you.
Dear Father in heaven, I love you,
    I really, really do!

I love you today,
I love you tomorrow,
I'll love you forever more.

With you by my side, to teach and to guide me…
How can I ask for more?

Dear Father in heaven, I love you, I really, really do!
Dear Father in heaven, I love you, I really, really do!

Always Value Your Parents and Grandparents

At the risk of sounding self-serving, I need to also remind you to highly value your parents and grandparents.

1. They are your heritage and history.
2. They are what makes up who you are. You are a part of them; so the way you treat them, in one way, is how you respect or treat yourself.
3. They have a lot of interesting experiences that would be interesting to listen to and learn about.
4. They know a lot of stuff that you don't, and you can learn from them.
5. You don't get any spares, and when they are gone, they're gone. That's it.
6. They still are a great resource for you—for help, wisdom, encouragement, and advice.
7. Your kids will take note of the time you spend with your parents and the way you treat them, and that will be the way they will treat you when you are old.
8. God commands us to honor and respect our parents.
9. There is a blessing for us if we honor and treat them with respect.
10. They love you more than you know and are always on your side.
11. They are great prayer resources, and God hears their prayers.

Always call home at least once a week. It's a proven fact that we tend to call home less the older

we get, and that's just wrong. It should be the other way around, because as we get older, our parents get older too. (Unknown)

Be kind to everybody, be grateful, say thank you every day. My parents taught me well. (Nichole Richie)

My parents taught me many of the things that people need in life to feel confident: practical things, such as managing finances, mucking out the goat barn, cleaning a house, doing repairs, mending a broken roof or a toilet. (Brice Dallas Howard)

Honor your parents by not judging them. Always give them the benefit of doubt. (Michael Jackson)

If you love your parents and grandparents, don't just say it, prove it. There should never be room for a doubt or question. (Me)

Honor your father and your mother, as the Lord your God commanded you, that your days may be long, and that it may go well with you in the land that the Lord your God is giving you. **(Deuteronomy 5:16)**

Listen to your father who gave you life, and do not despise your mother when she is old. **(Proverbs 23:22)**

Hear, my son, your father's instruction, and forsake not your mother's teaching. **(Proverbs 1:8)**

Grandparents are proud of their grandchildren, and children should be proud of their parents. **(Ephesians 17:6 CEV)**

But if a widow has children or grandchildren, let them first learn to show godliness to their own household and to make some return to their parents, for this is pleasing in the sight of God. **(1 Timothy 5:4)**

Honor Your Parents and Grandparents

Honor tends to be an old-fashioned or even archaic word these days that is not often used or even less understood. Basically, all honor means in this respect is to make one feel special, valued, important, above the rest. In some cases, it can mean to obey or not to question. As we grow older and our relationship changes over the years with our parents and grandparents, that doesn't mean that we don't need to honor or respect them, although the "How" we show or express it will be different.

There are many ways to honor your parents and grandparents. Although at times it might seem like a job or burden with everything else we have going in life, I have found it to be a real blessing that I enjoy and miss being able to do. I don't know if they always recognized it as such, but I always tried to show them my love and appreciation through helping them, talking with them, and wanting to do stuff with them. I really felt blessed to be able to do that for as long as I had been able to. I feel it's a way to pay them back for all the good that I've benefited from their lives, influence, and hard work. It's also a way I can pay it forward to coming generations, to not overlook the great blessing we have in our parents and grandparents.

A lot of people believe in karma. The Bible teaches it as "sowing and reaping." I just call it "paying it forward" or just being able to get out of something only what we previously had put into it. You will be in the place of a parent and hopefully someday a grandparent, or even a great-grandparent. So whatever honor and respect you sow into their lives, you, too, will one day receive the same kind of kindness and care from your children or grandchildren. However, if you can pick apart the way they did everything and come up with good excuses as to why they don't deserve your best, then one day when you need it the most, you, too, will receive a similar neglect and lack of care and love.

I once read a tombstone that said,

Pause, Stranger, when you pass me by,
As you are now, so once was I.
As I am now, so you will be,
So prepare for death and follow me.

An unknown passerby read those words and, underneath, scratched this reply:

To follow you I'm not content,
Until I know which way you went.

Here are a few ideas on what honoring looks like:

1. Let them know how much you Love them in words and action.
2. Make them look good by what you say and do. (Let them be proud of you.)
3. Recognize and show appreciation for the stuff they have done for you.
4. Take an interest in their stories and laugh at their jokes.
5. Tell them about what's going on in your life and what interests you.
6. Be excited about their accomplishments and be interested in their lives.

7. Try to understand them and why they do what they do and like what they like.
8. Be a good parent and show how much you Love their grandchildren.
9. Don't just presume upon their help, yet ask them if you need it.
10. Do what it takes to keep working on your marriage (make it work).
11. Treat them out once in a while.
12. Respect and follow their values especially when you're around them.
13. Try to fit into their lives once and a while.

Respect your father and your mother, and you will live a long time in the land I am giving you. **(Exodus 20:12 CEV)**

Every one of you shall revere his mother and his father. **(Leviticus 19:3 ESV)**

They must declare to the elders of his city, "Our son is stubborn and rebellious and pays no attention to what we say—he is a glutton and drunkard." **(Deuteronomy 21:20 GNB)**

Cursed be anyone who dishonors his father or his mother. **(Deuteronomy 27:16 ESV)**

If you honor your father and mother, "things will go well for you, and you will have a long life on the earth." **(Ephesians 6:3 NLT)**

Neither Ignorance nor Grace

Ignorance is not an excuse, and grace is not a license.

Situations in life often makes it seem that to do the wrong thing is really the right to do, or even that it's the only thing we can do. At times it can get hard, dark, or just feel like your back is against the wall and there is no real way out. Often it is a lot easier to do the wrong thing than the right. The people you are with or want to impress are doing it and wanting you to do it, and so it seems it's just easier to do it than have to explain why you don't want to or feel you can't. It might even be the most convenient thing or the most accessible when you are needing something quickly.

Nighttime reminds all of us that we all face things that are dark, are dreary, and seem hopeless. However, just when it seems to be the darkest, the morning breaks through.

New Beginnings always follow our darkest moments.

The Law says that "Ignorance is not an excuse," and the Bible says that we have plenty of opportunities to know what the truth is. *"It is because we have it within us and all creation reminds us of the truth and what we should be doing"* (Romans 1:20).

For most things in life, we have an innate knowledge of what is right and wrong or what we should or shouldn't do. Then to add to that, we raised you and your siblings to know the truth and right from wrong. So you have your upbringing, the Bible, a lot of good teachers on the TV and radio, churches everywhere, a natural understanding of what is right, a conscience, and nature, not to mention the Holy Spirit, and our influence and prayers—all working together to help you navigate through life and make the best choices. Knowing what is the right thing to do isn't the hard part, but having the guts or the character to do what is right is the hard part.

The Bible teaches us that as Christians, we are to hold ourselves to higher standards and live more responsibly than what we expect from those around us.

The more we know and the more we have, the more we are also responsible for what we know and have.

We are also responsible for the opportunities where we could have learned more or done more yet wasted it or didn't take advantage of the opportunity we had. I used to have people who would tell me that they didn't like my preaching, because they learned more of what they didn't know before and so they were now more responsible to live by it now. Yet I'd tell them that even if they would have stayed home, they would have still have been responsible for the information they were supposed to learn but didn't because they skipped church.

> *Where ignorance is our master, there is no possibility of real peace.* (Dalai Lama)

> *The grace of God does not give us the license to live however we want.* (Focus on the Family)

> *Beware of false knowledge; it is more dangerous than ignorance.* (George Bernard Shaw)

> *Since earliest times men have seen the earth and sky and all God made, and have known of His existence and great eternal power. So they will have no excuse when they stand before God at Judgment Day Yes, they knew about Him all right, but they wouldn't admit it or worship Him or even thank Him for all His daily care. And after a while they began to think up silly ideas of what God was like and what He wanted them to do. The result was that their foolish minds became dark and confused.* **(Romans 1:20–21 TLB)**

> *If you go the wrong way—to the right or to the left—you will hear a voice behind you. It will say, "This is the right way. You should go this way."* **(Isaiah 30:21 ICB)**

But you must remain faithful to the things you have been taught. You know they are true, for you know you can trust those who taught you. **(2 Timothy 3:14 NLT)**

Take hold of My instructions; don't let them go. Guard them, for they are the key to life. **(Proverbs 4:13 NLT)**

Push to the Future

Pride will keep you stuck in the past
and rob you from your future.

"Put your past in your past" (Timon and Pumbaa, *Lion King*).

Learn to be more proud of your potential than your past successes.

Learn to be more and not allow your "good enough," to be good enough for you.

Find a way to do more instead of being satisfied with what was already done.

Be less proud of your past or position than your potential or the possibilities that could still be achieved, discovered, or developed. Your past successes are good and worthy of celebration, but let them only serve to help you go further. If you did something great before, it means you know how to do something great again. You have the ability to use past successes to be stepping-stones for the future. If you allow things in your past to stop you from going forward and pursuing your future, then your future is held hostage or prisoner of your past. The problem is it keeps you trapped in status quo and looking backward and unable to see into the future you could have.

You will never know the potential you have or the future that you could attain with God's help if you stop there and allow yourself to be hindered by your past.

I believe you are great beyond your understanding and can accomplish more than you ever dreamed. I believe your successes are only just proof of the much greater potential that is within you.

The past is dead except for the life you give it. (Myles Monroe)

There is no passion to be found playing small—in settling for a life that is less than the one you are capable of living. (Nelson Mandela)

Good, better, best. Never let it rest. 'Til your good is better and your better is best. (St. Jerome)

Every person is born with a seed of greatness. (Myles Monroe)

In a car, the rearview mirror is small, and the front window is big because, although it is important to see where we have been, it is much more important to see where we are going. (Me)

I will bless you with a future filled with hope—a future of success, not of suffering. **(Jeremiah 29:11 CEV)**

I alone know the plans I have for you, plans to bring you prosperity and not disaster, plans to bring about the future you hope for. **(Jeremiah 29:11 GNT)**

The heart of man plans his way, but the Lord establishes his steps. **(Proverbs 16:9)**

Many are the plans in the mind of a man, but it is the purpose of the Lord that will stand. **(Proverbs 19:21)**

For we are His workmanship, created in Christ Jesus for good works, which God prepared beforehand, that we should walk in them. **(Ephesians 2:10)**

The Lord will fulfill His purpose for me; Your steadfast love, O Lord, endures forever. Do not forsake the work of Your hands. **(Psalm 138:8)**

The steps of a man are established by the Lord, when he delights in His way; though he falls, he shall not be cast headlong, for the Lord upholds his hand. **(Psalm 37:23–24)**

And I am sure of this, that He who began a good work in you will bring it to completion on the day of Jesus Christ. **(Philippians 1:6)**

Test What Is True and Don't be Gullible

Never take anything, except the Bible, as fact or true without having to check it out first. Test and prove everything before you go ahead and just accept it as true. Even what someone says is from the Bible, you should always check to be sure yourself before you accept it as true. Don't even believe people, the media, or anyone who says, "This has already been fact-checked, so you can trust what we are telling you…," or even this new group or that organization says it's true…

There are a lot of people who are wanting you to just blindly believe whatever they say. They come at you from all sides today. The media, phone calls, junk mail, social media, door-to-door salespeople, the guy at the dealership lot, the salesperson at the store, the doctor, the politician, even TV preachers will all try to tell you to believe them. Most of these people will want you to just blindly believe whatever they say, accept it as fact, or buy into whatever they are selling. Don't do it!

Don't overly trust anyone except God and your parents. In this day and age especially, everyone has to earn your trust, with you continually checking them out as you go. Over the years, even your mother and I have had good friends whom we overtrusted, and they took us for a few very expensive rides (one that we almost didn't recover from). I don't want to scare you, but you, too, will get taken for a ride once in a while. I guess that is just part of life these days. So don't be surprised when it happens, but as much as possible, try to develop a habit of always checking out everyone and everything ahead of time. Develop a sixth sense for judging people's intent. Always try to be smarter than they are. Just always check things out thoroughly, and never give anyone any more trust than what they have earned. This hopefully will save you a few sleepless nights, broken friendships, and some hard-earned dollars too.

And the people of Berea were more open-minded than those in Thessalonica, and they lis-

tened eagerly to Paul's message. They searched the Scriptures day after day to see if Paul and Silas were teaching the truth. **(Acts 17:11 NLT)**

Never let us be guilty of sacrificing any portion of truth on the altar of peace. (J. C. Ryle)

Most people would rather tell a friend a lie and keep their friendship than to risk losing their friendship by telling them the truth, especially if it's about something serious or life threatening. (Me)

Don't believe everything you hear. There are always three sides to a story: yours, theirs and the truth. (Unknown)

My dear friends, don't believe everything you hear. Carefully weigh and examine what people tell you. Not everyone who talks about God comes from God. There are a lot of lying preachers loose in the world. **(1 John 4:1 MSG)**

Teach me Your way, O LORD, that I may walk in Your truth; unite my heart to fear Your name. **(Psalm 86:11)**

Sanctify them in the truth; Your word is truth. **(John 17:17)**

Urgent or Important

*Focus on what is important, and avoid
the distraction of the urgent.*

Life will always be busy, and there will always be a hundred things trying to take your time and attention. You will drive yourself crazy running around in circles and/or never be able to get anything done unless you can judge between the good and the important. You have to prioritize your time, attention, and resources. Prioritize when and where you spend your time and what you devote your attention to. Always do what is most important first, not just the Urgent. There are a lot of good things for doing but not so good for the cost of doing them, and there are a lot of urgent things that would want to take our time and attention, but not all of them are really important to do, or especially to hurry off right now to go do them.

Making a list will help you. This will help you to focus on the important. Remember that most of the time the urgent didn't just happen, many times it's been going on for a long time. If it truly is urgent, it will still be urgent after the important is done, but after it's done, the important will still be important but not always so with the urgent.

Family is important	Buying toilet paper is urgent
Going to church is important	Finding the cat is urgent
Reading to your child is important	A crying Baby is urgent
Going to work is important	finishing your project is urgent
Daily exercise is important	A Band-Aid for a cut finger is urgent
Daily family time is important	Helping an upset friend is urgent
Keeping a good relationship is important	Resolving an argument is urgent

Taking care of your house is important	Fixing a burst water line is urgent
Getting your life right with God is very important	Looking good to others is urgent

I would like to be remembered as a guy who had a set of priorities, and was willing to live by those priorities. (George W. Bush)

If you show me your calendar and your bank statement I can tell you what you value the most in your life, because your priorities are where you spend your time and money. (Me)

Living in light of eternity changes your priorities. (Rick Warren)

We don't drift in good directions. We discipline and prioritize ourselves there. (Andy Stanley)

Decide what you want, decide what you are willing to exchange for it. Establish your priorities and go to work. (H. L. Hunt)

And do not seek what you will eat and what you will drink, and do not keep worrying. For all these things the nations of the world eagerly seek; but your Father knows that you need these things. But seek His kingdom, and these things will be added to you. **(Luke 12:29–31)**

But seek first His kingdom and His righteousness, and all these things will be added to you. **(Matthew 6:33)**

For where your treasure is, there your heart will be also. **(Luke 12:34)**

So teach us to number our days, That we may present to You a heart of wisdom. **(Psalm 90:12)**

Be Willing to Try Something New

How do you know;
you can't do it,
it won't make it,
that won't last,
I won't like it,
it won't work,
that won't help,
I will do bad at it,
it won't make a difference,
they won't come,
I won't be good enough,
it won't run,
they won't help you,
I will make a fool out of myself,
it won't be enough,
they will laugh,
I won't have any friends,
it won't turn around,
they won't like you,
I will be embarrassing
it will hurt me,
they won't buy it,
I won't win,
it will be too hard,
they will beat me,
I will never learn how,
it won't last,
they will say no,
I won't be able to finish,
it will taste bad,

you won't like it, **unless you try it first?**

> *So do not fear, for I am with you; do not be dismayed, for I am your God. I will strengthen you and help you; I will uphold you with My righteous right hand.* **(Isaiah 41:10)**

> *Remember not the former things, nor consider the things of old. Behold, I am doing a new thing; now it springs forth, do you not perceive it? I will make a way in the wilderness and rivers in the desert.* **(Isaiah 43:18–19 ESV)**

> *I can do all things through Him who strengthens me.* **(Philippians 4:13 ESV)**

> *There is no fear in love, but perfect love casts out fear. For fear has to do with punishment, and whoever fears has not been perfected in love.* **(1 John 4:18 ESV)**

Try something new. Go a different way. See if you can see or notice something different. Order something you never had before. Read a different genre of book. Try a different author. Help out with a different group, club, or class for a while. Plan a different outing from what you've ever tried before. Try to befriend someone who has no friends. Take up drawing or start painting. Try rock climbing or rappelling.

Not everything will work out, and you might not like everything you do, but you will never know what you like until you try it first. You will always be able to learn something new from every new experience. It will also make you a more experienced, knowledgeable, and more of a well-rounded person because of it.

I always like seeing where a new road leads or going to realtors' open houses just to see what someone else thought looked good.

I always enjoy trying new cultures and new foods. Some haven't worked out very well for me (like eating blackened shrimp in South America which was really rotten. But they did make an interesting meal with real bird's nests).

For several years, I worked part-time as a property inspector for the local banks and insurance companies. I really enjoyed that part of just being on the road and finding far out of the way places or inspecting interesting properties. The only main drawback was when I had the wrong address and inspected the wrong properties. I really freaked out some unsuspecting people to say the bank was foreclosing on their property when it was really someone else's property being foreclosed on, or when I would go into a house that was supposed to be empty and find someone sleeping in bed there… OOPS! But it was fun, embarrassing at times, and humiliating at others, but always interesting.

So be willing to try something new even if it's just for a while. You never know but what you just might like it!

Choose Joy and Peace

Joy is better than happiness, and peace is better than prestige.

I like it when you are happy. You're a lot of fun when you're happy. However, I would prefer you had a life of real joy and peace, instead of temporary happiness. Peace, real peace, only comes from knowing the Prince of Peace; and Jesus is the real joy giver. The closer you follow Him and the more you trust Him, the more peace and joy you will have.

Happiness is only a response to something else. It's like if I get a birthday gift, then that makes me happy. If after I have it for a couple of days and it breaks, then I'm sad, and that happiness it brought me is gone. When I see you drive up, I'm really happy, but then you tell me you can only stay a few minutes, and then I'm sad again, and all the happy feeling I previously had is gone. Happiness is just a temporary response in proportion to, and not exceeding, whatever brought on the happy feeling. However, Joy comes from inside of us and is not contingent upon a stimulus, nor is it a response to something else.

I can have real joy no matter what goes on around me or how I feel about my surroundings. Joy can even be the catalyst that helps me pull through very unpleasant or upsetting situations I might go through. I might get down, I might even become sad, something might even make me angry, but I won't stay down, because I still have joy that keeps me going. It's kind of like a float. If you take a float under the water, no matter how deep you take it, as soon as you let it go, it will make its way back to the surface again and once again find its place on top of the water. The bigger the float, the harder it will be to take it under, the faster it will again surface, and also the higher it will set itself above its surroundings. Yet even a little float, if it's made of the right stuff, will overcome its surroundings.

The Peace I'm talking about is from knowing that whatever screw-ups I've done or mistakes I've made, Jesus has forgiven me for them, and even made them right for me.

Peace doesn't mean my life will be easy or stress-free, but it does mean I know I've done my best, and I am trusting God with the rest. When you put yourself in that position, you know that no matter what happens, God is in control, and He will do what is best for you. Joy is a gift from God that brings you above whatever tries to bring you down, and Peace is from knowing God has your back.

Peace begins with a smile. (Mother Teresa)

Joy is the infallible sign of the presence of God. (Pierre Teilhard de Chardin)

Lord, make me an instrument of thy peace. Where there is hatred, let me sow love. (Francis of Assisi)

If God be our God, He will give us peace in trouble. When there is a storm without, He will make peace within. The world can create trouble in peace, but God can create peace in trouble. (Thomas Watson)

May the God of hope fill you with all joy and peace as you trust in Him, so that you may overflow with hope by the power of the Holy Spirit. **(Romans 15:13)**

The L*ord* *gives strength to His people; the* L*ord* *blesses His people with peace.* **(Psalm 29:11)**

May grace and peace be multiplied to you in the knowledge of God and of Jesus our Lord. **(2 Peter 1:2)**

To Date or Not to Date

I always said I didn't have any problem with you
dating. Just wait until you're…thirty or so.

We needed a sign at home that said, "No Boys Allowed."

A few things to remember before dating anyone:

1. Boys are bad.
2. Don't trust them.
3. They all lie.
4. Avoid being with them for as long as you can.

But if you can't, then at least always keep high expectations and standards for yourself as well as your date. Remember that character isn't important; it's crucial. Godliness is everything. Someone who is worth his salt would have these characteristics and ideals, too, and wouldn't want to put you into any situation that would hurt or bring your character into question. *"Do not be misled: Bad company corrupts good character"* (**1 Corinthians 15:33**).

You don't owe a date anything, not a kiss, not a date, nothing.
You set the ground rules on the date and approved of the destination beforehand.
Group dates and always in public places usually keep people more honest.
Avoid dark lonely places. They do nothing to build relationships, only regrets.
It's better to put the fire out than to live with regrets.
Be very direct and clear with what you mean. Guys don't get hints very well.
If he doesn't treat you right on a date, he is not worth trusting for anything more.

If you let him get away with disrespecting you now, he'll never value you more later.

Do what you need to do. You don't have to feel sorry about him or for him.

Always keep track of where you are and where you're going on a date.

Always have a couple of backup plans in mind in case things go wrong on a date.

If you need to, don't be afraid to hurt him if you feel in danger or threatened.

When danger is present, always pick being safe before being nice.

Eyes, nose, throat, and groin are good sensitive places to strike.

Even with a group, always be the smartest one in the group.

It is far better to be alone, than to be in bad company. (George Washington)

The best way to avoid being married to a jerk is to avoid dating one. (Me)

The naïve believes everything, But the sensible man considers his steps. **(Proverbs 14:15)**

A sensible person sees danger and takes cover, but the inexperienced keep going and are punished. **(Proverbs 22:3 HB)**

A Real Man Is Also a Gentleman

Although you might be mostly interested in someone who looks good (tall, dark, handsome, and extra buff, like me), one's Character, Actions, and Reputation are way more important and should actually be more attractive yet. There are a few good ways to know if your date is only handsome skin deep or if he is a real quality person. If he is one,

He should want to meet your parents to make sure it's okay with them before he would take you out on a date, and he should want to get their approval first.

He must meet you at the door and not just honk the horn or just wait for you in the car.

He does not only open the door for you, but he also walks between you and the traffic or between you and any danger.

He already knows that if it's a date, the guy pays for everything and you owe him nothing. Not a second look or even another call if you don't want to.

He will always protect your morals, character, and reputation, and never take you anywhere that would ever cause any of it to even come into question.

He will be someone who will value you above himself. To protect you and keep you safe. One who can show you respect and treat you as someone special.

He would never put you in an uncomfortable or unsafe situation.

He is someone who would stick up for you and not allow you to be embarrassed or made fun of by anyone, not friends, family, or even by strangers.

He is someone who would let you borrow his coat if you were cold and needed one.

He would be quick to drive you home in the middle of the date if you asked him to.

He is not one who would be too needy or clingy, nor would he overstay his welcome.

He would never seem like a "project" or a "social worker's case study."

He would not blame you for his immaturity, bad attitude, or regrettable actions.

He is someone who will always look for ways to be helpful and kind.

He is not someone who would appear to try to buy your attention or affection.

He is not someone who is in love with himself and can't stop talking about himself.

He is not a "selfie king" who is overly impressed with his looks or accomplishments.

He is someone who takes responsibility for himself and others.

He is someone who is complementary to you and others.

He is someone who would give up his seat for a woman or child needing one.

He is one who would be quick to notice someone in need and be quick to help them.

A good name is to be more desired than great wealth, Favor is better than silver and gold. **(Proverbs 22:1)**

So ought men to love their wives as their own bodies. He that loveth his wife loveth himself. **(Ephesians 5:28 KJV)**

Let your gentle spirit be known to all. **(Philippians 4:5)**

That the person dedicated to God may be capable and equipped for every good work. **(2 Timothy 3:17 NET)**

But keep away from youthful passions, and pursue righteousness, faithfulness, love, and peace, in company with others who call on the Lord from a pure heart. **(2 Timothy 2:22 NET)**

Who Is Good Enough for You?

I'm sorry to admit this to you; but, as far as I'm concerned and with how much I love you, there will never be anyone that I think is really good enough for my little girl. (Until after you are married, then I will do everything I can to make your marriage succeed and keep yas together.)

If there ever was a guy who could be good enough for you, I hope he has all my good qualities and none of my faults. If that is possible, let him first of all be someone who would love you with all of his heart and that second only to his love for God.

> *A daughter needs a dad to be the standard against which she will judge all men.* (Unknown)

> *No one in this world can love a girl more than her father.* (Michael Ratnadeepak)

> *But the Lord said to Samuel, "Do not consider his appearance or his height, for I have rejected him. The Lord does not look at the things people look at. People look at the outward appearance, but the Lord looks at the heart."* **(1 Samuel 16:7)**

"I Loved Her First"
Artist: **Heartland**

How could that beautiful woman with you
Be that same freckled-faced kid that I
    knew?
The one that I read all those fairy tales to
And tucked into bed all those nights
And I knew the first time I saw you with
    her
It was only a matter of time

I loved her first
I held her first
And a place in my heart will always be hers
From the first breath she breathed
When she first smiled at me
I knew the love of a father runs deep
And I prayed that she'd find you someday
But it's still hard to give her away

I loved her first
From the first breath she breathed
When she first smiled at me
I knew the love of a father runs deep
Someday you might know what I'm going through
When a miracle smiles up at you
I loved her first

There Is a Man Who Is Right for You

There is a young man out there whom we have been praying for since you were little. He is a man who God has picked for you. He is probably someone you don't even know yet (unless if at the time you are reading this you are married, then you do already know him).
Don't worry, God has a plan.
If you find someone who puts;
God first, and
you second, and
isn't afraid of hard work, and
is a man of honor and good character,
then I would be proud to stand up there with you.
True character is shown in how you act in any situation.
Actions do speak louder than words
It doesn't matter as much what he tells you,
as much as what he does under pressure and stress.
What does he do when no one else is around or is looking?
What does he do on the computer when no one can see the screen, and
how many "oops" does he have with bad websites popping up?
Is his browsing history open to be seen or does he keep erasing it?
Never pick someone that seems "Good Enough" or "Is Working on It," or "Just
Needs a Little Help."
He needs to already be the man he should be before you marry him. Never marry a project!
Character is something that you hold fast to inside and that people see in you on the outside. More importantly, it's something that God always can see.

> *But put on the Lord Jesus Christ, and make no provision for the flesh, to gratify its desires.* **(Romans 13:14)**

> *Better is a poor man who walks in his integrity than a rich man who is crooked in his ways.* **(Proverbs 28:6)**

> *The good person out of his good treasure brings forth good, and the evil person out of his evil treasure brings forth evil.* **(Matthew 12:35)**

- I want soo much for you to have a great marriage with someone you will be happy with during the tough times and not just the good times. I want someone who you will have every opportunity to grow old with and not have to go through a breakup and definitely not a divorce.
- It's not enough to just do the right thing to prepare and set your future marriage up for success. It's also important to pick someone who has been doing the same.
- Then it's not just picking a good one; it's picking the right one.
- It's not just preparing but finding the right timing too.
- It's not just someone you love but someone you respect.
- It's not just someone who looks good to you, but is he the right someone for you?
- It's not just someone you can be good for, but does he challenge you to be better?
- It's not just someone you marry but someone you make a lifelong covenant with.
- It's not just someone with whom you spend your life; it's someone you build a real life with.
- It's not just someone who you can enjoy living with but one you can't imagine living without.
- It's not enough to just be preparing yourself for but also be praying and trusting God for.

God has this all worked out for you if you are listening and following Him. He's been working on this for you for a long time. Trust Him. If you do it His way, I guarantee you won't be sorry.

> *When God takes out the trash, don't go digging back through it. Trust Him.* (Amaka Imani Nkosazana, *Heart Crush*)

> *It is presumptuous of me to wish to choose my path, because I cannot tell which path is best for me. I must leave it to the Lord, Who knows me, to lead me by the path which is best for me, so that in all things His will may be done.* (Teresa of Ávila, *Interior Castle*)

> *No matter how hard you try to fit the pieces together, sometimes it's beyond your control, so sit back and trust in His plans.* (Tilicia Haridat)

> *God can still do more for you and through you. You just need to trust in Him.* (Gift Gugu Mona)

> *Happiness doesn't come from being the one in control. It comes from trusting the One who is.* (Leya Delray, *Where Daffodils Bloom*)

> *I know what I'm doing. I have it all planned out—plans to take care of you, not abandon you, plans to give you the future you hope for.* **(Jeremiah 29:11 MSG)**

> *Let love be genuine. Abhor what is evil; hold fast to what is good.* **(Romans 12:9 ESV)**

"Daddy Dance with Me"

Artists: Krystal L. Covel, Mica Roberts, and Sonya Rutledge

Sung by Krystal Keith

I know what you see when you look at me
As we walk down the aisle
Little pink tutu, bows, and tennis shoes
In the wide eyes of your child
Those are all the memories you will cherish
    and you'll carry
No matter how much time has come and
    gone

Daddy, dance with me
I want you to see the woman I've become.
Daddy, don't let go
I want you to know I'll always need your love.
Today I became his wife
But I'll be your baby girl for life.

Don't know what to do when I look at you
Words can't say enough
What you've done for me
You gave me what I need
You were tender, you were tough
'Cause the world you built around me is the strength that will
    surround me
And protect me now that I am on my own

Daddy, dance with me
I want you to see the woman I've become.
Daddy, don't let go
I want you to know I'll always need your love.
Today I became his wife
But I'll be your baby girl

You gave me faith, you gave me life
You trusted me to live it right
And now you give your blessing on his love and mine.
Daddy, dance with me
I want you to know I'll always need your love.
Today I became his wife
But I'll be your baby girl for life.

Develop a Sixth Sense

Avoid Dangerous Situations and Places
Develop a keen sense of awareness wherever you go
Always keep your eyes open to your surroundings.
Keep track of all exits.
Look at the people around you, and take note of how they are acting.
Have your keys in your hand before you go to your car.
A key sticking out of your fist is a great weapon.
Always look in the backseat area of your car before you get in.
As you are passing the back of your car, give a little pull on the trunk lid just to make sure no one messed with it or is hiding in there.
Never waste time at your door. Do what you have to do and get in quickly.
If someone tries to stand in front of your car to stop you from going, don't stop just slowly keep your car going forward. Keep safe. Keep going.
Never open your door for anyone who you are unsure about (even a cop), and require them to show you some ID. Leave your door locked, and lower your window only a little.
If you are alone and get pulled over in an isolated area, ask the cop who comes up to your window (or call 911, and explain the situation to them) that you want to proceed to a populated, well-lit area.
If you are ever in an accident, take a lot of pictures and write down a lot of info. Unless there are a lot of neutral people around, stay in your car. First call the police, next call your insurance company, and then call me. Don't leave an accident. Wait for the police.
If someone tries to force you out of your car, put your car in gear, press on the gas, and run them over if necessary. It's better to go to jail than to be dead.
If someone tries to take you or force you into their vehicle, FIGHT, make a lot of noise, and NEVER GO WITH THEM. You are always less likely to be killed running away than going with them.

Always run zigzag away from a person with a gun, but get away from there fast.

If a person forces their way into your car and makes you drive, fasten your seat belt tight, and then as soon as you can, drive fast into a wall or concrete abutment or bridge. You will be hurt, but they will more than likely be at least knocked out or killed. Then get away from there and get help.

Always pray about everything and in every situation, and then trust God for everything. Listen to the voice of the Holy Spirit, and let Him guide you. Listen to that voice, and if it's telling you something is wrong or that you need to do something, then do it. It just might save your or someone else's life.

Common sense is not common. Not all places are safe, and not all people are trustworthy. So always be alert, always be wise, and never let your guard down.

> *The prudent see danger and take refuge, but the simple keep going and pay the penalty.* **(Proverbs 27:12 NIV)**

> *Whoever walks in integrity walks securely, but whoever takes crooked paths will be found out.* **(Proverbs 10:9 NIV)**

> *My prayer is not that You take them out of the world but that You protect them from the evil one.* **(John 17:15 NIV)**

> *Assuredly, the evil man will not go unpunished, But the descendants of the righteous will be delivered.* **(Proverbs 11:21)**

> *But keep on the alert at all times, praying that you may have strength to escape all these things that are about to take place, and to stand before the Son of Man.* **(Luke 21:36)**

> *Like a muddied spring or a polluted fountain is a righteous man who gives way before the wicked.* **(Proverbs 25:26 ESV)**

> *He said to them, "But now let the one who has a moneybag take it, and likewise a knapsack. And let the one who has no sword sell his cloak and buy one."* **(Luke 22:36 ESV)**

Friend or Acquaintance

Learn how to know the difference between acquaintance and true friends.

Friends are people who…
- **F**ight for you
- **R**espect you
- **I**nvolve you
- **E**ncourage you
- **N**eed you
- Never **D**eserts you and
- **S**tand by you

Have As Many Good Friends As You Can

Friends can be great blessings, adding to our happy times and helping in our troubles; but rarely do friends last a lifetime.

Some friendships do not last, but some friends are more loyal than brothers. **(Proverbs 18:24 GNT)**

A person who has friends may be harmed by them, but there is a friend who sticks closer than a brother. **(Proverbs 18:24 NB)**

There are many friends we will have in our lives. Some are just okay, and some we will think we can't live without. Friends come and go in our lives, yet it's your family that you are stuck with for the rest of your life. Be blessed by your friends. Enjoy your friends. Be a good friend to your friends, but don't be devastated as they come and go in your life. *"A friend is there to help in any situation, and relatives are born to share our troubles"* **(Proverbs 17:17 CEV)**. *"A friend is always loyal, and a brother is born to help in (during) time of need"* **(Proverbs 17:17 NLV)**.

Good people make good friends. Look for people whom you respect, who have great character, and who are the kind of people you want to be known as; and then make friends with them. *"Walk with the wise and become wise, for a companion of fools suffers harm"* **(Proverbs 13:20)**.

Your friends will come and go. Some will be good, some will be great, and others will prove to be a real detriment to you and those around you. There are some friends you will see often and make you wish you could see them less. There are some you will see rarely and make you wish you could see them more often. There are some you won't see for months or years apart and yet pick right back up like you were never apart, and there are others you will think you were very close to but they will turn on you or walk off from you without a second look. Some, no matter how hard you work to keep them, will still fade away to nothing. Some will bless you, and some will hurt you, but if you are wise, all will enrich your life in one way or another.

Your family circle will grow and change. Your inner circle will slowly change to an outer circle as your family dynamics change and children come, grow up, and then leave... But your family will be a gift for you that will last your entire life long.

Never trust anyone but Jesus completely and family next and then good friends.

We would be considered very blessed if we had enough good friends in our lifetime to carry our casket when we die.

A friend is someone who wants the best for you even if it doesn't include them.

We will have many acquaintances throughout our lifetime but very few close friends.

There are a lot of people we know of but very few we really get to know.

A friend isn't so much the one who come to your party; they are the ones who stay to help you clean up after everyone else has left.

You will never have good friends without being a good friend first.

"He who wants friends must first show himself friendly" (**Proverbs 18:24**).

Never sacrifice your family for your friends or focus more on the temporary over the permanent.

Have many friends but not at the expense of your character or your reputation.

If ever a friendship is to be more than a friendship, then it must first of all be a good friendship.

A friend who would tempt, lead, or pressure you to compromise your morals is not a friend at all.

Always guard your heart, and keep all your relationships in check.

Above all else, guard your heart!

> *In the End, we will remember not the words of our enemies, but the silence of our friends.* (Martin Luther King Jr.)

> *The bond that links your true family is not one of blood, but of respect and joy in each other's life.* (Richard Bach)

> *Guard your heart more than anything else, because the source of your life flows from it.* **(Proverbs 4:23 GW)**

> *Do not make friends with a hot-tempered person, do not associate with one easily angered, or you may learn their ways and get yourself ensnared.* **(Proverbs 22:24–25)**

> *Now when Job's three friends heard of all this evil that was come upon him, they came every one from his own place: Eliphaz the Temanite, and Bildad the Shuhite, and Zophar the Naamathite, and they made an appointment together to come to bemoan him and to comfort him… Then they sat on the ground with him seven days and nights, but no one spoke a word to him because they saw that his suffering was very intense.* **(Job 2:11, 13 CSB)**

Everyone Is Valuable and Is a Gift from God

Everyone is a blessing. There are those who are a blessing to see them come and others who are a blessing to see them go, but all are a blessing.

Everyone is valuable. "*Some are valuable as a good example of what to do, and others are valuable as a good example of what not to do, but all are valuable*" (Ruth Graham).

Some people are a great blessing for what they can tell us or teach us or what wisdom they can share with us. Others are valuable because they entertain us, make us smile, make us laugh, or help us to at least forget our troubles for a while. Yet other people are a blessing by things they discover, invent, make, or do. Some people are a blessing to us by the way they can help or encourage us. Then there are some friends who can motivate us to do something more or be better than what we would be otherwise. Still others just by being with us can make us feel better or make our life somehow better. Then there are those who could be a bigger blessing if they would just sit quietly and do nothing. Job's three friends were really good friends for him…at least until they opened their mouths.

Even people we don't like are valuable and should be treated with some manner of dignity and respect. As much as we can, we need to try to get along with everyone ("*Do your best to live at peace with everyone*" [**Romans 12:18 CEV**].) However, there will always be those who seem to do their best to make this difficult at best, and impossible if they can. That doesn't give us a right not to try, but there are those who are more valuable to be farther away from than to be around. For those, be very careful when you have to be around them, and do your best to stay away from all those who can easily push our buttons or cause us trouble.

Everyone was created to be a blessing. However, we are all masters of our destiny, and because of that, some have never achieved the full qualities for which God has created them to be. For those, we pray, yet they still have value, and if they would accept God's plan for their life, they could still fulfill the higher purpose and value for which He created them.

> *When Job's three friends, Eliphaz the Temanite, Bildad the Shuhite and Zophar the Naamathite, heard about all the troubles that had come upon him, they set out from their homes and met together by agreement to go and sympathize with him and comfort him.* **(Job 2:11)**

> *And as you wish that others would do to you, do so to them.* **(Luke 6:31 ESV)**

> *And I will bless those who bless you, And the one who curses you I will curse And in you all the families of the earth will be blessed.* **(Genesis 12:3)**

> *Blessed is everyone who blesses you, And cursed is everyone who curses you.* **(Numbers 24:9b)**

> *And Laban said, If you will let me say so, do not go away; for I have seen by the signs that the Lord has been good to me because of you.* **(Genesis 30:27 BBE)**

What Can I Do

Grandma J wrote it between fall of 1997 and March 23, 2020
The last half was added by me in 2020.

Lord, what would You have me do for
    You?
what would You have me do?
I love You and serve You and honor
    You too…
Now, what would You have me do?

That which I say unto thee shalt thou
    do…
That's what I want you to do.
To tell all the others that I love them too.
That's what I want you to do.

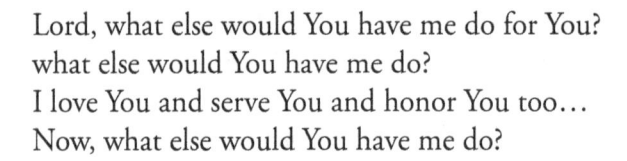

Lord, what else would You have me do for You?
what else would You have me do?
I love You and serve You and honor You too…
Now, what else would You have me do?

First, That which I've said unto thee thou must do…
For That's why thy Savior did die.
For My message of Love, care and hope for you,
And for they too thy Savior did die.

Lord, something else please have me do?
For You know that they scare me so?
To tell them of You they'd think me crazy too…
For I do much good, to church, I go…

It's for those who are separate and far from Me…
For those who bound and blinded by sin.
It is for all of those that I bleed and died, to free

For the lost and alone do I still long to win.

Lord, teach me to do what would You have me do?
Please, teach me to do what You'd have me do?
I love You and serve You and want to obey You too…
Now, teach me to do what You'd have me to do?

*****

> *Until the race is run, until the journey's done, until the crown is won, teach me thy way!* (Benjamin Ramsey)
>
> *Teach me to do Your will, for You are my God; Your Spirit is good. Lead me.* **(Psalm 143:10)**

Prayer Is How We Connect with God

Prayer is our Direct link to real power, real help, and every resource we could ever need.

Prayer provides the insight, clarity, and direction we so desperately need in times like these, for wise decision making.

I don't know what I would do or could do if I couldn't pray about things. It's not just my lifeline or my safety net; it is my daily help, encouragement, companionship, guidance, direction, motivation, and comfort. I have, through prayer, a connection with someone who knows everything and not only knows what happened but everything that led up to the situation at hand; and He even knows what is going to happen. He has unlimited resources, availability, and a never-ending love and desire to help me. Try prayer. It really makes a difference in everything.

Paul gives Christians the following command: *"Do not be anxious about anything, but in everything by prayer and supplication with thanksgiving let your requests be made known to God."* If we bring our requests to God in prayer, He promises to give us the *"peace of God, which surpasses all understanding"* **(Philippians 4:6 ESV).**

Most importantly, understanding our need for God's hand of provision, help, and protection. Even our president, seeing the need for help beyond your medical and science elite, saw the need to call America to pray. He issued the following proclamation for prayer, declaring March 15, 2020, as a National Day of Prayer, stating in part,

> *In our times of greatest need, Americans have always turned to prayer to help guide us through trials and periods of uncertainty… I ask you to join me in a day of prayer for all people who have been affected by the coronavirus pandemic and to pray for God's healing hand to be placed on the people of our*

> *Nation… As one Nation under God, we are greater than the hardships we face, and through prayer and acts of compassion and love, we will rise to this challenge and emerge stronger and more united than ever before. (President Donald Trump 2020)*

Prayer gives us an appropriate response to those that hurt us.

> *Pray for those who persecute you.* **(Matthew 5:44 NIV)**

Prayer helps us when we are scared, nervous, or anxious.

> *Do not be anxious about anything, but in everything, by prayer and petition, with thanksgiving, present your requests to God.* **(Philippians 4:6)**

Prayer is a way we can help anyone and everyone around us.

> *I urge, then, first of all, that requests, prayers, intercession and thanksgiving be made for everyone.* **(1 Timothy 2:1)**

Prayer gives us a means to learn from, copy, and become like Jesus.

> *But Jesus often withdrew to lonely places and prayed.* **(Luke 5:16)**

Prayer is available to us not for being good but just because He loves us.

> *We do not ask because we deserve help, but because you are so merciful.* **(Daniel 9:18)** *(Mercy means showing favor, compassion, and kindness.)*

Prayer connects us with someone who understands, cares, and can help us.

> *For we do not have a high priest who is unable to sympathize with our weaknesses, but we have one who has been tempted in every way, just as we are—yet was without sin. Let us then approach the throne of grace with confidence, so that we may receive mercy and find grace to help us in our time of need.* **(Hebrews 4:15–16)**

Prayer is how we confess our sins, accept His forgiveness, and are made new.

> *For everyone has sinned; we all fall short of God's glorious standard… People are made right with God when they believe that Jesus sacrificed His life, shedding His blood… He makes sinners right in His sight when they believe in Jesus.* **(Romans 3:23–26 NLT)**

Prayer is our access to great power and makes great things happen.

> *The earnest prayer of a righteous person has great power and wonderful results.* **(James 5:16)**.

Prayer is a mighty weapon against evil around us and against the attacks of Satan.

> *Watch and pray so that you will not fall into temptation. The spirit is willing, but the body is weak.* **(Matthew 26:41)**.

Prayer is how we can change everything.

> *If they pray to Me and repent and turn away from the evil they have been doing, then I will hear them in heaven, forgive their sins, and make their land prosperous again.* **(2 Chronicles 7:14 GNT)**

Prayer gives us strength to resist temptation.

> *Jesus warned His disciples to "watch and pray, lest you enter into temptation."* **(Matthew 26:41 NKJV)**

Prayer is our access to healing for ourselves and others.

> *Are any of you sick? You should call for the elders of the church to come and pray over you, anointing you with oil in the name of the Lord. Such a prayer offered in faith will heal the sick, and the Lord will make you well. And if you have committed any sins, you will be forgiven."* **(James 5:14–16 NLT)**

Prayer is where we receive understanding, mercy, and grace no matter what we've done or are going through

> *So then, since we have a great High Priest who has entered heaven, Jesus the Son of God, let us hold firmly to what we believe. This High Priest of ours understands our weaknesses, for He faced all of the same tests we do, yet He did not sin. So let us come boldly to the throne of our gracious God. There we will receive His mercy, and we will find grace to help us when we need it most.* **(Hebrews 4:14–16 NLT)**

Learning Happens Everywhere

*Every experience can enrich and build our
lives, even the bad experiences.*

I can't say that everything that I have ever done has turned out good, nor have I enjoyed every experience I have gone through. But I can say that I have always tried to learn something from every situation. I can even remember sitting in some classes in college that I thoroughly hated, some not just because of the content but for some the presentation was horrible too. However, even in those situations, my dad always told me, "You can still dig for treasure," and find something worth taking home or learning. Most treasure has to be mined or dug up.

No success or victory has ever been achieved without some measurable amount of loss, failure, or defeat.

Never waste an opportunity to learn something new.

Every experience is a learning opportunity.

I heard a saying "If you have to fall, then fall forward." That way, you're at least gaining ground.

Not every choice turns out to be right, but every choice can be a learning experience.

If you are always learning, even a bad situation can be a positive experience.

You can learn something from anything even if it's just to never do that again.

If something's important enough, you should at least try. Even if you think—the probable outcome is failure. (Elon Musk)

Success is not final, failure is not fatal: it is the courage to continue that counts. (Winston Churchill)

There are no secrets to success. It is the result of preparation, hard work, and learning from failure. (Colin Powell)

Just because something doesn't do what you planned it to do doesn't mean it's useless. (Thomas A. Edison)

I think that what my parents taught me about hard work, optimism and education still holds true. (Samuel Alito)

Let a wise person listen and increase learning, and let a discerning person obtain guidance. **(Proverbs 1:5 CSB)**

Take learning in your hands, do not let her go: keep her, for she is your life. **(Proverbs 4:13)**

Teach the wise, and they will become wiser; inform the righteous, and their learning will increase. **(Proverbs 9:9 CEB)**

I have always thought that I can learn something from anyone and any meeting I have had to be in. I would often visit my grandma and grandpa Gage, and when I would stay with them, I would have to go to their Catholic church with them. It was weird and in Latin, but I would learn about the respect for their faith. Anything that was in English was interesting. I didn't learn a lot, but I always came away with something. Over the years, I've also had to sit in a lot of boring meetings at work, and even so I have always tried to learn something even if I had to really search to find it. So I always came out ahead. If you try to do the same in every situation, then you will do nothing but get better and better. If that is even possible.

A Great Father for Your Children

Make sure that the man you choose will be the
kind of father you want for your children.

A good name is better than great riches. Kids will only do on the average half of the good they see in their parents and twice the bad, so pick the guy who has twice as many good qualities and half as many bad as you can tolerate to see your children emulate.

Is he a good example (1 Corinthians 15:33)?

*****

Does he make a good leader for you? For your children (Ephesians 5:22–23 KJV)? The husband is the head (of the family). Will he lead your family self-sacrificially?

Is he able to recognize your achievements and qualities and praise you for them?

"*Her husband also praises her*" (Proverbs 31:28 KJV).

Is he honest? Does he always tell the truth? "*Lying lips are an abomination to the Lord: but they that deal truly are His delight*" (Proverbs 12:22 KJV). Is he kind and forgiving?

Does he forgive you and let it go? "*Forbearing one another, and forgiving one another, if any man have a quarrel against any: even as Christ forgave you, so also do ye*" (Colossians 3:13 KJV). "*Put up with each other and forgive anyone who does you wrong, just as Christ has forgiven you*" (Colossians 3:13 CEV).

Is he content, or is he jealous of what others have, comparing himself to those around. "*Do not desire to possess anything that belongs to another person—not a house, a wife, a husband, a slave* (workers), *an ox* (truck), *a donkey* (car), *or anything else*" (Exodus 20:17 KJV).

Is he patient? Not a hothead. "*Don't even be friends with an angry man…*" (Proverbs 22:24–25).

| 373

Does he practice good self-control? Proverbs 23:20–21 says don't even be around those who don't.

Does he have roaming eyes and can't help but to watch the girls go by (Matthew 5:27–28)?

Does he demonstrate being a man with wisdom? *"He that walketh with wise men shall be wise: but a companion of fools shall be destroyed"* (Proverbs 13:20 KJV).

*****

A good husband is, indeed, difficult to find. But no matter how hard it is, you need to be patient and faithful enough to wait for the right one. Take note that marriage is the covenant union of two who will start a new important chapter for the rest of their lives. It is also the beginning of building a family. Therefore, don't only think of yourself, but also think about the future of your children and even your husband himself.

So Pray and trust God to lead you to the right one, and look for the qualities above. Remember to make yourself ready to be a good wife. As a woman of God, you also have to practice and develop the traits of a good wife too.

> *"Don't let anyone look down on you because you are young, but set an example for (those who are watching you)…in speech, in life, in love, in faith and in purity"* **(1 Timothy 4:12).**

A Wise Woman Will...

1. Never belittle her man or try to put him in his place.
2. Never talk down to her man even when she knows better.
3. Never ignore her man.
4. Never let her man feel that he is replaceable or second to anyone.
5. Never make her man think that she doesn't need him.
6. Never make her man feel he is less of a man or not as good as anyone else.
7. Never embarrass her man.
8. Never look away, watch TV, or text...while her man is talking to her.
9. Never manipulate her man.
10. Never be controlling of or act like the boss of her man.
11. Never laugh at her man's mistakes or failures.
12. Never put any person before her man.
13. Never be too busy for her man.
14. Never be inconsiderate of her man's feelings.
15. Never tell anyone anything negative or personal about her man.
16. Never neg or henpeck her man.
17. Always encourage her man.
18. Always let him know she's with him, on his side, on his team, and in his corner.
19. Always make him feel he's smart and has good ideas.
20. Always be attentive to her man and there when he needs her.
21. Always praise her man and make him feel he is her hero.
22. Always let him know she feels blessed to have him.
23. Always tell him she doesn't know what she would do without him.
24. Always be quick to recognize his good points and forget about his failures.

25. Always tell him she thinks he is wiser, stronger, better than…
26. Always let him hear her bragging to others on his accomplishments.
27. Always be a good listener for her man.
28. Always be careful to know when he's needing advice or when he's just needing someone to listen to him.
29. Always let him lead even if he fails and still be there to help when he does.
30. Always laugh at his jokes and praise him for his wisdom.
31. Always be quick to encourage him after he fails.
32. Always be sensitive of his feelings and hurts.
33. Always be her man's biggest cheerleader and best friend.

This is the way a wise woman will treat any man in her life who is important or special to her. It's just as important for her husband whether she just got married or has been married for fifty years, or for her brother, father, and grandfather too. God made us strong and even independent in many ways but yet at the same time very weak and emotionally fragile. There is very little we can do on our own to build our ego or self-esteem. I think that is why God said, "It's not good for man to be alone," because he needed a helper, an encourager, someone who would think he could do it and was the best. So like it or not, I think God intentionally made man dependent on the women in our life. If Eve didn't come along, I think Adam would probably still be sitting there in the garden, feeling overwhelmed with the task before him.

Be the Best Mother You Can Be

Don't just be a Christian around your kids. Be like Christ to them because it makes it so much easier for kids to make the right choices with that kind of parents.

As a parent, I believe this and have always tried to live by this, that children are always watching and learning from you. The decisions they make and the way they deal with things in the future will largely be based on what they learn at home. They will either do it the same way (or the way they thought you did it), or they will intentionally remember the way you did it to make sure they do it differently.

Children will statistically do only half the good they see you do. (So make sure they see you doing twice the good you want them to do.)

And they will do twice the bad that they see you do. (So make sure you are doing a lot less wrong or acceptable gray-area decisions than you would want doubled in their lives.)

I believe in you and know that you want to be the best mother. So learn from the best, learn all the things you saw your mother do right and all the things you saw and heard that your grandmothers did right, and copy them. Then read books on how to be the best mother, but most importantly, read the Bible, and learn what God says about it. I believe in you. Even on those bad days when it all goes wrong, I still believe in you.

Mother is the name for God in the lips and hearts of little children. (William Makepeace Thackeray)

A child's first teacher is its mother. (Peng Liyuan)

I remember my mother's prayers and they have always followed me. They have clung to me all my life. (Abraham Lincoln)

Men are what their mothers made them. (Ralph Waldo Emerson)

A wise woman builds her home, but a foolish woman tears it down with her own hands. **(Proverbs 14:1 NLT)**

Please, just one more thing: Bless my family; keep your eye on them always. You've already as much as said that You would, Master God! Oh, may Your blessing be on my family permanently! **(2 Samuel 7:29 MSG)**

Build Your Home, Strengthen Your Family

It's not about how much you have; it's more about what you do with what you have. I have seen families that live in cardboard shacks in tent cities who have love and peace and contentment; and I've seen families living in million-dollar mansions and have all the toys yet who are mean, nasty, and filled with hate toward themselves and others. So it's not about having money or nice things that make a family of peace and love, or a house a home—it's all a matter of the heart.

Being a wife and mother, you are never off duty. As you know, you never punch a time clock, nor do you work a nine-to-five as a mother. So with that in mind, you are never not affecting your marriage, children, or household in general. I know it happens. It's just life, but you can't let yourself just have "a bad hair day," because you are either building or tearing down your home. It's the same as it is with everything else. It takes twice as long to repair what was broken than it does to build it in the first place. Not only that, but when you give yourself too much freedom to express your frustrations, you tend to say or do things during those times, that you would never do or say at any other time, things you would later regret. Have a safety net set up for yourself when you know you are on your last nerve. I would suggest getting into a church activity or a women's group. Have a couple of friends or family members you can hang out with or call on to vent and get counsel from. Whatever you do, develop a safety plan so you don't do or say something that will hurt you or the people you love.

Just work hard to always keep your head and build your family and home, and never allow yourself the latitude to destroy what you know you really don't want to destroy. Then when the others in your family have their bad days, you will be able to help them be able to handle and work through their frustrations too.

You have to first be out of the water to be able to pull someone else out of the water. A person who can't swim can't help anyone from drowning. (Me)

A woman is like a tea bag—you never know how strong she is until she gets into some hot water. (Eleanor Roosevelt)

A strong woman builds others up because she knows what it's like to be torn down. (Anonymous)

The LORD's curse is on the house of the wicked, but He blesses the home of the righteous. **(Proverbs 3:33)**

A woman's family is held together by her wisdom, but it can be destroyed by her foolishness. **(Proverbs 14:1 CEV)**.

Homes are made by the wisdom of women, but are destroyed by foolishness. **(Proverbs 14:1 GNT)**.

Be the Best Wife You Can Be

As a wife and mother, always do what is best, not easiest, for your family. Always plan and build for the future first and present time second. Remember, the health, beauty, mood, and focus of the home all rest on your shoulders.

You are the partner, helper, encourager, and motivator of your husband. You build his self-esteem and character. He needs to know you are on his side and you believe in him. He needs you to be his biggest cheerleader and fan. Just as your biggest need, first and foremost as a wife, is to be loved by him, his greatest and biggest need as a husband is to receive your respect first and honor second. It really doesn't matter if you think "he doesn't deserve it" in so many ways. Find ways in which he does deserve it, and lavish it on him. He still must have it, if for no other reason, just because he is your husband (this is positional respect). Don't nag him, belittle him, or tear him down for his shortcomings or failures. Just keep building him up for his good points and successes, and even when he really tries hard to do what is right (whether or not he succeeds doesn't matter). Make sure what you praise him for is something real. Don't fake it, because he will know it, and that will work against you. Know for sure that your praise and respect will build him into a great man because not only do we need the praise and respect of our wives but when we get some for real, it becomes addictive to us and we'll do anything just to get more. Just keep doing it, and he will keep growing and becoming a better man. So much of what kind of man he becomes depends on you and what he hears from you. The way God made us men, we desperately want to be someone's hero and worthy of respect, especially to our family, and we definitely need it from our wife.

A Real Woman Builds Her Man Up with Her Love Instead of teasing Him Down. (Adam Cappa)

When a man realizes that a woman is his teammate and not his opponent, that's when his life changes. (Unknown)

A wise woman knows the importance of speaking life into her man. If you love him: Believe in him, encourage him, and be his peace. (Dansel Washington)

The wife must respect her husband. **(Ephesians 5:22–33)**

However, I want you to realize that Christ has authority over every man, a husband has authority over his wife, and God has authority over Christ. **(1 Corinthians 11:3 GWT)**

A wife must put her husband first. This is her duty as a follower of the Lord. **(Colossians 3:18–19 CEV)**

Be the Best Mother You Can Be

When you do your best as a wife and build your marriage or invest into your husband, it will overflow into your children. They will benefit more than you will ever know from a good relationship between their parents. The best thing you can give them is a great relationship between their parents. Beyond that, children need time more than things. To them love is spelled T-I-M-E. The other thing they really need is consistency, especially with things like feeling loved, keeping regular schedules, training, and realistic rules with consequences. But they also need someone to teach them. That will mostly have to rest on your shoulders.

Teach them that they are important and they can make a difference in this world.
Teach them that they were created with a purpose.
Teach them that they are never alone.
Teach them that they are special, unique, and one of a kind.
Teach them that they are loved to the extreme and can never do anything that will make them be loved less or anything that could even make it possible to be loved more.
Teach them that they are a part of a big family that loves them and loves God.
Teach them that we defend, support, and value every member of our family.
Teach them that they are smart, and beautiful, and awesome too.
Teach them that a boy is born a boy and a girl is born a girl and there are differences between them and we don't get to change it.

Teach them that we are Christians, and Americans, and we eat meat in our family.

Teach them that they are better than all the other kids who are popular or wanting them to join in their mischievous or bad behavior, so they can make a better choice than the crowd.

Teach them about empathy and how to care about others.

Teach them that we are responsible to do our part to help whoever may need our help with as much as we can help and for as often as we are able to help.

Teach them that wherever we go, we should leave it better than when we arrived.

Teach them that there is a way that our family believes and does things.

Teach them that drugs and alcohol and any other thing that could harm them are wrong and we don't do them no matter what society may currently think about them.

Teach them that right is right and wrong is wrong and the truth is always the truth.

Teach them that there is a difference between good and bad and it does make a difference.

Teach them that even when they blow it, we still love them and we believe in second chances.

Teach them most of all about God and take them to Church where they can get to know Him.

This will build your children with everything they need to be great men and women who will grow up to do something great and people we can all be proud of.

I know that it is popular to think that "a child should never hear the word *no* while they are young, because it might hurt their psyche." Or another one is a child should never have any kind of punishment for doing wrong and, for heaven's sakes, never spank a child. Or another one I've heard that Hillary Clinton made popular in her book that "it takes a village to raise a child." All those previous thoughts are very wrong and will cause your child a lot of irreparable damage if you buy into them. Children need to first learn the difference between right and wrong. The ding-a-ling doctor who said, "Don't spank," ended up losing all his kids sadly and tragically. So his advice was proven no good. Furthermore, if you don't set up strong parameters for them to keep them safe and know what is right or wrong, that could even end up being life-threatening to them. Then most importantly is they don't need the village or school district or government to help raise them. They only need a loving mom and a dad to do the job right.

Your mother and I tried to always have the philosophy that we are responsible to be the best parents we can be, not the best friends of our kids. We have to keep our children safe and healthy and not necessarily happy. We have to teach them what they need to be successful and good in whatever they do for their future, not just entertain them nor give them what they want. So if you, while you were growing up, thought we were not the best parents, maybe because we were not as fun as your friends' parents or didn't let you do the things you wanted. I'm sorry. I hope you are old enough now to understand why we did it the way we did. You may not agree with us but at least understand why.

> *I wonder if parents know that they are teaching their children to be unaccountable when they blame teachers for their kids failing. Be a parent. Be a part of your kid's life. Don't try to be your kids friend!* (Unknown)

> *I'm not your friend. I'm your mother. I'm here to give you the boundaries you need to become a functional, responsible adult. You may hate me now, but I don't care. It's my job to raise a responsible*

adult, not nurture bad habits in my teenage child. (Njfamily.com)

Teaching kids to count is fine, but teaching them what counts is best. (Bob Talbert)

Don't raise your kids to have more than you had. Raise them to be more than you were. (Anonymous)

Parenting is not giving your child everything they want. Parenting is not being your child's friend. Parenting is about preparing your child to be a useful and respectful person in society. (GloZell)

Parents are the ultimate role models for children. Every word, every movement, and every action affects them. No other person or outside force has a greater influence on a child than a parent. (Bob Keeshan)

Teach a child to choose the right path, and when he is older, he will remain upon it. **(Proverbs 22:6 TLB)**

I have chosen him to teach his family to obey Me forever and to do what is right and fair. If they do, I will give Abraham many descendants, just as I promised. **(Genesis 18:19 CEV)**

Teach them to your children. Talk about them all the time—whether you're at home or walking along the road or going to bed at night, or getting up in the morning. **(Deuteronomy 11:18–20, 6:7–8 CEV)**

Parents, don't be hard on your children. Raise them properly. Teach them and instruct them about the Lord. **(Ephesians 6:4 CEV)**

Be the Best Domestic Engineer You Can Be (Housewife/Home Care)

Beyond that, take care of your home. Keep it clean. It doesn't matter if it's a palace or a big box. It can be clean and inviting. Make it look pretty, pleasant, inviting, and nice. It doesn't have to be fancy or look impressive to be good. Just keep a standard of keeping it clean and looking nice. It changes the mood, the feel, the ambiance of the experience of being there. You are the boss of the house. And you are the boss of the food. It works good that way. Make the rule that everyone pitches in and makes the place look good before they can eat. No clean, no eat!

This is a struggle for all of us especially while we are raising kids, and if anything, I know that I tend to be a lot OCD on this. I do try to find a happy medium with the family on this. (I know, don't laugh.) I also know that my tendency to save everything I think I might need someday tends to work against me. (My life is complicated.) However, if I could learn how to do this differently, I know I would be able to do this better. I would like our home to be comfortable and inviting for whoever comes there. I've been in homes with almost nothing and only dirt floors, but the wife worked hard to sweep and clean what they had and make it nice. I know that if they can do that much with so little and make it nice, then it shouldn't be too much to think we can make our homes clean, comfortable, and inviting with the many nice things we have too.

You got this. You can do this, even if it's just one room at a time or one wall at a time. Remember, you set the standard in the home, and "making a house a home" starts with clean and comfortable.

Keep your house clean enough to be healthy but dirty enough to be happy. (Unknown)

Your neighbors will make judgments about you based on how your lawn and house look, and people who see you passing will judge you based on how clean you keep your car. It's not always fair, but it has always been true. Appearances matter, so make yours a good one. (Lou Holtz)

You cannot get through a single day without having an impact on the world around you. What you do makes a difference and you have to decide what kind of a difference you want to make. (Jane Goodall)

Your home is living space, not storage space. (Francine Jay)

By wisdom a house is built, and through understanding it is established; through knowledge its rooms are filled with rare and beautiful treasures. **(Proverbs 24:3–4)**

Luke 11:25 tells us to not just clean our house but also fill it with God.

Everything must be done in a fit (clean) and orderly way. (**1 Corinthians 4:14**)

Be the Best Cook/ Dietitian You Can Be

Fix the best and healthiest meals you can. No matter what it is, do your best.

I saw mothers in South America and in Haiti who had nothing to eat and no money to buy anything and yet still did the best they could to find some rice or leaves or other things to cook for their family. I have no idea what it was, but it tasted good.

That is one thing that I am thankful for—that all you girls are good cooks. When we were first married, your mother couldn't cook at all, except for desserts; and we had desserts for every meal. I do mean "for" the meal (haha). I used to tease her that our first meal was a recipe she found on the Elmer's Glue bottle, but the dessert was good. However, it wasn't too long before she was an awesome cook, and most of the time, I would rather have her cooking than any restaurant food. I know you are a very good cook too. And I am proud of you for that. Just make sure you're keeping healthy as an important goal with your food you eat and feed your family. Even if they complain, still make your family eat lots of veggies and salads. Be creative and avoid as much as possible prepackaged and restaurant food. It might be easy and quick, but it's not best. As much as you are able, always do your best for your family.

> *Sorry, there's no magic bullet. you gotta eat healthy and live healthy to be healthy and look healthy. End of story.* (Morgan Spurlock)

> *The doctor of the future will no longer treat the human frame with drugs, but rather will cure and prevent disease with nutrition.* (Thomas Edison)

> *Investing in early childhood nutrition is a surefire strategy. The returns are incredibly high.* (Anne M. Mulcahy)

There is nothing unhealthy about educating youngsters about nutrition. (Pierre Dukan)

Research shows that what works and is healthy for adults also works well for children, if adjusted to be age-appropriate. Children, like adults, do not suffer from a deficiency of white sugar, white flour, junk food, or processed foods. A growing child as well as an adult is hurt by junk foods and benefited by healthy foods." (Gabriel Cousens, MD, *Conscious Parenting: The Holistic Guide to Raising and Nourishing Healthy, Happy Children*)

Then God said, "Look! I have given you every seed-bearing plant throughout the earth and all the fruit trees for your food." **(Genesis 1:29 NLT)**

Since everything God created is good, we should not reject any of it but receive it with thanks. **(1 Timothy 4:4 NLT)**

Dear friend, I hope all is well with you and that you are as healthy in body as you are strong in spirit. **(3 John 1:2 NLT)**

You say, "I am allowed to do (or eat) anything"—but not everything is good for you" (to eat). **(1 Corinthians 6:12 NLT)**

Set the Best Mood You Can

Do the best you can to set the mood of the home. Love, Peace, Happiness... Make it that way. As a wife and a mother, you have the ability to set the mood. No matter what anyone else chooses, you have the final say on what that home will feel like. Yes, it is easier if everyone is on board, but the old saying is true: "If Mama's happy, everyone is happy!" It's a gift and a calling, or like Munk always says on his detective show, "It's a blessing and a curse."

Your family all need your skill to make it a place of peace and love and acceptance...

Philippians 2:14–15 says we need to do what we do without complaining, grumbling, or arguing about it. **Proverbs 17:22** says we need to have a joyful attitude and it will keep us healthy. **First Peter 5:7 and Philippians 4:6** say we need to give God whatever we worry about so we don't have to. **Philippians 4:8** says we need to keep our mind full of good things and not bad. **Colossians 3:23** says we need to do our work as if we were working for God Himself and not to people. Why we should do this is because that is the attitude Jesus had (**Philippians 2:5–11**) and He is our example.

I don't know if I'm very good at this or not. I don't know. I do tend at times to let my emotions lead me (too much) and maybe wear my feelings on my sleeve a little much. But the way I try to do this is through being funny. I like laughing, and I like making others happy. That is why I have had all the "Dad jokes" through the years. If I could think of a way to make you laugh when you are feeling down or pick up everyone's mood by saying or doing something funny, I would feel I did a good thing.

I think I could have done this better by showing my happy feelings more and hiding my downtimes better, and maybe a joke book or two could have also helped. Hey, by the way, one of my deaf friends wanted to know if you heard the guy yelling outside last night, complaining about his neighbor's dog. I said I didn't. He said, "Me neither." Haha, did I make you laugh?

A strong positive mental attitude will create more miracles than any wonder drug. (Patricia Neal)

If life seems jolly rotten, there's something you've forgotten! And that's to laugh and smile and dance and sing. (Monty Python)

The enormous power to change your home and your children's behavior is in your hands, parents. (Nurit Levi)

Create a good habit of staying home for family nights, focus on simple entertainment for children. (Ronald Valentino)

Kind words are like honey—sweet to the taste and good for your health. **(Proverbs 16:24 GNT)**

If you are cheerful, you feel good; if you are sad, you hurt all over. **(Proverbs 17:22 CEV)**

Don't burn out; keep yourselves fueled and aflame. **(Romans 12:12 MSG)**

Be the Best You That You Can Be

Last but not least, please TAKE CARE OF YOURSELF. Keep yourself healthy, eat healthy, get enough rest, exercise, keep learning, and be careful not to forget to do what it takes to make yourself or what it takes to keep yourself spiritually, morally, and physically healthy too.

Always challenge yourself to be better. You can influence others, but you can control and change yourself. You're the daughter of a Marine, so you, too, can "be all you can be." URAH!

I know for me that I would have done much better and been better off now if I had kept with my exercising routine. Of course, I was a Marine, and so I was in pretty good shape from that. Then I was a long-distance cyclist and loved doing regular bike trips, biking as much as a thousand miles a week. Do you remember how often I would take you biking? When you kids were young, we had bikes and bike trailers for the youngest one or for cousins who were not as used to biking and were not able to keep up. We had tagalong bikes that one of us would have connected to one of the bikes, and we would all do a fourteen-to-twenty-four-mile bike ride together. I thoroughly enjoyed it. Being with my family like that, doing something and going places, was lots of fun. Sara and I would go. I think it was a 40-to-60-mile trip once a week or so (a hilly country road to the beach and back). Then I would do 150-mile trips by myself a couple of times a month or more.

However, I was told I wasn't doing right by you kids and I needed to stop. So after a while, I believed it, and regretfully, I did. I gave up biking, and I really shouldn't have listened to those who just wanted to tear down what we were doing. Did you enjoy it? Was it a good memory for you? If so, I am sorry that I gave up on us and our special time. It would have helped us as a family stay in a lot better health and keep in shape.

I also had a membership at a major health club and would go to work out regularly, and I enjoyed that, but I was told that was selfish and I shouldn't be leaving my family to do something like that…and I listened to the naysayers again. And quit working out. If I would have been smart enough, I could have kept in good shape, and so avoided a lot of the health trouble I have today.

So please remember not to listen to the people who want to bring you down to their level. **Proverbs 24:5** says it is wise to strengthen our bodies and work on our health. If you are doing something good and right, if you are trying to take care of your health and your future, then don't stop doing what is good, unless you are trading it to do something even better. Learn from me on this, but don't follow me. **First Timothy 4:8** says that it is profitable to take care of yourself, to get in shape. So get healthy, and stay healthy. You are the only one like you that I have and I don't want to lose you!

When you are doing your best, your family wins, but when you give up or lower your standards, your family falls apart, and everyone suffers. This is what a Proverbs 31 woman is all about.

> *Press forward. Do not stop, do not linger in your journey, but strive for the mark set before you.* (George Whitefield)

> *Why not simply honor your parents, love your children, help your brothers and sisters, be faithful to your friends, care for your mate with devotion, complete your work cooperatively and joyfully, assume responsibility for problems, practice virtue without first demanding it of others, understand the highest truths yet retain an ordinary manner? That would be true clarity, true simplicity, true mastery.* (Laozi)

> *Bottom line, your body is a temple, and you have to treat it that way. That's how God designed it.* (Ray Lewis)

> *Unless the LORD builds a house, the work of the builders is wasted. Unless the LORD protects*

a city, guarding it with sentries will do no good. **(Psalm 127:1 NLT)**

Jesus knew their thoughts and said to them, "Every kingdom divided against itself will be ruined, and every city or household divided against itself will not stand." **(Matthew 12:25)**

As for me and my household, we will serve the Lord. **(Joshua 24:15)**

Keep your house and family in order. **(1 Timothy 2:8–3:13)**

I Am Here to Help You Raise Your Children with Strong Family Connections and Values

No one can be enough, work enough, teach enough, or nurture enough to raise kids the way we might want them to be raised. Even if we alone work twice as hard at it, we'd still only get half the effect we were wanting. Hillary Clinton knew that and thought that the government would make the best parents for raising children, but she was wrong. Traditionally and biblically, the Family is the best suited for the task. Children need a safe home with a loving father and mother (one of each). They do best with siblings; and the more loving and supportive the extended family is, especially grandparents, the better. Kids do best when they know how they are connected to something much bigger than themselves, *that they are loved and important.*

Kids are more able to stand up to peer pressure and make good choices when they have a strong connection to their family and are able to say,

> *This is the way our family believes or does it.* (Me)

> *Children are great imitators. So give them something great to imitate.* (Me)

Teaching kids to count is fine, but teaching them what counts is best. (Bob Talbert)

I am very thankful that you kids were raised with two sets of grandparents who loved yas. I know that they were far from perfect; and I know, on a bad day, you kids could sure pick them apart. Yes, they could have been better in many ways, but like they say, "You can't pick your relatives." They might not have been perfect, but they were good! I thank God for them and that they loved God, loved all their family, and were good examples for you kids to be around. And they were safe. All in all, with what is out there, I'd say you guys scored pretty high on getting good grandparents. Then the bonus is getting to have some good memories of a couple of your great-grandparents and having time you spent with them. If you think about it, make sure you let each of the grandparents you have left know you appreciate them and are thankful for them. One of these days, too soon I'm afraid, you will run out of chances to do that. I wish I had another chance with my grandparents. I loved them soo much, not for what they did (they never really did any of the fun stuff with us) but just because they were my grandparents, and I had the world's greatest grandparents.

> You can pick your seat.
> You can pick your cloths.
> You can pick your nose.
> You can pick your friends.
> But your family, you're
> just stuck with them.
> So choose carefully at
> what you do get to pick
> And pick a good one.

A grandparent is a little bit parent, a little bit teacher, and a little bit best friend. (Unknown)

Young people need something stable to hang on to—a culture connection, a sense of their own past, a hope for their own future. Most of all, they need what grandparents can give them. (Jay Kesler)

What children need most are the essentials that grandparents provide in abundance. They give unconditional love, kindness, patience, humor, comfort, lessons in life. And, most importantly, cookies. (Rudolph Giuliani)

Some of the world's best educators are grandparents. (Dr. Charlie W. Shedd)

From your heart as long as you live. Teach them to your children and grandchildren. **(Deuteronomy 4:9b)**

Oh, that their hearts would be inclined to fear Me and keep all My commands always, so that it might go well with them and their children forever! **(Deuteronomy 5:29 NIV)**

*And you and your children and grandchildren must fear the L*ORD *your God as long as you live. If you obey all His decrees and commands, you will enjoy a long life.* **(Deuteronomy 6:2)**

For I will speak to you in a parable. I will teach you hidden lessons from our past—stories we have heard and known, stories our ancestors handed down to us. We will not hide these truths from our children; we will tell the next generation about the glorious deeds of the Lord, about His power and His mighty wonders. **(Psalm 78:2–4)**

Start children off on the way they should go, and even when they are old they will not turn from it. **(Proverbs 22:6 NIV)**

"As for Me, this is My covenant with them," says the LORD. *"My Spirit, who is on you, will not depart from you, and My words that I have put in your mouth will always be on your lips, on the lips of your children and on the lips of their descendants— from this time on and forever," says the LORD. "Arise, shine, for your light has come, and the glory of the LORD rises upon you."* **(Isaiah 59:21–22)**

Tell our children! Let it be told to our grandchildren and their children too. **(Joel 1:3 CEV)**

It's Who You Are That Counts

Not because of what you've done but because of who you are.

I love you! As a professional interpreter, this is a pet peeve of mine. This phrase is probably used hundreds…maybe even thousands of times a day. I love…my dog, my cat, my kids, my girlfriend, my selfies, chocolate, running, football, sweet tea, my TV show, pizza…. and, oh my goodness, the list goes on and on. What exactly are we saying when we say we love something? Does it mean that we place the highest value or the most meaningful emotional connection we have on that thing or person? If so, do we mean that to me that pizza has the same value as my family? Or my dog is just as dear to me as my wife? But when I tell you, "I Love You," I mean you are one of the most valuable things in my life. (I don't love things. I like things and love people, but you know what I mean.)

No matter what you do, where you go, or how old you get, you will always be my daughter, and I will always love you.

Before you could cook or read, before you could ride a bike or even walk, before you could sing or talk, before you sit up or smile, before I could even hold you or see you, you were already my daughter, and I already loved you.

Everything since then has just been frosting on the cake.

Sometimes, it is easy for us to get confused between *human beings* and *human doings*. We are not valuable because of our doings but because of our being. And you are not loved because of what you do but because of who you are. Thank you for being my daughter.

> *I hope that my daughter grows up empowered and doesn't define herself by the way she looks but by qualities that make her an intelligent, strong, and responsible woman.* (Isaiah Mustafa)

> *To a father growing old nothing is dearer than a daughter.* (Euripides)

No one in this world can love a girl more than her father. (Michael Ratnadeepak)

The happiest moment of my life was probably when my daughter was born. (David Duchovny)

When my daughter says, "Daddy, I need you!" I wonder if she has any idea that I need her billion times more. (Stanley Behrman)

See what great love the Father has lavished on us, that we should be called children of God! And that is what we are! The reason the world does not know us is that it did not know Him. (**1 John 3:1 NIV**)

And I will be your Father, and you will be My sons and daughters, says the L<small>ORD</small> *Almighty.* (**2 Corinthians 6:18 NLT**)

We love because He first loved us. (**1 John 4:19**)

Find the North Star and Let It Lead You to Safety

No matter where you are, what you do, or how lost you think you are, if you can find your way to the cross, you can find your way home. Jesus is the way no matter how lost you get. If you lose your way, just look for the cross. He'll always lead you home.

You can remember that the sun rises in the east and sets in the west, so depending on the time of day, look where your shadow is pointing in relation to the position of the sun. In the morning, your shadow will basically be going west and in the evening basically to the east.

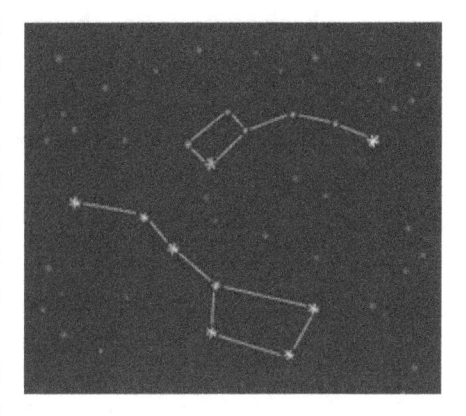

When you were young, I tried to teach you how to tell directions if you were lost. You could use geographical markers. Look at a map, or remember where mountains or tall buildings or strange trees are located. If you can find them, you can get an idea where you are and how to find your way.

When you are in a woods, you can look for the side of the tree that most of the moss is growing on, and in general, it grows mostly on the north side of trees.

In a general way, all streams flow toward the equator. So in the north, if you follow a stream, you will be somewhat heading south, and you will always find a town or city somewhere along every river if you follow it far enough.

The problem with those means of telling directions is that they are very general and not very exact.

You can use a compass to find magnetic north; and if you are good at using it, here in the northern hemisphere, you will be able

| 403

to find where you are in reference to the "North Pole," to a pretty close to an exact location. Yet the further north you travel, the less accurate the use of a compass is because magnetic north is constantly changing.

That's why people who navigate on the sea use the North Star because it has not moved or changed in thousands of years of people using it. It's our "True North."

So when people say you need to find your North Star, they are saying to find what is right and doesn't change over time or doesn't vary depending where you are. To know where you are, you should know where you are heading and not just a general direction of north.

In this life, Jesus is the only thing that doesn't change. Don't base your life on a moving target. Everything the people in this world believes in—their philosophies, theories, concepts, and schemes—is constantly changing. *"But the word of the Lord endures forever"* (1 Peter 1:15; Isaiah 40:8). You can set your life by Him and not be disappointed. The things that people will tell you is right is like chasing the waves of the sea (Ephesians 4:14). They are never the same twice, constantly changing and all the time telling you to take what they say as true. We can avoid making a shipwreck of our lives by "*fixing our eyes on Jesus*" (Hebrews 12:2). He is Our North Star. This song "True North," a song by Twila Paris, sums up our need for Jesus as our guide:

"True North" Song

We lost our bearings,
Following our own mind
We left conviction behind…
How did we ever wander so far
And where do we go from here?
How will we know where it is?

True North
There's a strong steady light
That is guiding us home…

We need an absolute
Compass now more
Than ever before.

> *As for God, His way is perfect: The LORD's word is flawless; He shields all who take refuge in Him.* (**Psalm 18:30**)

> *Everyone then who hears these words of mine and does them will be like a wise man who built his house on the rock. And the rain fell, and the floods came, and the winds blew and beat on that house, but it did not fall, because it had been founded on the rock. And everyone who hears these words of mine and does not do them will be like a foolish man who built his house on the sand. And the rain fell, and the floods came, and the winds blew and beat against that house, and it fell, and great was the fall of it.* (**Matthew 7:24–27**)

Never Be Afraid of Hard Work

Doing your best the first time is better than having to do it over again.
Just good enough is never good enough.
Never be satisfied with seeing a job half done.
If there is a need that you can meet then do it.
If it is out of place, then put it away.
If it is a mess, then clean it up.
If it is broken, either fix it, sell it, or throw it away.
If there is something that needs to be done, then do it.
If you can help, then help.
Anything worth doing is worth doing your best
Make it better because you were there.
Doing your best once is better than doing it halfhearted and having to fix it later.
If you always do your best, you will never need to be ashamed

"If you're doing your best, you won't have time to worry about failure" (H. Jackson Brown Jr.)

Do your best, and let God do the rest.
I have always tried to take pride in my work and do my best no matter what I was doing. I received much fulfillment in working that way over the years. Each time I had to do something, I would try to see if I could do it better. Each building I would build, I would try to make it a little better than

the last one I built. Even if I had to just put better windows in it or a better grade of shingles, I would use more nails than what code called for, and I would use the heavier tar paper just because it was better. Many times I would do things that no one else would ever know, but I did and God did. It was the way I would want it, so I built it for someone else the way I liked it done.

Often your mother or your grandfather would say, "No one knows you are even doing it that way," or "You would make more money not including those extras." But I felt that God knew and if nothing else He appreciated it.

> *And whatever you do or say, do it as a representative of the Lord Jesus, giving thanks through Him to God the Father.* **(Colossians 3:17 NLT)**

> *Whatever you do, work at it with all your heart, as though you were working for the Lord and not for people.* **(Colossians 3:23 GNT)**

> *Whatever the activity in which you engage, do it with all your ability.* **(Ecclesiastes 9:10a)**

> *Never be lazy in your work, but serve the Lord enthusiastically.* **(Romans 12:11)**

> *The slacker craves, yet has nothing, but the diligent is fully satisfied.* **(Proverbs 13:4)**

You Are Very Blessed

If you woke up this morning in a bed, you are very blessed.
If you have your health and strength, you are very blessed.
If you live in a house that is shelter from the rain and protection from the storm, then you are very blessed.
If you have food to eat today, you are very blessed.
If you have a change of clothes, you are very blessed.
If you have those blessings, you are way richer than over 80 percent of the world's population.
Most of the people of this world would think they won the lottery to have what you have problems and all.
You are very blessed!
Yes, we all must work hard and do what we can do to have and maintain what we have, but we must understand that anything beyond that is just a blessing from God.
Have we thanked God for all those many blessings He has given?

I sometimes think about how unfair life can be. I have worked hard most of my life working at times, three jobs at once to just to make ends meet. Yet when I see all the new trucks in town, I know that several of them are owned by people who don't work hard at all and don't take care of their families. Here I am driving my old truck. It's not fair. I look at my old lawn mowers or tractors and see the new ones my neighbors have. It's just not fair. I look at the jobs that many of my friends have. They work close by and are home by 5:00 p.m. They are appreciated and respected. Yet I put on tens of thousands more miles on my car than they do each year. I work with people who are not popular, and so my work is misunderstood and often goes unappreciated. It's just not fair. When we choose who we want to compare each part of our lives to, it's easy to say there are a bunch of people who have it better than we do and say that life is definitely not fair. However, would we want to trade everything around us with everything around them? Most of the time not! We really would only want to pick and choose the things we want and not the things that we don't want. Most of the time, we would take their truck but not their payments. We would take their house but not their crazy family.

Even in our worst situation or most difficult of times, if at all possible, we just need to think of the things we have for which we can be thankful. No, it won't change our current situation we are in, but it will change us even while we are in our current situation. I'm not saying it's not tough or difficult. I'm just saying even now you are very blessed even with this trouble you are in. I have been in countries where the people have no bed to sleep in or houses to live in. They might be living in boxes or under pieces of tarps. Many don't have good health; they might be missing a leg from a landmine or have open wounds without any medical help. I've seen the kids starving with bloated stomachs and watched where a mother would mix dirt or sawdust in with the rice just to make it go further. I saw children with rags for clothing carrying dirty water for their family to drink or sorting through the dump to recycle a thousand plastic bottles for a few cents for their family.

Yes, it might hurt, it might be scary, but thank God you still have a lot to be thankful for.

I know I have a lot I'm thankful for if nothing more than just because you're my daughter.

"Gifts from God"
(Feat. Chris Lane)

Back when I was a kid
I thought gifts from God only came from church
But the more that I live
The more I learn, it's not always the way it works
Sometimes you don't see it till your looking back
When ya didn't get what ya thought ya had to have
'Cause He had a bigger plan than the one you had
Yours didn't work out and aren't you glad?
When you take a look around it ain't hard to find
Everybody's got things that money can't buy
If the ones ya love are sitting right beside ya
Then I'd say ya got a lot
The best things in life are straight from His hands
It's like we're raising kids on a piece of land
A little piece of mind when the day is done
Where ya think that comes from?
That's gifts from God
Ah yeah
It makes ya thankful for the
    hills that we climb
For the waves that we ride
For the lows and the highs
For the wrongs made right
For the songs we sing
For the dreams we dream
Makes ya thankful for
    everything
Hallelujah, every day's a gift from God

Hallelujah, every day's a gift
Hallelujah, every day's a gift from God
Hallelujah every day's a gift
(Hallelujah) Where ya think that comes from?
That's gifts from God
(Hallelujah) You know that's gifts from God
(Hallelujah) Every day's a gift from God
(Hallelujah) Every day's a gift
Gifts from God

Gifts of Love and Affection

Life is full of gifts. Some we really want, some we know of, and some we totally missed.

There are gifts that we have been given that we wanted and finally got just to realize they are not as wonderful as what we were led to believe, or they quickly break and are discarded. Then there are gifts that we are given that we never desired or thought of before or even appreciated much when we received them yet turned out to be the best gifts ever. Then there are those gifts that we never even recognized or noticed that we were given yet may have been given to us at great cost. All gifts that are given to bless us are worthy of appreciation. Gifts show that someone is thinking of us, remembering us, wanting to bless us. They show that someone desires to make our life better, easier, happier, or a little more fun.

With each gift I give you, please know I am missing you, thinking of you, and wanting you to know just how much I love you. This is the same reason that God has given us gifts too.

God's gifts He gives us are so awesome they are beyond description (2 Corinthians 9:15).

The Bible says that our Heavenly Father gives us the gift of eternal life (Romans 6:23);

The gift of salvation by grace through faith (Ephesians 2:8);

and the gift of the indwelling Holy Spirit (Acts 2:38).

Our children are a gift from God (Psalm 127:3)

Our ability to work and enjoy the rewards of our labor is also a gift (Ecclesiastes 5:19).

James said, *"Every good gift and every perfect gift is from above, and comes down from the Father of lights"* (James 1:17).

Romans 4:17 says He "gives life to the dead," and

Romans 8:11 promises life to our mortal bodies through His Spirit who dwells within us.

Always "Love the giver more than the gift."
(Unknown)

Yesterday is history, tomorrow is a mystery, today is God's gift, that's why we call it the present. (Joan Rivers)

Love is, above all, the gift of oneself. (Jean Anouilh)

You don't choose your family. They are God's gift to you, as you are to them. (Desmond Tutu)

My father gave me the greatest gift anyone could give another person, he believed in me. (Jim Valvano)

The greatest gift that you can give to others is the gift of unconditional love and acceptance. (Brian Tracy)

Don't Forget Your Mom

Remember to show your love to your mother.

One thing I've always noticed when my family or your mother's family would get together during the holidays is that all of the women would go out to the kitchen to help. I don't know what they were talking about, because when I would go out there to help (myself), they would always stop talking and shoo me out. (Go figure.) It was always a bonding time for them, talking, laughing, helping, and sharing. It was always a great way to build relationships.

For me, you know I always try to show my mother (your grandmother) my love and respect. I'm always quick to do whatever she needs help with and try to include her in everything I can. She is always welcome and often invited to meals, cookouts, and outings with us. I just naturally try to take care of her house, yard, vehicle as just a natural part of my routine. I try to watch out for her health and make sure she gets to the doctor when needed. I try to do special things for her, and I make sure I always give her a hug and tell her I love her every time I leave her house, even though she lives next door.

I figure that she took care of me for the first part of my life. I have no problem doing that for the last part of her life.

You never know when you will have missed your last chance to do something nice for or affirm your love for someone.

> *It was your mom's turn to carry you when you were young. It's your turn to carry her when she grows old.* (Kelly Roper)

All that I am, or hope to be, I owe to my angel mother. (Abraham Lincoln)

Mothers never retire, no matter how old her children are she is always a Mom, always willing to encourage and help her children in any way she can! (Catherine Pulsifer)

Love your parents and treat them with loving care. For you will only know their true value when you can only see their empty chair. (Anonymous)

No matter how old I get or how many children I have, I will always be my mother's child. (Kelly Roper)

But if a widow has children or grandchildren, they should learn first to carry out their religious duties toward their own family and in this way repay their parents and grandparents, because that is what pleases God. **(1 Timothy 5:4 GNT)**

When your mother is old, show her your appreciation. **(Proverbs 23:22b GNT)**

Don't neglect your mother when she grows old. **(Proverbs 23:22b CEV)**

Make your parents proud, especially your mother. **(Proverbs 23:25 CEV)**

So give your father and mother joy! May she who gave you birth be happy. **(Proverbs 23:25 NLT)**

Be Very Responsible with Your Money on Good Days

If you do, then the rainy days will be taken care of too.

Watch your finances closely. Be very careful with the way you handle your money. I am not talking about valuing it more than your family or making it a focus or a big goal in life. Just learn to be skilled at handling your money and make it go as far as it can. Make up a budget that will work for you, and stick with it. It will keep you safe in hard times and build your future for better days to come. The more detailed you are and the closer you follow your budget, the better off you will be.

Try to find money you can set aside to invest regularly. If you just invested $10 a week at 7 percent interest for thirty years, your $15, 653.57 you invested would end up being worth $53,148.91. In forty years, it would be worth $114,502.08. If you could find a 12 percent for forty years, you'd have $519,310.86… And that's only for faithfully investing $10 each week.

Whatever you do, make a plan and stick with it. It could make all the difference in the future.

Live as if this is your last day to live, and plan as if you were going to live a hundred more years.

This is a difficult thing for everyone. It takes work and self-discipline and time. Your grandparents didn't make a lot of money and never had much, but they had done this very well. They also went through several recessions, were laid off, and had to scramble to just to keep from losing everything and keep food on the table. Yet they budgeted and saved.

They were always helping in every special fundraiser that came around as well as always gave their tithes every time the offering plate was passed. They even helped people in need directly when they heard of anyone in need. They always were careful to spend less than they made, always keeping everything paid off. They never owed anyone anything but the bare minimum and for as short of a time as possible. They never bought any extras and going out to eat was something that was very special, rare, and cheap MickyD's, Taco Bell, or Pizza. It might have happened six to ten times a year at the most. We always had enough clothing but not much extra. Then they saved and invested as much as possible.

Your great-grandpa Jackson raised a family during the Great Depression and had to work three jobs around the clock and even gave sacrificially to keep his church open while many other churches closed. He ate things like lard and ketchup sandwiches (the food of the depression). They raised most of their food and canned everything that could be canned. Yet the most impressive thing was that he always supported missionaries even to the end of his life. After he died, we found more missionaries that he was sending money to regularly support than many large churches support. Always **think, plan, give, save,** and stick to it.

God 10 percent
housing 50–60 percent
savings 10 percent
food 10 percent
Transportation 10 percent
entertainment 3–5 percent
others 3–5 percent

**Make all you can,
Save all you can,
Give all you can.
(John Wesley in the 1790s)**

If we command our wealth, we shall be rich and free. If our wealth commands us, we are poor indeed. (Edmund Burke)

A simple fact that is hard to learn is that the time to save money is when you have some. (Joe Moore)

If you would be wealthy, think of saving as well as getting. (Benjamin Franklin)

You must gain control over your money or the lack of it will forever control you. (Dave Ramsey)

Keep your eyes on the price when spending, don't regret later to find that you have nothing for tomorrow. (Auliq Ice)

Go to the ant, you sluggard; consider its ways and be wise! It has no commander, no overseer or ruler, yet it stores its provisions in summer and gathers its food at harvest. **(Proverbs 6:6–11 NIV)**

That I may give wealth to those who love Me. I fill their treasuries. **(Proverbs 8:21 NHEB)**

Wisdom can make you rich, but foolishness leads to more foolishness. **(Proverbs 14:24 CEV)**

The plans of the diligent lead surely to abundance, but everyone who is hasty comes only to poverty. **(Proverbs 21:5 ESV)**

Be sensible and store up precious treasures—don't waste them like a fool. **(Proverbs 21:20 CEV)**

Give with a Generous Heart

You need to work everything into your budget, but don't forget to include regular acts of generosity.

Giving is something I have learned to enjoy doing. When your mom and I were first married, we learned to tithe even when it really didn't make sense. We gave until it hurt, and then we gave some more. Then we learned to give to others in need as well as our tithe and then add missions… There were times when we were taken advantage of by people who had much more than we had, but believe it or not, I learned it's okay. I gained wisdom, because I learned that I give to God not the person or group we handed the items or check to and He's keeping track and will pay me back, not those people. I think that is how we have been able to survive so many storms and financial difficulties. We honor God, and God is blessing us.

> *You cannot do a kindness too soon because you never know how soon it will be too late.* (Ralph Waldo Emerson)

> *If you can't feed a hundred people, then just feed one.* (Mother Teresa)

> *We make a living by what we get, but we make a life by what we give.* (Winston Churchill)

> *The value of a man resides in what he gives and not in what he is capable of receiving.* (Albert Einstein)

> *You have not lived today until you have done something for someone who can never repay you.* (John Bunyan)

No one has ever become poor by giving. (Anne Frank)

A generous person will prosper; whoever refreshes others will be refreshed. **(Proverbs 11:25 NIV)**

Good will come to those who are generous and lend freely, who conduct their affairs with justice. **(Psalm 112:5 NIV)**

Whoever is generous to the poor lends to the Lord, and He will repay him for his deed. **(Proverbs 19:17 ESV)**

Give to the one who begs from you, and do not refuse the one who would borrow from you. **(Matthew 5:42 ESV)**

I'll Be Here to Help You Finish Your Work When You're Too Tired to Finish It Yourself

I believe you can do anything you set your mind to doing.

However as much as I can, as much as I am able, I will always try to help you, in any way, anywhere, and with anything I can that you might need my help with.

I have always wondered why God didn't give me three arms and three hands. Sometimes, just one more hand would mean so much. It would not only make some difficult jobs easier, but it would make some jobs possible.

When your grandpa was around, I would always just hang out with him to help him and be there if he needed me, hold something, get something, maybe for another idea, or just to keep him company. He would always do the same with me when he was around. Man, how I miss him! The Bible tells us, "*And if one falls down, the other helps, but if there's no one to help, tough*" (**Ecclesiastes 4:10 MSG**). Sometimes, just having someone there who cares makes the difference. As much as I can, I will be there for you because I really care.

> *The only mistake you can make is not asking for help.* (Sandeep Jauhar)

> *I may not be the kind of person you want me to be, but I will always be there for you.* (Alfusainey Jallow)

Never confuse people who are always around you, with people who are always there for you. (Gee Linder)

But I am poor and needy; yet the LORD thinks upon me. You are my help and my deliverer; do not delay, O my God. **(Psalm 40:17)**

Give us help from trouble, for the help of man is useless. **(Psalm 60:11)**

Because You have been my help, therefore in the shadow of Your wings I will rejoice. **(Psalm 63:7)**

Trust Only Those Who Are Trustworthy

There are those you can trust; but be careful who you trust, with what, and how much you can trust them.

Be careful who you spill your guts with or share your deepest secrets with. Even very few BFFs are good to open yourself up to that much, because things change and friends tend to be during seasons of life and trusted confidants can someday use your secret against you.

**Always;
Love everyone,
Help many,
Trust few.**

Don't live your life alone and afraid of everyone, and yet don't live carelessly and recklessly. Don't set yourself up to be needlessly hurt and taken advantage of.

It's okay to let people earn your trust, and I guess you have to give them some trust to prove themselves with, and then later you can give them a little more, and so on.

Just don't blindly over trust anyone, except God!

You can always trust Him!

Over the years, I can't tell you how many times we have been burned by trusting the wrong people or overtrusting someone we thought felt about us like we felt about them. Some were very good people. Some were very close people. Some I doubt ever gave their betrayal a second thought or even noticed. There were a couple of different times that my closest friends lied about us just to have something interesting to say that might make them look good to my superiors. Tore me up. I didn't think I would be able to survive it. Some hurts were so deep it has taken years to not wish something on them. (If not a real conscience, then at least a good case of boils or hemorrhoids or something like that would be nice too.) The worst thing about it is for many of the closest friends who hurt us, we still had to work together and forgive them and be friends with them.

For some, all we could do was put on a good act on our part, and it was never really the same again or easy, but with God's help over the years, the pain of the incident slowly healed. Several I could name that you would know, and we do care for them today, although it still isn't the same, and we do miss those close days of the past.

So even when someone hurts you, just remember most people are stupid and don't really know what they are doing (like Jesus prayed on the Cross, as written in Luke 23:34). Most won't even know it hurt you, but try to forgive them and ask God to help you through the situation.

> *Dear friend, if you've gone into hock with your neighbor or locked yourself into a deal with a stranger, If you've impulsively promised the shirt off your back and now find yourself shivering out in the cold, Friend, don't waste a minute, get yourself out of that mess. You're in that man's clutches! Go, put on a long face; act desperate. Don't procrastinate—there's no time to lose. Run like a deer from the hunter, fly like a bird from the trapper!* **(Proverbs 6:1–3 MSG)**

> *Don't trust anyone, not even your best friend, and be careful what you say to the one you love.* **(Micah 7:5 CEV)**

> *It is better to trust the* Lord *for protection than to trust anyone else.* **(Psalm 118:8 CEV)**

> *My relatives and my closest friends have stopped coming. My house guests have forgotten me.* **(Job 19:14 GWT)**

Remember How to Love

In everything you do and say, in every way you interact with people, make sure you allow love to be seen.

Use things but help people
Like things and love people.
Discard things but care for people
Hold things loosely but hang on to people
Get frustrated with things but be patient with people
I think even a bad person is more valuable than a good animal.

If your car is sliding and you're either going to hit an animal or a person, always pick the animal. Even if it's a stupid person, still they are more valuable than an animal.

There have been times when I have had a problem seeing this. Sometimes, it's much easier to find my solace with an animal or a thing or more for me in just doing something. People can disappoint you, frustrate you, let you down, and even turn against you. However, things cannot be there to comfort you or care for you when you are sick. Things cannot help you when you need a hand or direction or an encouraging word. People are what is made in the image of God, and God rewards us for taking time with people, and only people will go to heaven with us.

So value what really counts, even if they get on our nerves sometimes. People really are the ones who count. Everything else can only come in second at best.

> *Love people who hate you. Pray for people who have wronged you. It won't just change their life… It'll change yours.* (Mandy Hale)

> *The value of our lives is measured by our capacity to love others.* (Wayne Gerard Trotman)

Define yourself—not by how much you are loved, but by how much you love others. (Connor Chalfant)

The way we relate with people is the same way we relate with God. (Sunday Adelaja)

A new command I give you: Love one another. As I have loved you, so you must love one another. By this, all men will know that you are My disciples, if you love one another. **(John 13:34–35 NIV)**

But speaking the truth in love, [that we] may grow up into Him in all things, which is the head, [even] Christ: **(Ephesians 4:15)**

My little children, let us not love in word only but also in deed. **(1 John 3:18)**

And over all these virtues put on love, which binds them all together in perfect unity. **(Colossians 3:14)**

If I Could, I Would Give You the World

If I could…
if I would…
would you?
could you?
then understand just how much I love you?

I wish I could give you
all that I desire for you
I would not only give you all the
things you would like and desire
I would give you all the experiences
that would bring you Joy and great memories
I would also bring you all the best friends
who would challenge and inspire you
I would take you to places
that people dream of
if I could I would give you
the Sun and the Earth and the moon and the stars
but all I have to give you I do
And that's my love
I love you forever

Just a Few Thoughts I've Been Wanting to Share with You…

I hope my thoughts will continue to bring you comfort and encouragement for a long time to come. Please see my heart and feel the reality of all my love that I have for you.

I know it might take some time to get through these pages, and some might seem unpleasant or even in a way intrusive or overly blunt. Please forgive me if that is how it seems to you. It is not my intent to give you a big lecture but a daddy-to-daughter talk, maybe a long overdue talk but a talk from love and concern for you.

Please keep this, and let me talk to you whenever you need to know what I think about something or how I feel about a situation or maybe how I would handle a situation. I tried to get everything I could think of that I wanted to say to you in these pages. I also tried to follow each thought up with the reasons I would do it that way or why I believe the way I do. The scripture wasn't intended to be a continual sermon. You growing up in a pastor's home, I think you got enough of those. However, it is the reason I try to do everything I do and the way I try to do it. I'm not trying to say I succeeded at doing it right or that I even did it in a way that totally honored God in everything I did, and for all those times, I truly say, "I'm sorry. Please forgive me!" But it truly was my heart's desire to do it right and to serve God to the best of my ability and bring honor to His name in everything I have done throughout my life. As a husband, a father, a grandfather, a son, an uncle, a cousin, a pastor, a builder, an interpreter, a teacher, and in the many other hats I have worn through the years—and you have had to put up with watching me, helping me, and maybe even being embarrassed by me—I have tried to show God's love and honor Him through it all.

*****

I don't know why things have turned out the way they have. I wanted, hoped, and truly believed that things would have been different. As a young man, I believed I would be the answer to some young woman's dreams and be her everyday hero, her Prince Charming, her knight in shining armor. I would find her and marry her and be the best husband to lead her, protect her, and impress her; and she would thank God for me every day… Then I got married…

*****

I, as a young man, would help with other people's kids. I would babysit neighbors' kids and cousins and even my own little spoiled brothers… I could easily see their mistakes, and I knew what I would do as a father someday. I would be the best father, and my kids would think I was the greatest and want to be with me… I wouldn't make the mistakes that I saw everyone else making. I was even thinking about writing a parenting book to help other misguided and struggling parents. My kids would grow up knowing they were loved. They would feel so fulfilled and satisfied with their home. All their friends would want to stay at our home just to experience the awesome, peaceful, loving home we had… Then we had kids and well…

*****

I have been told by many relatives that even as young as two to three years old, I was always known for finding a stool or chair, and I would pull it into the center of the room and climb up on it and start acting like I was preaching. (*"I am your Creator, and before you were born, I chose you to speak for Me to the nations"* [Jeremiah 1:5].) Even before I could talk, I'd be jabbering there like an old-time Pentecostal preacher. Somehow, I always knew I wanted to be a preacher. Even through my more rebellious teenage years, somewhere in the back of my mind, I still knew that is what I was supposed to be and wanted to be someday.

I knew how to be a good pastor. I loved people. I cared where they were going, what they were doing, and where they would spend eternity. I studied under some of the greats, at some of the best colleges. I saw God do great things and learned everything I could about building a church and being a good pastor. I was at the top of my class, and I knew how to do it. I saw the mistakes that many other pastors were making and why their churches were not growing. I was also a general contractor for many years, and so I knew the building trade. I knew how to build a wonderful church building and had drawn up blueprints on a couple of different churches I wanted to build. I knew God was going to bless our endeavor because I was doing it to honor Him. (*"If someone aspires to be a church leader, he desires an honorable position"* [1 Timothy 3:1].) Then I moved the family to Wisconsin feeling this was where God wanted us to be and knowing the church was going to be growing into a mega church really soon (*"And the Lord added to the church daily those who were being saved"* [Acts 2:47].) Surveys, outreach events, tracts and Bibles, community events, food giveaways, community home repairs, and… Well, I do still really enjoy preaching and caring for people, and I'm faithfully preaching each week…but…

*****

I always wanted to help orphans and kids in need. My grandparents were foster parents. My mother was a foster child before she was adopted. It's also an important theme in the Bible. God requires us to care for them ("*Religion that is pure and uncorrupted in the eyes of [our] God and Father involves taking care of orphans and widows in their distress*" [James 1:27 AUV]). He says we have to defend them ("*To defend the cause of orphans*" [Isaiah 1:17]). He said we have to make sure they're treated fairly ("*Give justice to the poor and the orphan*" [Psalm 82:3–4]). And we are guilty if we don't ("*But they refuse to defend the cause of orphans*" [Isaiah 1:23–24]). So I have a lot of motivation and desire to care for kids who need someone. We went to classes. Talked with many people who were doing it already. Read books about it and learned what to expect and how to do it right. We got our license and took in many kids over the years. When we moved out here to Wisconsin, I added on the house, and I set it up to take in many kids. We had several kids over the years, and then…well, we were never told about everything that could happen and what the system might do to people like us, I guess…

*****

I don't know why many things happened. I know in looking back over the years, I guess I didn't know as much as I originally thought I did. I did some things foolishly thinking that they would all work out good in the end. Other things, I soon found out that I wasn't as prepared for everything that might happen as I thought I was. Some I was at fault for trusting people that I shouldn't have or even having people turn against me that I thought never would. I would even say that some situations happened because I thought everyone else in the family would just naturally see things the way I saw them and just naturally have the same belief or drive I had to do the work or see things happen that I had wanted, but…

*****

Am I hurt over the way things have turned out? Yes, it hurts; and at times, I'd have to admit, it hurts really bad. I would also have to admit that I have been upset with God on more than one occasion wanting to know "Why!" ("*My God, my God, why have You aban-

doned me? I have cried desperately for help, but still it does not come" [Psalm 22:1 GNT].) But do I blame God over it all? NO, I don't. ("*Life isn't always fair*" [Ecclesiastes 9:11].) I don't think life is going to be fair, and although I don't like it, I'm not surprised when things don't turn out right. It's like the message you have heard me preach many times over the years, "This ain't Heaven yet!"

I do have many things I think are good in my life. I have been faithful. I have survived many shutdowns, depressions, recessions, national disasters, plagues, pandemics, and illnesses. I have been saved from dozens (if not hundreds) of close calls in my life. Many of which could have and even should have taken my life. Although I have had to live with a lot of physical problems and chronic pain for much of my life, I haven't had it as bad as some, and yet I have done more than most people who've had to deal with a lot less. Even though I have not had the fancy house, cars, farm equipment, or lifestyle that many others seem to have, we may not have had all the extras, but we have always had enough and never had to go without. We even were able to help a lot of other people along the way. Yet to me, the most important success in my life is my family! I have a wife. I've been married most of my life to the same woman, and we still love each other. I have a bunch of kids who most of the time will admit that I'm their father. We also have several grandkids who think I'm awesome. The main thing is that I LOVE my family more than I can ever tell.

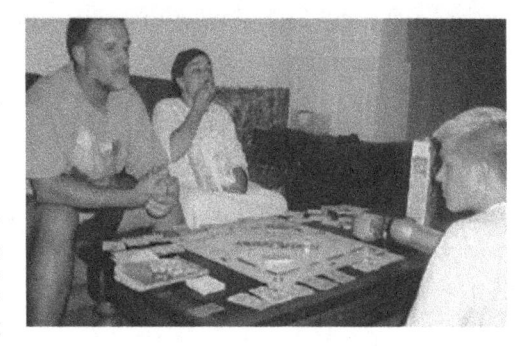

Many times I have remarked about how thankful I am that my family is all healthy, smart, and good-looking—a little weird sometimes, but that's okay too. We have gone through soo much together, and we are still together (although the distance is more than I can bear at times) and still love each other and like to be together (although it happens way too rarely). And then there is my greatest achievement, the apex of my success, my opus, my grand crescendo—my daughter.

You are my greatest achievement. You are my life in which I get to live on beyond myself. You have great ability, intelligence, and potential; and I love you so much more than you'll ever know!

As long as there is you, no one will ever be able to convince me that I didn't do anything right.

My only real fear, and my only real concern, is one that compels me to ask you for a favor. The one real concern that often wakes me up in the middle of the night is a fear, I'm afraid, of losing you. I don't want to lose you! I'm not talking about not knowing where you are or you moving away from me. Although that bothers me, too, but what I really mean is, after everything is said and done here, PLEASE make sure you are ready so we can be together again. One of these days I'm going to run out of things to say as well as the time to say them. One of these days, the only thing I will have to say is either, "See you in the morning," or "Goodbye." And whichever one it is, is totally up to you. I LOVE YOU soo much I couldn't stand it if we would have to say, "Goodbye!" just because you wouldn't just give your life to Christ so we could be together again. I believe with everything that is happening in the world right now, we are probably living in the last days, so much so that I have been very concerned that I might not get a chance to get this to you in time. This stuff that is happening in the news around here and the world everywhere looks just like what you have heard me preach many, many times while you were growing up. Constant tension between countries; increase in the threat of war; collapse of countries (including this one); economic chaos; the talk of new global cashless currency; pandemics, talks of a global government; AI; nanobot technology; microchip implanting; the possibility of a new civil war based on morality, religion, and personal thought…they're all in there, and they're all happening now.

I'm not asking you to live perfectly. I'm just asking you to live FORGIVEN.

It's not that I'm asking you to be perfect; I'm just asking you to live FORGIVEN. We have all blown it. "We are all screw-ups" **(Romans 3:23)**. We all are sinners. We have all made a mess of it all. I have, your mother has, your uncles aunts and cousins all have, and even your grandparents have all the way back through each generation failed God in one way or another. It doesn't matter what you've done. If it's not what God said or wanted, He just calls it SIN. It doesn't matter what or how bad or how much or how often… It's all just the same to Him, SIN. Nothing is so bad that it's worse than the others or so insignificant enough that God doesn't count it… We are all just sinners. Good, bad, best, worst, all of us are just Sinners, Separate from God, and needing a Savior to make all our mess-ups right again. We are all living as if we were on a fast train oblivious to the fact that the breaks are out and the bridge ahead has collapsed. For the most part, we don't even know how desperate we are for a hero or a Savior to save us.

I'm not saying this because I think you are so bad or have intentionally walked away from God. It's just that when we pick a different way for our life other than the way of God, it all ends badly. No matter how good we think it is at the time, it won't get us to heaven. *"There is a path before each person that seems right, but it all ends in death"* **(Proverbs 16:25 NLT)**.

As a matter of fact, our eternal home is what we have earned with our life here on earth, and God is obligated to give us what we have earned. *"For the payoff of sin is death…"* **(Romans 6:23a NB)**. It is a law just like here. A company is, by law, required to pay you what you have earned while working for them. That wouldn't be so bad, but this is the sum total of our life debt. No matter how good we are and despite all the good things we can do or how bad we've been, our life all just totals to sin and death. You see, it's an Old Testament law that Adam and Eve first messed up and put the entire family in terrible debt because of their action, forever. Yeah, they were conned by Satan but by turning their back on God and destroying what He did for them in favor of the promises of Satan's lies. There is only one way to pay the penalty of the life we've lived and pay off the debt that

Adam and Eve put us in, and that's by eternal death in hell, but that is exactly why Jesus came.

Jesus is not just an example of a good way to live and get your life right. He said that He was the only way to God. *Jesus answered, "I am the way and the truth and the life. No one comes to the Father except through Me"* **(John 14:6)**. We couldn't pay for it, be good enough, or earn it, or do enough good things to earn it even if we worked hard at it every day and lived to be a thousand years old. Fortunately for us, Jesus wants to give it to us for free, just for the asking. *"The gift of God is eternal life in Christ Jesus, our Lord"* **(Romans 6:23b NB)**.

The way to seal the deal is just to ask Him for it. That's what He said—just ask Him, and He would do it for you. Ask Him to apply the price He paid for your forgiveness (His death on the Cross), and tell Him you give up your way for His (you want Him to be your Lord and Savior). Then follow Him (start praying and reading the Bible, learning about Him). That's it. That's all there is to it. Totally Free. And as the woman said, *"If it's free, it's got to be good!"*

That's what I want. When all is said and done, I just want to know that I'll see you in the morning. I want to know, for sure, that you are putting it right and heading to heaven, and we'll be together again there.

The only thing left to ask you is, "**When?**"

Remember what is going on now. Life is getting cray. People are crazy today. The world is getting crazy. World leaders are calling out for a "one world government." Crazy terrorist countries are saying they are going to take over the world and they are making the weapons to get them there. Countries are making viruses that can shut down the world and maybe even kill everyone…

I know you agree with me that it's important and something you should do. The only thing now is to ask, "**When?**" **Why not now?** Why not get ready, be ready, and stay ready? And why not start today?

God says, *"When the time came, I listened to you, and when you needed help, I came to save you"* **(2 Corinthians 6:2 CEV)**. That time has come. This is the day for you to be saved.

For now our salvation is nearer than when we first believed. **(Romans 13:11)**

I hope you are already ahead of me on this and are already ready and good to go. If so, That Is Awesome! **Please stay that way. Stay ready.** If that is true, then whatever the future holds, we can know for sure that we'll be together in the morning.

> *"For I am sure that neither death nor life, nor angels nor rulers, nor things present nor things to come, nor powers, nor height nor depth, nor anything else in all creation, will be able to separate us from the love of God in Christ Jesus our Lord"* **(Romans 8:38–39)**.

> *Please take this as a big love letter from a dad who is a little overprotective, who is a little long-winded, slightly unpredictable, maybe a little crazy, and who is definitely crazy about you. Read it over and over again. Keep it. If there is something that stands out to you, please try to understand why I said it and why I believe it. Please read the verses to understand why I believe the way I do or do things the way I do. Then too, where I should or could have done it different or better, Please forgive me for my shortcomings, failures, and any harm you may feel I have caused. I've said all this just to make sure that you know, that I do, always have, and always will, Love you more than you will ever know.*
>
> *And never forget that you will always be my little girl.*
>
> *Love you the most,*
>
> *Dad*

"My Dear children, let us not love with words or tongue but with actions and in truth" **(1 John 3:18).**

The only thing left to say is
You are awesome!
You are my daughter,
And I'm so proud to be your dad
And I'm crazy about you!
I LOVE YOU!
I LOVE YOU THE MOST!
I ALWAYS HAVE, ALWAYS WILL!
And I want to SEE YOU IN THE MORNING!

About the Author

Kip was born and raised in a middle class christian home, just one hour north of Detroit. His father served in the Army during the Korean conflict, then came back to marry his mother. Then after 40 years, retired from General Motors automotive. His mother was a stay at home mother of five boys. They were married just shy of 60 years before his father died of cancer. Kip after graduation from high school joined the Marine Corp. After that, he began pursuing his education and credentials as a pastor. There he met his wife-to-be and was married the following summer in 1984. It wasn't long before God blessed them with their first child, all the while ministering in their church as youth pastors at that time, working a secular job, and completing some further education. With everything else going on, Jolene and Kip felt led to become licensed foster parents and took care of mostly hard to place kids for the next 20+ years. Later God began to move him in another direction of ministry and back to college, this time to study American Sign Language and Deaf culture ministries. Within that field of ministry, Kip worked in many different situations and met many interesting people. One occasion that was very memorable was being able to interpret for President GW Bush.

After many years, God started stirring pastor Kip's heart, and once again feeling God's leading, they moved to southwestern Wisconsin to plant and pastor a small congregation. There they have continued there raising their 4 daughters and one son. Later they adopted 2 more special children from afar. Jolene and Kip continue to reach out to people through their ministry. Kip works as an Educational Interpreter in the local school system. Kip and Jolene also operate a small cattle and sheep farm, and still make themselves available to those in need.

Kip wrote this as an over committed father, still wanting to "do it right" and be the best father He can be to the amazing kids God has given him (who are now adults themselves). He says "I still believe (as most parents) that although times keep changing, so does our involvement, influence and relationship with our children is constantly changing. However, some aspects of parenting are never done. I was desperately wanting to find some help or a tool to help me continue building the relationships (or maybe even to help find the areas that need mending) with my kids, to help me be able to share some of the important things of life I have learned and those things that have helped me along the way. It was from this desire to be able to express my love and concern for my daughters that "A Few Thoughts From Dad" was birthed, and hopefully will turnout to be a big blessing to my daughters and maybe your relationship with your daughter might be blessed from it too."

CPSIA information can be obtained
at www.ICGtesting.com
Printed in the USA
BVHW070313310123
657438BV00001B/10

9 781639 039609